Helping Patrons
FIND THEIR
ROOTS

ALA Editions purchases fund advocacy, awareness, and accreditation programs for library professionals worldwide.

Helping Patrons
FIND THEIR
ROOTS

A GENEALOGY HANDBOOK
FOR LIBRARIANS

Janice Lindgren Schultz

ALA
Editions

AN IMPRINT OF THE AMERICAN LIBRARY ASSOCIATION

Chicago   2018

JANICE LINDGREN SCHULTZ retired in 2013 as manager of the Midwest Genealogy Center in Independence, Missouri. She has served on many History Section committees of the Reference and User Services Association, and she chaired its Genealogy Committee, Local History Committee, Genealogy Preconference Planning Committee, and the History Section. Schultz has also served as president of the Missouri State Genealogical Association and the American Family Records Association. She has been a speaker at various genealogy conferences, the Missouri Library Association, and the Association of Tribal Archives, Libraries, & Museums.

© 2018 by the American Library Association

Extensive effort has gone into ensuring the reliability of the information in this book; however, the publisher makes no warranty, express or implied, with respect to the material contained herein.

ISBN: 978-0-8389-1644-5 (paper)

Library of Congress Cataloging-in-Publication Data
Names: Schultz, Janice Lindgren, author.
Title: Helping patrons find their roots : a genealogy handbook for
    librarians / Janice Lindgren Schultz.
Description: Chicago : ALA Editions, an imprint of the American Library
    Association, 2018. | Includes bibliographical references and index.
Identifiers: LCCN 2017031641 | ISBN 9780838916445 (pbk. : alk. paper)
Subjects: LCSH: Reference services (Libraries)—United States. |
    Genealogy. | Genealogy—Library resources—Handbooks, manuals,
    etc. | United States—Genealogy—Handbooks, manuals, etc. |
    Genealogical libraries—United States.
Classification: LCC Z711.6.G46 S38 2018 | DDC 025.5/2—dc23 LC record
    available at https://lccn.loc.gov/2017031641

Cover design by Karen Sheets de Gracia. Images © Adobe Stock.
Interior design and composition by Dianne M. Rooney using Palatino and Univers typefaces.

♾ This paper meets the requirements of ANSI/NISO Z39.48–1992 (Permanence of Paper).

Printed in the United States of America

22 21 20 19 18   5 4 3 2 1

CONTENTS

PREFACE

I retired as the manager of the Midwest Genealogy Center in Independence, Missouri, in 2013. I enjoyed many aspects of the job, but whenever I needed to hire new staff I was in a turmoil. I wasn't sure if I should hire someone who was excellent in library skills but had no knowledge of genealogy, or find someone who was knowledgeable in genealogy but needed training in library procedures. Recognizing the right candidate was always a challenge. The right combination didn't always present itself. Staff training was an ongoing procedure, even when the employee was a perfect fit.

You may be faced with the same conundrum. Finding and training employees is a difficult part of a manager's job. But what if you are the one who needs training? When the task comes to finding training for yourself, it is important to take the initiative and begin the journey. All aspects of management, from training to collection development, can be a challenge in genealogy librarianship. But with guidance, I'm sure you will be up to the task.

Genealogy librarianship involves knowing your subject, discovering how to help a patron get started in research, finding good websites and print resources, and uncovering networking opportunities. My experience in the genealogy field has given me insight into the skills needed by you and your staff in working with family historians. Genealogy resources have changed over the years and will continue to change. The journey you begin will continue to be a learning experience. During my career, my mind was opened to many new avenues of knowledge, and I'm sure yours will be too. I hope you enjoy the trek.

What Is Genealogy?

Your worst fears have been realized. You are alone at the reference desk and suddenly someone asks a question about genealogy. It is a topic that can have an unprepared reference librarian shaking with fear. Genealogy is a popular subject today. We see commercials on network television for Ancestry.com and can watch shows such as *Who Do You Think You Are? Finding Your Roots,* and *Genealogy Roadshow.* This "genealogy thing" has people curious about their heritage. It sounds so easy. Is it?

Historically, genealogy had a focus on royal lineages or in legitimizing a claim to land, wealth, or power. But since the 1970s, this popular pursuit has found Americans trying to discover their personal history. They want to know their origins, or as we sometimes say, their "roots." We are a nation of immigrants and come from all different backgrounds. Many of us are asking, "From where did my ancestors originate?" The plethora of information on the Internet has made the pursuit easier than ever, causing many to feel they can go about this venture on their own. Can they? Or do they need the guidance of a librarian, or perhaps a professional genealogist? Are we prepared if they ask us, the librarians, how to do genealogical research? We consider ourselves information specialists, but if we don't know the basics of genealogy to give assistance to our customers, we are doing them, and ourselves, a disservice.

Many in the United States are far removed from their immigrant ancestors and their memories, and thus far removed from the names and stories of those ancestors. But for many, there comes a time when the mystery of their forebears is one they desire to solve. It happens to people at various times in their lives, but when it happens it often becomes a passion. The first explosion of interest in family origins on the American continent coincided with the bicentennial celebration of our nation's founding and the publication of Alex Haley's *Roots* in 1976.[1] The subsequent presentation of *Roots* on network television in the form of a miniseries added to its impact. Libraries, archives, and historical and genealogical societies were amazed by the burgeoning number of researchers wanting to trace their family history. I have fond recollections of the early days in my career in a genealogy library. Patrons were lined up outside the library, waiting for the front doors to open. When finally allowed to enter, they would walk hurriedly into the building to obtain one of the microfilm readers and begin their genealogical research for the day.

In 2010 Americans saw the first airing of *Who Do You Think You Are?* a network television show using famous personalities in search of their ancestry. First aired in the United Kingdom by the BBC in 2004, *Who Do You Think You Are?* took the British by storm. The program's popularity spawned similar shows in other countries and eventually made it to the United States. Henry Louis Gates Jr. also used celebrities in filming *Faces of America*, which aired on PBS. When genealogy hit prime time, another surge of interest hit libraries and archives, as well as the Internet, and another generation of genealogists was born.

Who am I? Where did I come from? It is the quest for the answers to these questions that helps us discover who we are. Somehow, we feel our own identity is linked to our ancestors. When we were young, our identity was linked to the smaller world of our parents, grandparents, siblings, aunts and uncles, and cousins. We didn't venture much out of that realm. Much of our security and even a sense of family pride depended on our relationships with these people. As we have aged, our world has become wider and our experience with the world vaster. Now we have learned that, in addition to our living relatives, we had family who came before those still living—those who are now long deceased. These are called *ancestors*. Our curiosity about older generations of our families is but an extension of our search for identity and security. The memories we collect tell us who we are.

Learning about history also arouses our interest in family history. When I first visited the World War I museum in Kansas City, Missouri, I began to wonder about my own family's participation in that war. Did they play a part in that world event? What were their lives like during that time? We read about other wars, economic hard times, epidemics, and other historical events and wonder how our family fits in. Sometimes answers come as we sit around picnic tables at family reunions, or at weddings and funerals as we visit with relatives. As grandparents, aunts, uncles, and parents reminisce about the past, children begin to learn the stories of their family of long ago. However, in today's mobile and disjointed world, children are often unaware of near kinfolk or perhaps even the identity of one of their parents. When we don't have family stories to enrich our understanding of our forebears, the answers to questions about our ancestors' lives and roles come only through discovering those relatives in books and original records.

Learning about our ancestors helps us understand ourselves better. The process of genealogical research and its discoveries helped a friend of mine in such a way. Here is her story in her own words:

> My parents divorced when I was three years old. I was left in the custody of my father. I felt as though a dark, mysterious, unknown chasm lay ever before me in my life. I knew nothing of my mother's family tree, having been raised by my father and a stepmother. In fact, I questioned why God had given me such a birth mother, as her life was not very exemplary. Then, with a friend's help, we spent two years delving into the genealogy of my mother's side of the family. During that study, a longtime family mystery was solved and a new world was opened to me.
>
> I found I had four great, great, great, great-grandfathers who fought in the American Revolutionary War. A great, great, great-grandmother in Kentucky who birthed thirteen children, rode horseback throughout the mountains working as a midwife, and healed the locals with herbal remedies.

> I saw beyond my mother's generation to a well-respected
> family of founding forefathers and brave pioneers. A JOY
> filled my heart as the dark chasm was crossed, and the light
> of knowledge found in those genealogy books, microfilm,
> and on the computer changed my life forever.[2]

Through genealogical research we discover inherited traits that affect our own personality or health. As I look at photographs of my grandmother in her early years, I can see features which link with mine. Knowing that our hair or eye color and other physical traits were influenced by ancestors helps us recognize how firmly tied we are to past generations. This link to the past provides a measure of stability in a world filled with transient values and heroes. Our research may also benefit us by providing an early warning of health problems we or our children could inherit that might be avoided by taking timely precautions. This potentially unknown aspect of one's health history may be the impetus for beginning a genealogy research project. The surgeon general of the United States has created a free online tool for recording family health history to share with one's relatives. Entitled "My Family Health Portrait," it can be accessed at https://familyhistory.hhs.gov.

Who Are Genealogists?

A genealogist can be anyone: male or female, young or old, and of every ethnicity. In 2008 Scott Lucas, a doctoral candidate at Emporia State University, surveyed genealogists at three libraries: a public library, a proprietary library, and a historical/genealogical library. Lucas determined that the average genealogist is female and over 40, and often over 50, years old. The genealogical researchers surveyed had achieved a higher education level than the average person, and most traveled less than fifty miles to their research site. Members of the National Genealogical Society (NGS) often traveled farther and more often than members of other national historical organizations.[3] But this data does not limit the scope of those who pursue an interest in genealogy. The motivation to begin a genealogical journey can draw people of all ages, ethnicities, and genders. Genealogists are also avid in their avocation. In my many years as a genealogy librarian, I saw family history enthusiasts who came into the library every day. Others came once a week or once a month, but we considered them regular users of the library as we developed professional relationships with them. A frequent once-a-month visitor to the library once came with her husband to the facility, which was not a usual occurrence. The husband had the day off from work and decided to accompany his wife for what he thought was a couple of hours of research and then he would join her for lunch. About noon he wandered to the microfilm reader where she was busily engaged in her exploration. He asked her if she was ready to eat lunch. She kindly told him, "We do not each lunch when we come to the library." That was the last time he accompanied her on a research trip.

Where Does It All Begin?

We all have unknown facts in our family history. As we ponder those unknowns, it is helpful to discover what we already know. We find that out by writing down the known aspects of our forebears. The basics of beginning a genealogy project are as follows:

- Write down everything you already know (birth, death, and marriage information—also called vital records) about yourself, your parents, grandparents, and so on.
- Ask your immediate and extended family for information about themselves or their parents, grandparents, and so on.
- Look for documents in your own home or in the possession of your relatives.
- Search out documents that tell more about your ancestors in books, original records, and on web pages.

Genealogy, simply defined, is the study of one's family origins. More specifically, it is the history of a line of descent of a person, family, or group of ancestors. This can also be called *ancestry*. In genealogy, we seek to find ancestors. *Ancestors* are those family members who lived before you. Your parents, grandparents, and great-grandparents are your ancestors. You are a descendant of those ancestors. A *descendant* is one who lives after someone else. One's children, grandchildren, and great-grandchildren are descendants. A record of one's ancestors is called a *pedigree*. Anyone who is related to you but is not in your direct line of descent such as an aunt, uncle, or cousin is considered a collateral or allied relative.

Is It Genealogy or Family History?

A genealogist is concerned about his or her blood line. That individual's interest in research would be to discover his or her genealogy. Those who are interested in the full scope of their family with its collateral lines would be searching for family history. I will be using the terms *genealogy* and *family history* interchangeably. Each person determines the scope of his or her research. Everyone has their own specific goal in mind and decides when that goal has been completed.

Genealogy, as it has already been defined, is the study of a person's lineage. We search out the names of parents, grandparents, and great-grandparents and list them on a chart. We then continue to search for the names of the children of each generation, as well as the persons those children married. Since names are often repeated in each generation, dates and places of events in which those names are recorded help define each person. A genealogy, in its truest sense, identifies ancestors or descendants by showing their names, event dates, event places, and relationships.

Family history, on the other hand, is a study of our ancestors' or descendants' lives. Once the family historian has reconstructed a lineage using names, dates, and places, he or she then searches for stories, artifacts, records, social history, and other information that describe the activities and experiences of family members. Family history explores how people interacted with other family and community members, how they earned a living, and what they experienced and believed. Family historians search for any resource that will permit them to reconstruct their ancestors' lives within the world in which they lived. Within a family history, our forebears become defined not only in terms of names, dates, and places but also by what they did during their lives. We are looking for biographical information, but we are not creating a biography, per se.

Trying to define genealogy becomes increasingly more complex in our society today. In July 2011 the *New York Times* printed an article entitled "Who's on the Family Tree? Now It's Complicated."[4] The author points out the difficulty of defining relationships, family, and genealogy with children born via sperm donors, surrogate mothers, and same-sex partners as parents. "Some families now organize their family tree into two separate histories: genetic and emotional." These researchers face the same challenges that adoptees have had for many years. There may be unknowns in one's family tree that will never be discovered. Deciding on the scope of the project is a necessary first step when beginning a genealogical project.

Beyond Genealogies

Genealogists often become collectors of names. I have encountered many genealogy patrons who are proud of the number of names in their genealogy computer program. But a pursuit that consists solely of finding the names of ancestors does little to acquaint us with those forebears and the world in which they lived. Knowing the facts of birth, marriage, and death seldom satisfies the drive to relate our lives to the experiences of our progenitors. This is where family history comes in: it is the study of how ancestors lived and their relationships with people and institutions. The pursuit of family history helps us completely understand the names on our pedigree as individuals and makes them seem real to us. Compiling our genealogy is the first step in discovering the history of our family.

Until the late 1970s, few genealogies told the story of a family. Most consisted of traditional lineage and ancestor or descendant charts. But over the last forty years, more and more books use genealogies as a framework upon which to stretch the fabric of individual and family lives or family history. These latter publications are devoted to describing, interpreting, and comparing ancestors' lives with those of their contemporaries and of their descendants—us.

Family historians find out about ancestors' lives from interviews, family records, and other documents that teach us how historical events affected and changed (or did not change) the lives of our forebears. Knowing about our ancestors' health, the size and structure of their families, and how long they lived or from what they died will also help us to better understand them. Our ancestors were not passive observers of their time; they were involved in the world around them—politics, strikes against employers, controversies over religious or racial issues, and the founding of new towns and cities. Where did they stand, and how did they act out their feelings? The answers to these questions will help us understand history from a personal perspective that is seldom presented in textbooks. Many history teachers are now incorporating genealogy and oral history into their curriculums in order to help their students understand more about history. To learn even more, we can compare our ancestors' lives to those of their neighbors and even to contemporaries in other parts of the country. Like us, our progenitors were the products of their own place and time in history. We cannot relate to them unless we understand what it was like in their day.

Resources for Genealogy and Family History Research

The Records

The major obstacle to finding one's ancestors is knowing where to look for records about their lives. Sometimes these records can be found at home or with relatives. But often, we need to search books and records preserved in libraries, archives, historical societies, or government offices. Many documents, both digitized copies of the originals and transcribed records, are found on the Internet. Wherever one may look, the goal of genealogy research will be an understanding of one's ancestors and the places they lived, as well as the roles of local institutions in their lives as revealed through the records of those ancestors' interactions with those institutions.

Generally, a genealogist will search among three types of records to reconstruct the family's history: family records, the research results of others, and original records. These records may be found in someone's personal possession, in a records repository, in a research facility, or on the Internet. In this chapter, the three types of records are introduced to help you better understand the process your customers will use in re-creating their ancestors' lives. Each of these record types is explained in greater detail in subsequent chapters.

Research begins in the records you and other family members have. One should also conduct a survey to discover what other researchers have published or contributed to genealogical indexes, computer databases, or the Internet about one's family. Additionally, one can fill in the remaining gaps in a family's story by using original records such as censuses and birth, marriage, or death records.

Family Records

Family records are the certificates, heirlooms, stories, and other bits of family history found in one's own home or the homes and memories of one's relatives. Besides documents, they include the oral histories gathered by interviewing family members and their friends, neighbors, and coworkers. Although some people may have gaps in their memories of the past, many of their recollections may be true. Oral records must be evaluated for accuracy, as must any other sources used.

Published Records

When researchers take information from original and oral records, evaluate and enhance it, and then publish it, we have another type of resource: published records. Some genealogists have taken all the names and other personal data from vital records, cemetery records, and other original records and published them as research tools for others to use. An example is *The Original Lists of Persons of Quality . . . 1600–1700*.[5] The compiler created transcripts of original records which he found in the Public Records Office in England which list the names of people who legally left the shores of England for America. It is a wonderful source for those looking for ancestors who were colonial immigrants from England.

Such published research may have been contributed to genealogical or historical societies, libraries, newsletters or periodicals, or published in books. Although the term *research* evokes visions of dusty volumes on library shelves, it can also include the Internet, computer databases, card indexes, and pedigree and family chart files kept at local genealogical or historical societies and libraries. It is simply the research of other persons that has been made available to the public.

There are many other types of published sources that genealogists use: family and local histories, biographies, newspapers, and genealogies are examples. They describe events that generally took place many years before the history or genealogy was written. They may be based upon research found in original sources but are a later interpretation of those sources. Some of these family histories, genealogies, and biographies may have been published as books or Internet pages, while others may have remained in typescript or manuscript form.

Newspapers are printed matter that contain material that was generally current at the time of publication. One can find accounts of marriages, obituaries, local gossip, and other events and ephemera happening at the time. These publications are sometimes still in a paper format, but they are more likely to be preserved on microfilm or in electronic form.

Original Records

Under the term *original records* fall documents created by public (government) or private agencies to describe your ancestors or their activities. Birth certificates, marriage licenses, and wills probably come to mind as you think about original records. You will learn that churches, businesses, and clubs, as well as national and local government agencies, created many records that detail parts of your ancestors' lives.

Less frequently used sources can also be applied in family research. Court records will inform you of trials or lawsuits that involved your family. The minutes of town or religious councils may name your ancestors as participants in local events. Even if your family is not mentioned in records, such records will at least indicate what was happening in the community that may have touched your ancestors' lives.

Original records may be created at the time of an event or much later. Their purpose is the same no matter when they were created: to witness that an event took place and list those people involved. The birth and marriage records found at many county courts are examples of original sources. Sometimes an agency or institution will create a document that describes contemporary events, as well as some that took place many years before the document was created. These are original records, too. For example, a driver's license lists a person's birth date but was created many years after the person's birth. A death certificate describes the date and place of death, but it also contains information about the date and place of the deceased's birth or marriage. A census shows us where a family lived and those persons who were in the household, but it may also list the ages and birthplaces of these persons.

Reference Sources

Reference sources such as gazetteers, history books, and encyclopedias, both in print and online, are important in researching and writing a family history. These sources describe the places where ancestors lived and what happened during their stay there. Reference books may also explain where to look for original records or other resources. For example, *The Handy Book for Genealogists*[6] is a book you might use to learn more about the records created in the places where your ancestors lived. Even though it has not had an update since 2006, it is still a viable source. To find the location of a town or village, use a gazetteer. To locate the nearest historical society, you might look in the *Directory of Historical Societies and Agencies in the United States and Canada*.[7] The following chapters will help you identify reference books and published resources that will make the search for records easier and your interpretation of them more precise.

The Internet

The Internet is often the starting place where genealogists look today to find information. No longer must one have to find a repository for the information he or she is seeking. Finding information online has become easier and sources more plentiful. The Internet makes available an entire world of knowledge at one's fingertips. You can find transcriptions of records, digitized original records, compiled pedigrees, and numerous databases containing information. The Internet has not changed the principles of sound genealogical research, however, so evaluating each source you find on the Web is the key to good documentation.

Evaluating the Accuracy of Sources

Regardless of the sources you consult, be critical of their accuracy. Were original sources prepared by eyewitnesses? Did the people interviewed have a chance to see the events they describe? Were they near the people who were eyewitnesses? Do published sources agree with what you know from research in original records or from reading the books of knowledgeable authors? Do you note a bias in any resource that might make it less accurate? Let's look at an example of this concept. John and Joe are driving their separate cars. John is driving through an intersection and Joe is turning left at the intersection but coming toward John in the opposite direction. John's car hits Joe's car. There are three witnesses to the accident. Nancy was in her car immediately behind Joe. Jim was just coming out of a coffee shop on the corner when the accident occurred. Melissa was standing at the corner talking on her cell phone. Joe and John both have firsthand knowledge of the event, but either one's account may be biased because they were intimately involved. Nancy, Jim, and Melissa each saw the accident, but none saw it from the same perspective. Let's say a newspaper reporter interviews just one of the witnesses for a story. Will she be able to report it accurately? Can we rely on the newspaper article for complete and accurate information?

Any source may provide correct or incorrect information. Original sources created by eyewitnesses when the event occurred are preferred because they have a higher probability of being accurate. Sources created after an event should not be discounted, however, because they may be more accurate than some contemporary ones. Should you prefer the testimony of living witnesses over contemporary written sources? That depends on the accuracy of your informant's recollections. The key to success in using oral history is the verification of testimony. People's memories only contain what they have observed, heard, or felt. Sometimes they have been given false information by others. On some occasions, they may not have observed an event accurately, storing incorrect data in their memories. Then, too, there is always the danger that they have simply forgotten the facts, and attempts to recall them have created a less-than-accurate image of the past. In the previous scenario, will Joe or John or any of the witnesses relate an accurate account of the accident? At the same time, remember that most official documents are simply the observations of human beings recorded for future use; therefore, official printed documents can be erroneous too. Through careful interviewing and subsequent verification, the recollections of living witnesses become essential elements in discovering a family's story.

Verifying the Evidence You Gather

To verify any record, written or oral, you should compare it with at least two other sources. If you conduct an oral history, have the person comment on events surrounding the incident of interest to you and compare the description with what you can find in local newspapers or other sources. Interviews with other witnesses to the events can also be used to verify what the first informant said.

What do you do if none of the sources agree with each other? If you were called to jury duty in your community, you would face a similar challenge. The defense and prosecution would present the jury with their views of events and outcomes. Often each side's story conflicts with the other. Whom do you believe? It generally boils down to one's evaluation of the reliability of the witnesses and evidence. The issues are the same in genealogical and historical research. In genealogy, we refer to the Genealogical Proof Standard as the basis for accepting documents or testimony as fact. There will be more about this standard in chapter 6.

When the evidence gives conflicting information, researchers generally prefer the sources created nearest the event in question and have more confidence in records based on testimony from eyewitnesses. If you do not have eyewitness testimony, then you must consider how close the relationship was between your informant and an eyewitness to the event. It is likely that a son's information about his parents' marriage would be more accurate than a great-grandson's information. Generally, sources created near the time of an event are the best sources to use.

In researching and preparing a family history, one will find many different, and often conflicting, pieces of information. Finding the resources and using them to their best potential are the most difficult part of genealogical research. In the pages that follow, you will learn which sources to use, how to find them, and how to interpret them. Genealogical research is fun and addictive, but it is also intensive work. However, on the journey researchers will discover things about themselves and their heritage, preserve the past, and leave a legacy to their family. That's priceless.

LESSON ONE

1. Review the definitions for *ancestor, descendant,* and *pedigree.*
2. What is the difference between genealogy and family history?
3. What are the basic steps in conducting a genealogy project?

NOTES

1. Alex Haley, *Roots* (New York: Doubleday, 1976).

2. Interview with Judith Hawley, January 2017.

3. Scott Anthony Lucas, *The Information Seeking Processes of Genealogists* (Emporia, KS: S. A. Lucas, 2008), 41.

4. Laura M. Holston, "Who's on the Family Tree? Now It's Complicated," *New York Times*, July 5, 2011, A-1.

5. John Camden Hotten, *The Original Lists of Persons of Quality, Emigrants, Religious Exiles, Political Rebels, Serving Men Sold for a Term of Years, Apprentices, Children Stolen, Maidens Pressed, and Others Who Went from Great Britain to the American Plantations, 1600–1700: With Their Ages, the Localities Where They Formerly Lived in the Mother Country, the Names of the Ships in Which They Embarked, and Other Interesting Particulars, from Mss. Preserved in the State Paper Department of Her Majesty's Public Record Office, England* (Baltimore, MD: Genealogical Publishing Co., 1962).

6. *The Handy Book for Genealogists*, 11th ed. (Baltimore, MD: Genealogical Publishing Co., 2006).

7. *Directory of Historical Societies and Agencies in the United States and Canada*, 15th ed. (Madison, WI: American Association for State and Local History, 2002).

Genealogy 101

Taking the Journey into the Past

Accurate genealogical research is based upon the principles illustrated in the steps mentioned in the last chapter. Genealogy begins with the present and goes backward in time to the past. One should use sources that are reliable. Eyewitness or firsthand accounts are best. You have heard of the undesirability of hearsay evidence in courts of law. Instead, attorneys want the most reliable and credible firsthand witnesses to win their cases. Similarly, if we are going to create a reliable pedigree, we need to use reliable sources. We also need to avoid confusion by going backward in time and gathering sources along the way. Often people will find their surname in history, perhaps a signer of the Declaration of Independence, and desire to know if that person is a part of their family line. It is very difficult to start in the past and go forward in time because it becomes very complicated. Each generation had children, and those children had children. Soon the genealogical line becomes like a spreading tree—there are so many branches to trace that one is left in frustration. It is far easier to move from now back to the past. Each generation provides clues to the previous generation. For example, if one finds an ancestor on a census record, the document will give each person's age and where they were born. If John Smith, an eight-year-old child in Indiana, has a father who is thirty-one and was born in Massachusetts, then you know to look for the father as a child thirty-one years earlier in Massachusetts records.

Research begins with an analysis of what is already known. By starting with the living generation and working backward, the researcher will learn how much is already known about members of ancestral families in each generation. A generation begins with a family unit: father, mother, and children. There does not have to be a marriage for it to be a family unit and a generation. The next generation begins when those children marry and have their own families. Try to encourage your patron to avoid becoming a name collector—a person who records names and dates and nothing else. Even worse is finding a pedigree online and adopting it as one's own pedigree without the benefit of analysis and critical evaluation. In the pursuit of finding the names of our ancestors, we need to take the time to get to know each one and learn about the environment and community in which he or she lived.

As we go backward from the present to the past, one should begin recording the names of each generation on a pedigree chart, into a genealogy software program, or an online family tree. The research should begin by identifying the family members you already know. When using a printed chart (see figure 2.1), it is best to use a pencil to record the information. When I was the manager of the Midwest Genealogy Center, we kept a stack of blank pedigree charts at the service desks. When conducting a reference interview with someone seeking genealogical data, for example, the pedigree chart and the dialogue that occurs are a good basis for beginning the interview and finding out what information the patron already knows. The interview would proceed somewhat like this:

1. What is your full name? What is your first, middle, and last name (also called a *surname*)? All surnames should always be recorded in all-uppercase letters. (Recording surnames in uppercase letters helps alleviate confusion when a surname could also be a given name, such as Anthony.) Women will record their maiden name as their surname. All the women in a pedigree will be recorded with maiden names.

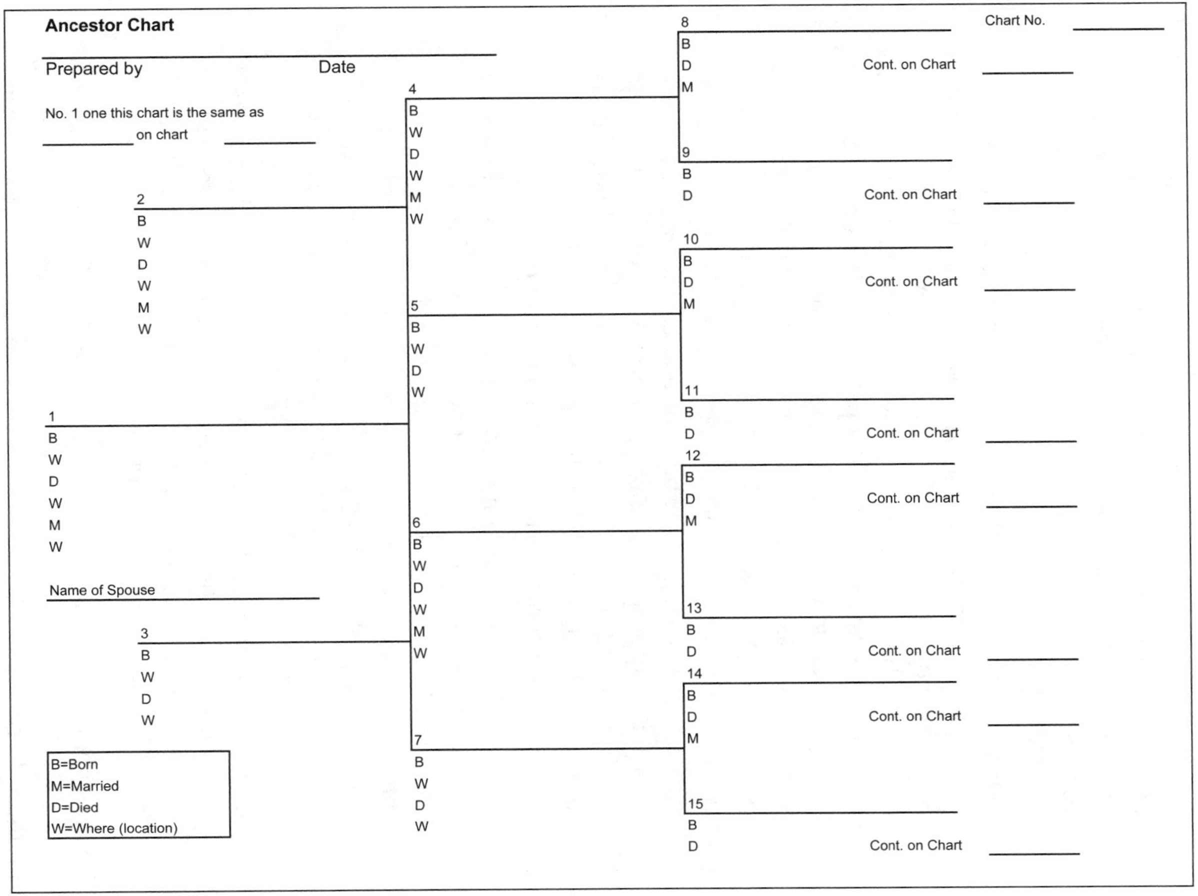

Ancestor Chart

Prepared by _____ Date _____

No. 1 one this chart is the same as
_____ on chart

2
B
W
D
W
M
W

1
B
W
D
W
M
W

Name of Spouse _____

3
B
W
D
W

B=Born
M=Married
D=Died
W=Where (location)

4
B
W
D
W
M
W

5
B
W
D
W

6
B
W
D
W
M
W

7
B
W
D
W

8
B
D
M

Cont. on Chart _____

9
B
D

Cont. on Chart _____

10
B
D
M

Cont. on Chart _____

11
B
D

Cont. on Chart _____

12
B
D
M

Cont. on Chart _____

13
B
D

Cont. on Chart _____

14
B
D
M

Cont. on Chart _____

15
B
D

Cont. on Chart _____

Chart No. _____

FIGURE 2.1 Printed ancestor chart

2. If someone is filling out his or her own pedigree chart, the next piece of information will be that person's date and place of birth. I don't ask that information during a reference interview because I don't want to seem intrusive. It can be added by the individual later.

3. What is the full name of your father? On a numbered pedigree chart, you are number one and your father is number two. Males from this point forward will be the even-numbered people on the chart. The females will be the odd-numbered individuals. Write the information about the patron's father on the number 2 line, including his place and date of birth (if known), the date and place of his marriage to the patron's mother (if a marriage occurred), and the date and place of his death (if appropriate).

4. What is the full name of your mother? She will be number three on the chart. Write down her full maiden name. Again, write down the appropriate known information of her birth and death. You will note that on a printed pedigree chart, the date and place of marriage is not shown under the mother's name. It will only be recorded under the father's name.

5. Continue to go back in time, recording the full name of each individual ancestor—first, last, and middle names. Record the dates and places of births, deaths, and marriages, where known. The information the patron is lacking for individuals and names of ancestors in past generations will soon be noticeable and will be the information the patron will seek in the genealogical research process. (See an example of a completed chart in figure 2.2.)

6. In a traditional pedigree, the names recorded are the names in one's blood line. Those who were adopted can choose to record the adoptive family's line, if that is most meaningful, but one's biological family is the true pedigree.

Note the pedigree of Harry Truman in figure 2.2. Truman was born 8 May 1884. Genealogists often record the date European style—day, month, and year. Whatever style you choose in recording the information, make sure that you spell out the name of the month. Writing out the name of the month will eliminate confusion should you choose to write the date format differently than another person might expect. On a Swedish church record my grandfather's birth is recorded 10–12–82.

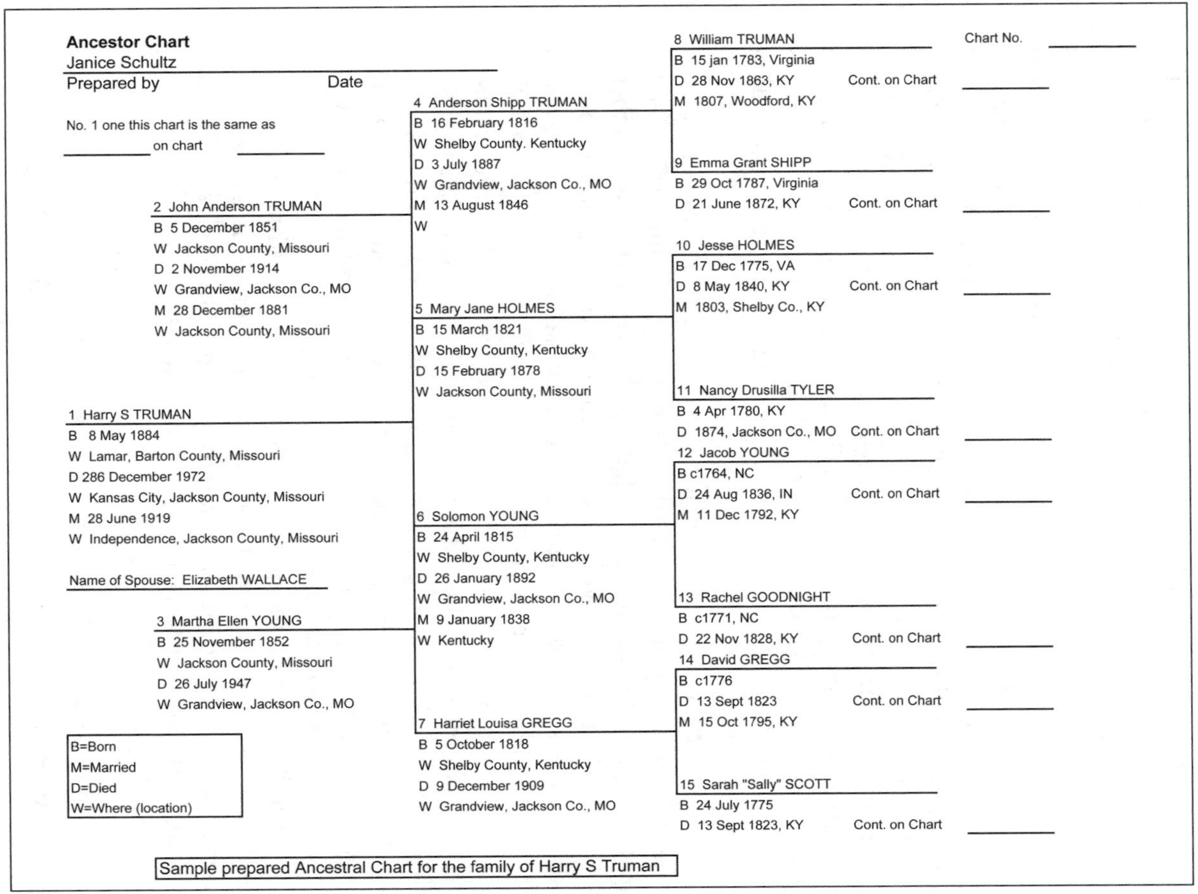

Ancestor Chart

Janice Schultz

Prepared by _____ Date _____

Chart No. _____

No. 1 one this chart is the same as _____ on chart _____

```
8 William TRUMAN
  B 15 Jan 1783, Virginia
  D 28 Nov 1863, KY                    Cont. on Chart
  M 1807, Woodford, KY

4 Anderson Shipp TRUMAN
  B 16 February 1816
  W Shelby County, Kentucky
  D 3 July 1887
  W Grandview, Jackson Co., MO
  M 13 August 1846                     9 Emma Grant SHIPP
  W                                      B 29 Oct 1787, Virginia
                                         D 21 June 1872, KY         Cont. on Chart

2 John Anderson TRUMAN
  B 5 December 1851
  W Jackson County, Missouri           10 Jesse HOLMES
  D 2 November 1914                       B 17 Dec 1775, VA
  W Grandview, Jackson Co., MO            D 8 May 1840, KY          Cont. on Chart
  M 28 December 1881                      M 1803, Shelby Co., KY
  W Jackson County, Missouri

5 Mary Jane HOLMES
  B 15 March 1821
  W Shelby County, Kentucky
  D 15 February 1878
  W Jackson County, Missouri           11 Nancy Drusilla TYLER
                                         B 4 Apr 1780, KY
1 Harry S TRUMAN                         D 1874, Jackson Co., MO    Cont. on Chart
  B 8 May 1884
  W Lamar, Barton County, Missouri     12 Jacob YOUNG
  D 286 December 1972                     B c1764, NC
  W Kansas City, Jackson County, Missouri  D 24 Aug 1836, IN       Cont. on Chart
  M 28 June 1919                          M 11 Dec 1792, KY
  W Independence, Jackson County, Missouri

6 Solomon YOUNG
  B 24 April 1815
  W Shelby County, Kentucky            13 Rachel GOODNIGHT
  D 26 January 1892                      B c1771, NC
  W Grandview, Jackson Co., MO           D 22 Nov 1828, KY         Cont. on Chart

Name of Spouse: Elizabeth WALLACE     14 David GREGG
                                         B c1776
3 Martha Ellen YOUNG                     D 13 Sept 1823            Cont. on Chart
  B 25 November 1852                      M 15 Oct 1795, KY
  W Jackson County, Missouri
  D 26 July 1947
  W Grandview, Jackson Co., MO

7 Harriet Louisa GREGG
  B 5 October 1818
  W Shelby County, Kentucky            15 Sarah "Sally" SCOTT
  D 9 December 1909                      B 24 July 1775
  W Grandview, Jackson Co., MO          D 13 Sept 1823, KY         Cont. on Chart
```

B=Born
M=Married
D=Died
W=Where (location)

Sample prepared Ancestral Chart for the family of Harry S Truman

FIGURE 2.2 Completed ancestor chart

19

He was born the 10th of December in 1882 (European style), not the 12th of October as some Americans might think. This could have caused a problem for me when I recorded the information onto my pedigree, but I knew his date of birth, so I was not confused. But you don't want to confuse others looking at the pedigree later. Do them a favor and write out the name of the month. It is also important to include four digits for the year in which the event occurred. You and your patron will be looking for records in various centuries, so don't confuse the situation for others who might look at the ancestor chart later and wonder which century a two-digit number stands for.

Going back to figure 2.2, you will note that all of Harry Truman's vital information is recorded—birth, death, and marriage. His wife's name is included as "spouse," but her pedigree and vital information are not shown.

Harry Truman's father was John Anderson Truman, number 2 on the chart. Harry's mother, Martha Ellen Young, is number 3. Harry's paternal grandfather, his father's father, is two times two, or number 4. His father's mother is two times two plus one, or number 5. Each person's father's number is double the number that person is on the chart, and the mother's number is doubled plus one. Should the researcher decide to continue recording names in the Truman line after William Truman, number 8 on the chart, then another chart would be prepared with William Truman appearing on line one of the second chart. The first chart would be chart number one and the second would be chart number two. At the top of the second chart the researcher would write "No. 1 on this chart is the same as No. 8 on chart 1."

Another way to record the pedigree is on an Ahnentafel chart. *Ahnentafel* is a German word that means *ancestor table*. It is a very easy, basic way of organizing one's family pedigree. In the Harry Truman example, the Ahnentafel chart would look like this:

1. Harry Truman
2. John Anderson Truman
3. Martha Ellen Young
4. Anderson Shipp Truman
5. Mary Jane Holmes
6. Solomon Young
7. Harriet Louisa Gregg
8. William Truman
9. Emma Grant Shipp
10. Jesse Holmes
11. Nancy Drusilla Tyler
12. Jacob Young

13. Rachel Goodnight   15. Sarah Scott

14. David Gregg

The numbers would continue for as many generations as there is information. You may see charts like this as you look at other people's genealogies. Knowing what those numbers mean will help you understand the information as it is presented.

As you help the patron enter information into the ancestor chart, what the patron thinks he or she knows may or may not be correct. I always use a pencil when entering information onto my working sheet to facilitate subsequent erasures and changes. Whenever data is lacking, the discovery of the life events for those people becomes the research objective:

- Where and when were they born, and to whom and when were they married?
- What were their lives like?
- Who were their parents?

By making the discovery of information about a specific person's research goal, a genealogist can define the scope of his or her efforts in terms of the relevant time period and locality. This is where the patron will begin the research process. To supply whatever data is missing or lacking is the goal.

As mentioned earlier, having some blank pedigree charts handy for the reference interview is a good idea. You can find blank charts at no cost online.

- Ancestry.com offers various printable charts at www.ancestry.com/trees/charts/ancchart.aspx?/.
- The Midwest Genealogy Center also offers various forms at www.mymcpl.org/genealogy/family-history -forms. The forms can be printed blank, or one can fill in the data and then print the form to include the inserted data.
- A site called Ancestors, www.byub.org/ancestors/ charts/, contains various forms. They, too, can be printed blank or filled in.

Developing Family Group Records

After helping the patron fill out a pedigree chart, the next step is to fill out family group sheets, which are also called family unit charts, family group records, or biological unit charts. (See figure 2.3.) You may have noticed that the pedigree chart showed only the patron's direct lineage. But families in each generation usually had more than one child, which create additional branches of the tree. Ask the patron to fill out a family group sheet for each generation in his or her pedigree. Record the name of the father with the dates and places of birth, death, and marriage, and that of the mother with the dates and places of her birth and death. There is a place under each person for the names of parents and other spouses. Record the children in the places provided under the parents' names, in birth order. The information for their births, deaths, and marriages should be recorded, along with the name of each child's spouse (if known). Record only the children who were a result of that union. If there were multiple marriages or partners, include each family unit on a separate family group sheet with the names of the children who were a result of that union.

A good example of using family group sheets for organizational purposes is shown in this example of my husband's great-grandmother, Ella Windt. She is recorded on four family group sheets. The first shows her as the oldest child of Klaas and Christina Windt. (See figure 2.4.)

The second shows her as a spouse to Fred Williams, listing their only daughter, Evelyn. (See figure 2.5.)

The third family group record shows Ella with her second husband, Louis Kunst, and the four children who were a part of that

FAMILY GROUP SHEET

HUSBAND

	DATE (DAY-MONTH-YEAR)	LOCATON (CITY/TWP-COUNTY-STATE-COUNTRY)
Birth		
Marriage		
Death		
Burial		
Father's Full Name		
Mother's Full Name		
Other Wives' Names		

WIFE

	DATE (DAY-MONTH-YEAR)	LOCATON (CITY/TWP-COUNTY-STATE-COUNTRY)
Birth		
Marriage		
Death		
Burial		
Father's Full Name		
Mother's Full Name		
Other Husbands' Names		

CHILDREN

	DATE (DAY-MONTH-YEAR)	LOCATON (CITY/TWP-COUNTY-STATE-COUNTRY)
	B	
(Child #1)	M	
	D	
	Spouse	
	B	
(Child #2)	M	
	D	
	Spouse	
	B	
(Child #3)	M	
	D	
	Spouse	
	B	
(Child #4)	M	
	D	
	Spouse	
	B	
(Child #5)	M	
	D	
	Spouse	
	B	
(Child #6)	M	
	D	
	Spouse	
	B	
(Child #7)	M	
	D	
	Spouse	

FIGURE 2.3

Family group sheet

FAMILY GROUP SHEET

HUSBAND   Klas H. WINDT

	DATE (DAY-MONTH-YEAR)	LOCATON (CITY/TWP-COUNTY-STATE-COUNTRY)
Birth	February 1852	Netherlands
Marriage	1883	Netherlands
Death	.	
Burial		
Father's Full Name		
Mother's Full Name		
Other Wives' Names		

WIFE   Christina WOLBERS

	DATE (DAY-MONTH-YEAR)	LOCATON (CITY/TWP-COUNTY-STATE-COUNTRY)
Birth	March 1860	Netherlands
Death		
Burial		
Father's Full Name		
Mother's Full Name		
Other Husbands' Names		

CHILDREN

	DATE (DAY-MONTH-YEAR)	LOCATON (CITY/TWP-COUNTY-STATE-COUNTRY)
Ella K.	B 30 May 1883	Vriesland, Netherlands
(Child #1)	M1 25 September 1902	Grand Rapids, Kent Co., Michigan
	D 22 March 1978	Grand Rapids, Kent Co., Michigan
	Spouse (1) Fred WILLIAMS; (2) Louis KUNST; (3) William Van Asselt	
Christian	B April 1885	Netherlands
(Child #2)	M	
	D	
	Spouse	
Garrett	B February 1887	Netherlands
(Child #3)	M	
	D	
	Spouse	
Herman	B April 1891	Netherlands
(Child #4)	M	
	D	
	Spouse	
Klas	B April 1891	Netherlands
(Child #5)	M	
	D	
	Spouse	
Hendrick (Henry)	B January 1894	Michigan
(Child #6)	M	
	D	
	Spouse	
Hendricka	B Nov 1899	Michigan
(Child #7)	M	
	D	
	Spouse	

FIGURE 2.4

Completed family group sheet

FAMILY GROUP SHEET

HUSBAND   Fred E. WILLIAMS

	DATE (DAY-MONTH-YEAR)	LOCATON (CITY/TWP-COUNTY-STATE-COUNTRY)
Birth	7 May 1877	Sylvan, Osceola, Michigan
Marriage	25 Sept. 1902	Grand Rapids, Kent, Michigan
Death	28 Aug. 1913	Mountain Home, Washington, Tennessee
Burial		
Father's Full Name	Warren WILLIAMS	
Mother's Full Name	Lora NORTON	
Other Wives' Names		

WIFE   Ella K. WINDT

	DATE (DAY-MONTH-YEAR)	LOCATON (CITY/TWP-COUNTY-STATE-COUNTRY)
Birth	30 May 1883	Netherlands
Marriage		
Death	22 Mar. 1978	Grand Rapids, Kent, Michigan
Burial		
Father's Full Name	Klas WINDT	
Mother's Full Name	Christina WOLBERS	
Other Husbands' Names	Louis KUNST, William VAN ASSELT	

CHILDREN

		DATE (DAY-MONTH-YEAR)	LOCATON (CITY/TWP-COUNTY-STATE-COUNTRY)
Evelyn May	B	17 Feb. 1904	Grand Rapids, Kent, Michigan
(Child #1)	M		
	D	Nov. 1987	Grand Rapids, Kent, Michigan
	Spouse	Herbert MEYERS	
(Child #2)	B		
	M		
	D		
	Spouse		
(Child #3)	B		
	M		
	D		
	Spouse		
(Child #4)	B		
	M		
	D		
	Spouse		
(Child #5)	B		
	M		
	D		
	Spouse		
(Child #6)	B		
	M		
	D		
	Spouse		
(Child #7)	B		
	M		
	D		
	Spouse		

FIGURE 2.5

Completed family group sheet

union. (See figure 2.6.) You will notice that there are two people named Louis Kunst; father and son. We commonly refer to people within the same family who bear the same name as senior and junior, or maybe II. In your genealogy, you need not insert the suffix, as each person is recorded and identified by the years in which they lived or flourished. For example: Louis Kunst (1877–) refers to Louis senior, the father of Louis (1908–).

The fourth family group sheet shows Ella with her third husband, William Van Asselt. (See figure 2.7.)

There were no children who were a part of this union. By looking at all of the family group records, you can easily see which child is a result of which marriage.

Make a habit of citing the source of the information for each entry in the space provided for sources at the bottom of the family group record. If there is insufficient space, continue your notes on the reverse side. A brief entry or a footnote is all that is needed. If the information about a person or event has come from a death certificate, your source would read: "Information about father from death certificate from [name of state] Department of Health, [date]." Knowing the date the information was received or found and the name of the information provider will guide others to the source you used. The source you use will also help others determine the validity of the information you have placed in your pedigree or family group record. Advise your patron to make it a practice to record the source of the information every time a name, place, or event is recorded. For those using genealogy computer software, ample space is provided for notes and sources.

LESSON THREE

Fill in a family group sheet for one of the family units in your pedigree. Use figure 2.3 or print a chart from an online source.

Organizing Data

The use of paper genealogy forms is waning among genealogists. It is much easier, and often more convenient, to use a genealogy software program for recording and organizing your family records. Since the software will reside on one's computer hard drive, the data cannot

FAMILY GROUP SHEET

HUSBAND **Louis KUNST**

	DATE (DAY-MONTH-YEAR)	LOCATON (CITY/TWP-COUNTY-STATE-COUNTRY)
Birth	1877	Michigan
Marriage	19 Sept. 1907	Grand Rapids, Kent, Michigan
Death		
Burial		
Father's Full Name	Adrian KUNST	
Mother's Full Name	Mary VAN OEVEREN	
Other Wives' Names		

WIFE **Ella K. WINDT**

	DATE (DAY-MONTH-YEAR)	LOCATON (CITY/TWP-COUNTY-STATE-COUNTRY)
Birth	30 May 1883	Netherlands
Marriage		
Death	22 Mar. 1978	Grand Rapids, Kent, Michigan
Burial		
Father's Full Name	Louis KUNST	
Mother's Full Name	Christina WOLBERS	
Other Husbands' Names	Fred E. WILLIAMS, William VAN ASSELT	

CHILDREN

		DATE (DAY-MONTH-YEAR)	LOCATON (CITY/TWP-COUNTY-STATE-COUNTRY)
Louis	B	1908	Michigan
(Child #1)	M		
	D		
	Spouse		
Christine	B	1912	Michigan
(Child #2)	M		
	D		
	Spouse		
Edward	B	1916	Michigan
(Child #3)	M		
	D		
	Spouse		
Eleanor J.	B	22 Aug. 1923	Michigan
(Child #4)	M		
	D		
	Spouse		
	B		
(Child #5)	M		
	D		
	Spouse		
	B		
(Child #6)	M		
	D		
	Spouse		
	B		
(Child #7)	M		
	D		
	Spouse		

FIGURE 2.6

Completed family group sheet

27

FAMILY GROUP SHEET

HUSBAND   William VAN ASSELT

	DATE (DAY-MONTH-YEAR)	LOCATON (CITY/TWP-COUNTY-STATE-COUNTRY)
Birth	30 March 1880	Michigan
Marriage		
Death	1965	Michigan
Burial		
Father's Full Name		
Mother's Full Name		
Other Wives' Names		

WIFE   Ella K. WINDT

	DATE (DAY-MONTH-YEAR)	LOCATON (CITY/TWP-COUNTY-STATE-COUNTRY)
Birth	30 May 1883	Netherlands
Marriage		
Death	22 Mar. 1978	Grand Rapids, Kent, Michigan
Burial		
Father's Full Name	Klas WINDT	
Mother's Full Name	Christina WOLBERS	
Other Husbands' Names	Fred E. WILLIAMS, Louis KUNST	

CHILDREN

	DATE (DAY-MONTH-YEAR)	LOCATON (CITY/TWP-COUNTY-STATE-COUNTRY)
	B	
(Child #1)	M	
	D	
	Spouse	
	B	
(Child #2)	M	
	D	
	Spouse	
	B	
(Child #3)	M	
	D	
	Spouse	
	B	
(Child #4)	M	
	D	
	Spouse	
	B	
(Child #5)	M	
	D	
	Spouse	
	B	
(Child #6)	M	
	D	
	Spouse	
	B	
(Child #7)	M	
	D	
	Spouse	

FIGURE 2.7

Completed family group sheet

be changed or compromised by anyone else, unless they have access to that computer. The best feature of today's software is that one can connect to major online websites that give clues to where one might find more information for an ancestor. For instance, in my genealogy program I have selected FamilySearch.org as a site from which I would like to get clues. Adding photos is another feature found in most software options. There are several programs available, though it is impossible to list here the names of all the available genealogy software:

Ancestral Quest (www.ancquest.com) is available for purchase but also offers a basic version of their product as a free download. It allows you to create your family tree, cite your sources, create multimedia scrapbooks, do research on the Internet, share your information on the Web, publish a family book, and record unlimited events for each person in your tree. It also offers a portable version to take with you on a flash drive or other portable electronic device.

Family Tree Maker (www.mckiev.com) was formerly produced by Ancestry.com and is now offered by Software MacKiev. The software will give you hints that will link you to online clues, will sync to your Ancestry.com online tree, offers a variety of colorful charts, and gives you access to online maps.

Legacy Family Tree (www.legacyfamilytree.com) offers a free download or gives the option of a deluxe version for purchase. The deluxe version offers several reports, mapping, easy source citation, ability to attach any type of document, research guidance, and linking to FamilySearch.org and Ancestry.com.

Roots Magic (www.rootsmagic.com) is available for purchase but has an "essentials" version that is available as a free download. The program offers six main screen views, gives web hints to genealogy records on FamilySearch and MyHeritage, offers numerous printed reports, the ability to publish your family book in print or online, create sharable CDs, and offers a portable option via your flash drive.

All genealogy software programs speak the same computer language—GEDCOM, an acronym which stands for Genealogical Data

Communication. This allows one to change to another software program if one chooses to upgrade or if the program chosen is not to one's liking. One can also share that information with other family members, no matter what program they might be using.

Putting data into one of the programs is simple. Just enter a name and the dates and places of vital records into the software program. You can add a spouse, parents, and children to that person's record. Each person is linked to another person. The benefit of using software is being able to generate a variety of reports from your data. One can easily create a pedigree or family group sheet depending on the option selected. Many of the programs allow the user to input photographs. Should the user want to create a genealogy book, most programs will format the data into simple sentences, generate a table of contents, and create an index. Genealogy programs come and go, so you may have to search online for the most current genealogy software programs. Cyndi's List (http://cyndislist.com/software) has a list of genealogy programs, but it includes some which are no longer being produced, so look carefully at the choices. Dick Eastman's blog, *Eastman's Online Genealogy Newsletter* (http://blog.eogn.com), often has reviews of genealogy software. Search his past newsletters for "software reviews" to find reviews of the latest programs. You can also search past newsletters for the name of a specific software program you may be considering.

Using an online family tree has become an increasingly popular option for many genealogists. An online tree has several advantages: you need not invest in a software program with the constant need to upgrade the product, it is able to be viewed by others in the genealogical community, and the information is able to be viewed by the creator of the tree wherever he or she may be, giving access to the data when one is at a research facility with computer or Wi-Fi access. Some popular options are the following ones:

- Ancestry.com offers an online family tree to its subscribers. As one builds the tree, Ancestry gives clues to sources within its site where those names occur. Nonsubscribers may also create a tree, but they cannot view the data within the hints. The option is not available within AncestryLibraryEdition (ALE).

- FamilySearch.org allows individuals to create a free account for building an online tree with hints to records on its site.

- MyHeritage.com offers a free account to create a tree and search records. But to view the complete documents one must subscribe to the site.

- Findmypast.com also allows you to build a family tree online for free. To view the hints one must subscribe to the site.

The list of other online family trees is numerous, and as usual, sites come and go. A list of online family trees can be found at www.cyn dislist.com/family-trees/online-family-trees. Each site password protects a person's personal pedigree.

Nothing, however, is perfect. Online family trees can be a good way to record and share information, but there are inherent problems. The trees are only reliable if those who created them are good researchers who have checked the facts and included only documented information. The online trees are a great place to get clues, but I never rely on them as fact. They should not be used as a cited source within your pedigree. One must carefully analyze the clues to ensure the information you see is correct. You will often find conflicting data.

Oral History

We can discover information and stories about our family from other family members. Oral history is a process of collecting stories from living people about their own experiences or about their memories of people they have known. An interviewer will record the information of the person being interviewed by taking written notes or by an audio or video recording. The process begins by choosing the subject of the interview. It is a good idea to interview all your older family members while they are still living—parents, grandparents, aunts, uncles, siblings, and cousins. The availability of older family members depends on how old one is when he or she begins researching and which family members are still alive.

Before the interview, determine the information desired and formulate questions to achieve the goal. The goal may be to learn about one's family's experiences during the Great Depression. Perhaps the interviews will center around everyone who knew one specific ancestor and recording those stories which relate to him or her. Maybe you want to record a person's life story. Whatever the purpose or focus of the interviews, one should try to stay on target and select interviewed subjects accordingly. Questions should be prepared in advance, but the interviewer should be flexible. The interviewee may go off on a different tangent, but if it is deemed worthwhile, let the conversation continue. If the direction of the interview is not going in the right direction, steer the interviewee back on course.

The knowledge that living people have about ancestors and past events cannot be duplicated. Tidbits about people's habits, interests, physical traits—all of these can add a great deal of information about those names on our pedigree. Take the case of my husband's grandmother, Evelyn Meyers. She shared information about her own grandparents, long ago deceased. She stated, "Grandpa was very small and dear. Grandma should have been a man—very large and meaner than dirt to grandpa. If he didn't mind her, she hit him over the head with an iron frying pan."[1] Where else can you find that kind of information? Even though I never saw a photograph of her grandparents, with that description I can now picture them in my mind and I can imagine their personalities.

An example of oral histories in the making can be found at the StoryCorps website at http://storycorps.org. StoryCorps is an initiative to record the living history of America through a partnership between National Public Radio and the Library of Congress. Since 2003, this organization has been traveling the country in Airstream trailers and recording the oral histories of everyday people. Visit the StoryCorps website to read more about the project, hear the stories, and discover their list of "Great Questions." Just click on "participate" and scroll down to their great questions. The Library of Congress also has an online Veterans History Project at www.loc.gov/vets, which records the stories of American military veterans. You can find numerous websites that give examples of oral history questions and guidelines for conducting oral history interviews. Since the URLs constantly change, it is best to use a search engine using "oral history" as your search term to find these sites.

Here is a selected bibliography of publications that talk about oral history in depth:

Bryson, Anna, et al. *The Routledge Guide to Interviewing: Oral History, Social Enquiry and Investigation*. London: Routledge, 2014.

Delaplane, Kristin. *Storytelling: How to Write an Inspiring Memoir, Oral History, or Family Genealogy*. Tucson, AZ: Our American Stories, 2015.

Hunter, Nick. *Talking about the Past*. Chicago: Heinemann Library, 2015.

MacEntee, Thomas. *Preserving Your Family's Oral History and Stories*. St. Agnes, South Australia: Unlock the Past, 2014.

Schmidt, Josiah. *2000 Questions for Grandparents: Unlocking Your Family's Hidden History*. Emmetsburg, IA: Schmidt General Publishing; Lexington, KY: Lulu, 2014.

Smith, M. J. Rutherford. *Colouring in the Leaves: Questions to Ask Family Members When Interviewing Them about Their Personal History*. Toronto, ON: Ontario Genealogical Society, 2010.

Smith, Nicka. *The Ultimate Family History Interview Primer*. United States: Nicka Smith, 2016.

Sommer, Barbara W. *Doing Veterans Oral History*. New York: Oral History Association, 2015.

Family Heirlooms

Treasures in one's family's attic or family heirlooms can give clues about ancestors. Information about our family's history can be found in attics, basements, filing cabinets, home offices, or even historical societies. These items may be in your own possession or in the hands of close relatives. Taking the time to ask family members what heirlooms they possess can be fruitful. The following are just some of the sources for which you might look:

Family Bibles contain information on births, marriages, and deaths. The information found in these treasure troves needs to be analyzed carefully. Look at the handwriting and the ink color. If a family immediately went to the family Bible to record a death or birth, then the information is probably accurate. But if the recordings of many events that cover a period of years is in the same ink and in the same handwriting, that information may have been recorded years after the events shown and you might find inaccuracies. Finding the current owner of the Bible can be an adventure. My husband and I tried to track down such an heirloom after hearing the story about his great-grandfather's sister who was supposedly in possession of it. We gave up the search when we found out her children and husband had predeceased her and there were no potential heirs. We were told she was not on speaking terms with her siblings, so we could only assume the item was lost to the family.

Letters, diaries, and memoirs can be excellent resources for discovering life events, migrations, relationships, church memberships, and glimpses of everyday life.

- Diaries were often begun with a significant event in someone's life, such as starting out in a covered wagon on a journey to Oregon. What did he or she see along the way? What new sites, plant life, and animals were seen along the trail? We have all heard of the *Diary of Anne Frank*. While in hiding from the Nazis during World War II, Anne Frank wrote in her diary of her fears and hopes and of her observations of the people around her. She gave the world a glimpse of life within the walls of that secret place and allowed us to sense what she was feeling. The diaries of our ancestors will most likely never be seen beyond one's own family, but they can be one of the most valuable and precious possessions we can discover. The chances of finding the diary written by one of your ancestors are slim, but you might find a diary of someone who has had similar experiences. Alexander Street Press, a book publisher and library database vendor, has developed several databases containing diaries of common individuals, such as their database *North*

American Immigrant Letters, Diaries, and Oral Histories. This product describes through primary-source documents the unique experience of those who immigrated to the United States and Canada. The benefit of an online product is being able to describe the type of diarist, by age, sex, and location, and then reading about the similar experiences they had to help interpret the time in which your ancestor lived and the events they experienced. To find repositories which might have diaries, one can search the National Union Catalog of Manuscript Collections online at www.loc.gov/coll/nucmc, or one can search WorldCat through its library database or online at http://worldcat.org.

■ In this world of computers and online resources, we seem to have forgotten the impact that letters had in lives of the past, but it was a way families stayed in touch when separated by distance or geography. Everyday events were shared, expressions of love were given, and life's major mileposts are shared—births, deaths, and marriages. What follows is a portion of a letter written by my grandfather, who immigrated to America in 1901 when he was eighteen years old, to his sister in Sweden on April 23, 1945:

> *Dear Sister!*
>
> *I write some lines to let you now [sic] that we still are alive in spite of it is a long time ago I wrote. We are all well. Melvin, Alan, and Arvid are in the war but no one is in Europe. Alan and Arvid have been out nearly 2 years. Melvin went away after New Years [sic] Eve. Arvid wrote that he perhaps will bee [sic] back soon. I think he is ill. But he hasn't said anything himself. But Alan has told me. They have seen each other several times, but Alan is futher [sic] north now so they can't meet more. I don't remember if I mentioned that Norma has a boy. He is more than 2 years. Melvin also has a boy be his [sic] only 8 months.*

Thanks to a grandson of that sister, a translated copy of the letter made its way back to me. My grandfather never returned to Sweden after immigrating, but letters and photographs were frequently shared across the ocean.

- Memoirs are recollections of a person's past. Laura Ingalls Wilder shared her memories of the past in a fictionalized account for children. She recalled washdays and the making of soap and head cheese. She told of an encounter with an Indian while in that little house on the prairie, and the presents she and her sisters received that Christmas. Memoirs can be a great discovery among family mementos and can give a glimpse of life long ago.

Yearbooks from elementary schools, high schools, and colleges and universities can be a good source of photographs of one's forebears. Yearbooks tend to stay in families because they are considered a cherished link to the past and there is a reluctance to throw them away, even if the books are never opened again. They show a picture of each student, giving the researcher a visual image of an ancestor. There may also be an indication of the organizations or sports in which the student was involved. Church yearbooks and fraternal society or church membership annuals often contain photographs, not only of an individual, but of entire family groups. Many yearbooks have been digitized by Ancestry.com in quite an extensive collection.

Photographs can be a treasure trove—if they are labeled or identified in some way. How frustrating it is to find a box of old photographs, only to have no identification of the people involved. In family photograph collections, not only will one find pictures of individuals, but also photographs of houses, snowstorms, floods, or anything else which was of significance to the photographer. Talk to extended family members about the photographs they may have in their possession and ask if you can scan them. A portable scanner is an excellent investment to capture the images of precious photographs.

There are many other types of documents you might find in the possession of family members—deeds, military papers, marriage licenses, naturalization records, school report cards, old driver's licenses, and insurance papers, to name a few. Each of these documents will give names, dates, places, and other clues to add to one's genealogy.

Timelines

Keeping track of the many generations of our ancestors can be difficult. Pedigree charts and family group sheets are vital to an effective research project, but timelines can also help in genealogical research. Timelines contain a list of events in chronological order and can give clues of locations for finding additional information. For example, I discovered that one of my ancestors started out life in Ohio and moved to Michigan as a young man. He also married in Michigan and had his first child there. Then he and his wife moved to Iowa where two more children were born. A few years later they were back in Michigan and two more children were born. Then, back to Iowa and another two children. Their last child was born in Kansas before returning to Michigan. However, their trek did not stop there. They moved to California late in life and both died there. Look at this example of a timeline below:

Timeline for Sylvester McGeorge

1826	Born, Ohio
1852	Married Sidney Colyar, Cass County, Michigan
1853	Son Perry born, Cass County, Michigan
1857	Son Leonard born, Iowa
1859	Son Ambrose born, Iowa
1861	Daughter Clarinda born, Cass County, Michigan
1865	Son Oscar born, Michigan
1867	Son Wilbert born, Iowa
1872	Son John E. born, Iowa
1875	Son Sylvester K. born, Kansas
1880	Residence, Montcalm County, Michigan (federal census)

1884   Residence, Montcalm County, Michigan (Michigan
        state census)

1900   Residence, Solano County, California (federal census)

1907   Death, Solano County, California

Without a timeline, knowing where to find records for this family
would be very difficult. I spent years trying to find where Sylvester
might have been buried in Michigan. Once I learned that he resided in
California in 1900, I searched cemetery records in Solano County. That
is where I found the burial for him and his wife.

Timelines can also put an ancestor into historical perspective. One
can develop a timeline which shows events that were happening at
certain times during your ancestors' lives. This can help determine factors that influenced their lives and what events they might have been
involved in. One can use a print almanac of American history or a history database to find the events that were happening during specific
years of an ancestor's life. National and international events as well as
wars, inventions, disasters, the names of elected individuals, and other
interesting facts can be found using one of those sources. Combining
the timeline of one's ancestor and a timeline of historic events helps
determine the types of sources one might use to find more information
about one's forebears.

Sylvester McGeorge Timeline *(Including Historic Events)*

1826   Born, Ohio—Completion of the Erie Canal

1852   Married, Cass County, Michigan—Completion of the
        Michigan Southern Railway

1853   Son Perry born, Cass County, Michigan—Construction
        begins on the canal and locks in Sault Ste. Marie

1857   Son Leonard born, Iowa—Panic of 1857, causing bank
        failures

The timeline above includes historic events which happened at the
same time as specific events in the life of Sylvester McGeorge. Not only
do we now have the personal events and milestones in his life, but we
also know what was happening in the world around him. If I wished
to write an account of this family, I would now have some historical

events to help my reader visualize my ancestor's place in history. Sylvester McGeorge did not just live—he lived in the world around him.

Genealogy Libraries

Genealogy patrons enjoy research, whether it be on the Internet or in a library. Your public library may have a genealogy department containing collections for your immediate area. Your library may have formed a partnership with the local genealogical society, and may even have allocated space for a genealogy section or room within the library building. Sometimes genealogy researchers have a need for resources you do not have in your library. Interlibrary loan may be the answer, but it is also helpful to know the resources of other libraries to which you may refer the researchers.

There are some libraries that specialize in genealogical research. The largest one is the Family History Library (FHL) in Salt Lake City. While it is a private library, all are welcome to research there free of charge. The library offers books, databases, microfilm, and digital records. Volunteers and reference specialists are always available to lend assistance. The FHL also has Family History Centers in various communities worldwide, and the FHL also gives that status to libraries that become partners with it.

The Library of Congress (LOC) in Washington, DC, has a Local History and Genealogy Reading Room. The LOC has numerous genealogy and local history books, databases, manuscripts, microfilms, newspapers, photographs, and maps on-site. Users of the collection must obtain a research card before they can begin their research. Interlibrary loan is available for some of the materials in the collection, but items in the Library of Congress's special collections can be used only at the LOC. Its interlibrary loan FAQs can be found at https://www.loc.gov/rr/loan/loan-news.html.

The National Archives and Records Administration (NARA) is a repository for federal records. In addition to the main NARA branch in Washington, DC, and its Archives II location in College Park, Maryland, there are twelve additional NARA research facilities around the country. Their record holdings are declassified federal records. Do not expect to find vital records (i.e., birth, death, and marriage records) at these research locations. Examples of federal documents are census, immigration, federal naturalization, and bankruptcy records. Each local repository has documents that were created in its region and are housed there. Each field branch also offers free database access to Ancestry.com, Fold3, ArchivesUSA, the U.S. Serial Set Digital Collection, and several others.

The Daughters of the American Revolution (DAR) Library is a private research facility in Washington, DC. Their library contains numerous genealogy books and records such as genealogies, cemetery readings, marriage records, and membership applications. Each application contains a pedigree from the applicant reaching back to her patriot ancestor. A visit to the library, which is free, allows researchers to use ALE, Fold3, Findmypast, HeritageQuest, and other databases. These special libraries, and other must-visit libraries can be found in *Family Tree Magazine*'s compiled list of "Nine Libraries to Visit before You Die," which was published in 2008. You can view the list at www .familytreemagazine.com/article/9-libraries.

Your local historical society is another library facility of which you should be aware. Historical societies have the mission to preserve history in the town, county, or state in which they are located. The history of a community incorporates the history of those who lived and worked there, as well as larger historical events. Your patrons may find information about their families in one of these facilities. They most certainly will gain a better appreciation for the area in which their ancestors lived by researching the local history. As you are most likely aware, the *American Library Directory*[2] is an excellent reference source for determining the location of all types of libraries and discovering the subject areas they collect. Knowing your own collection and the collections of other libraries around you will help you to better serve your genealogy patrons.

The Internet and Internet Databases

Genealogists today often start their research with a visit to Ancestry .com or other online sites. Ancestry.com advertises on network and cable television, and out of curiosity, many try it. An individual can find numerous records online, and many successfully find a host of ancestors. Will one find everything on the Internet? As a librarian, you should know that the answer to this is no. Someday we may find that all information is digital and available on the Web. Until that time, the Internet is only one of the tools people will use in researching their family. I look at a genealogy project as a research project. Knowing the types of resources and their availability is important in pursuit of a thorough finished product.

Our journey into the past begins with discovering what we already know, charting our pedigree, and forming our ancestors into family units. Then we discover what others might know and what documents they might have in their possession. Then, creating a timeline puts one's ancestors in historical perspective. Next, we discover the types of records available and begin the search. In the next chapter, you will learn more about the records and resources available. The adventure in helping your genealogy patrons is beginning!

NOTES

1. Oral history interview with Evelyn Meyers by Janice Schultz, March 1983.
2. *American Library Directory: A Classified List of Libraries in the United States and Canada, with Personnel and Statistical Data* (New York: R.R. Bowker, annual).

CHAPTER THREE

Finding Genealogy Records

In the last two chapters, we have discussed the basics of doing genealogy research and the types of records one might use. This book will assume you are helping patrons with beginning American genealogy. A discussion of European and Canadian sources will occur in chapter 5. Research does not simply involve going to an Internet site, putting in a name, and seeing what comes up in the search results, though for many that is the extent of their research. There are so many other sources where one might find clues to one's family history. Some of those sources may be found on the Internet, while others may be found solely in courthouses, libraries, cemeteries, or family attics. Limiting one's research to the Internet alone is limiting one's final product. I am not saying you should not use the Internet. It has made genealogical research much easier, and the plethora of records found there brings the world of family history to one's desktop. But using many types of sources from many types of formats can result in more rewarding and viable conclusions. Using documents helps genealogists discover information about their ancestors that may be found in places that are simply not accessible online. Knowing those sources that help identify and verify a lineage is important. This chapter will discuss the types of records you can use and where they are initially created.

Vital Records

Vital records are birth and death records, but marriage records are also often considered to fall in this category. All are an important element in genealogical research. These three events are the minimal information we hope to find for each ancestor. To find a vital record, one must determine which government entity is the holder of such documents. Birth and death records in the twentieth and twenty-first centuries are housed at the state level. The first step in finding these documents is to determine when the state started keeping records. For the most part, both birth and death record-keeping were started about the same time. The easiest way to determine the onset of reporting is to find the website for the state's department of health. There are several websites that offer speedy document delivery for a fee. However, I have found that VitalChek (www.vitalchek.com) is a good website to find established dates for the record desired. Look for the words "health," "gov," and the abbreviation of the state in the web address to ensure you are on the official site if you wish to order a document online.

Birth certificates play an important part in our lives today. We can't register a child for public school, obtain a driver's license, or register for Social Security without one. A birth record is proof that a birth occurred, and it indicates the date of birth and the names of the parents, including the mother's maiden name. If the parents were not married at the time of the child's birth, the father's name will usually be listed as "unknown" unless he was willing to be responsible for financial support. If the child was adopted, the certificate will have been altered to show the adoptive parents as the parents of the child. The original birth certificate is the adoption file, which is most likely sealed, private information and is unavailable for viewing or purchase. Some states have open adoption records that allow adult adoptees to obtain their original birth certificates, but the majority of states have closed records.

Birth records at the state level should be available, for a fee, for your own birth or for that of a deceased ancestor. State your relationship to the person in question, and your reason for wanting to obtain the record. Most states will accept genealogy research as a legitimate reason. It is important to determine that the date of birth is within the established time frame. If the state's record-keeping began in 1910 and you request a birth certificate of someone who was born in 1900, the state will keep the money you submitted and let you know that they did not find the record. An exception is a delayed birth certificate. If an individual needed a record of birth later in life to obtain a passport or to register for Social Security and a birth certificate was never created, a delayed birth certificate could be issued. The person was required to submit several sources of information to prove his or her age, such as a family Bible record, a church christening record, or the testimony of family members. Delayed birth certificates are found in the same location as other birth certificates. You are unlikely to find twentieth and twenty-first-century birth records online.

What if the birth occurred before state record-keeping began? Counties kept records before the state began its commencement as a record holder. Doctors and midwives were responsible for reporting the event and county clerks were required to register the event, if a law to do so was in place. Even though both are dated, I like to use *Ancestry's Red Book*[1] and *The Handybook for Genealogists*[2] for finding the dates of county record-keeping. The *Red Book* and the *Handybook* both give information about each state in the country: when it became a state, a map of the counties, a brief history, and the availability of records at the state and county levels of record-keeping. To find the onset date of county records using the Internet, try the FamilySearch Wiki (www.wiki.familysearch.org). County records are housed at the courthouse in one's county seat, possibly the county's historical society, and/or the state's archives.

Figure 3.1 shows page 393 from *Ancestry's Red Book* indicating the commencement dates of records in Adair County, Missouri. You will

Map	County Address	Date Formed Parent County/ies	Birth Marriage Death	Land Probate Court
B4	Adair 106 W. Washington Kirksville 63501 *Courthouse burned 1865.*	1841 Macon	1883–93 1841 ———	1841 1841 1841

FIGURE 3.1

Page 393 from *Ancestry's Red Book* indicating
the commencement dates of records
in Adair County, Missouri

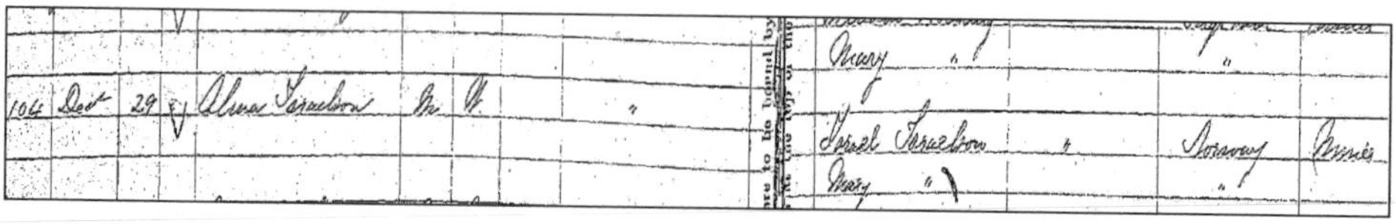

FIGURE 3.2

A birth record for the author's grandmother,
Alma Israelson, who was born in Quincy,
Houghton County, Michigan

often find these early (pre-twentieth-century) birth records on an Internet site such as FamilySearch (http://familysearch.org) or Ancestry .com and AncestryLibraryEdition (ALE). (From this point, ALE will be inherently included in references to Ancestry.com.) What you find on the Internet may be a digital copy, transcription, or an index or list of births. Figure 3.2 shows a birth record for my grandmother, Alma Israelson, who was born in Quincy, in Houghton County, Michigan.[3] Her name is shown on the left with her birth month (December) and day (the 29th). The year (1881) is not shown here but is written at the top of the page. Shown also are her parents' names, Israel and Mary Israelson, with their places of birth, which in both instances was Norway. Israel's occupation as a miner is also given. In this record the mother's maiden name is not listed.

Will the information on the birth record be accurate? The information provided for the legal name; the date, time, and place of birth; the weight and length of the child; and the doctor's name should be accurate. The mother's name will most likely be accurate, and the information she provides about herself—her age and place of birth—will be as accurate as she wishes it to be. She may have stated she was sixteen when she might have been fifteen years old. The information about the father will be as accurate as the information she knows or wishes to share.

Other documents which can give you information about births are death records, Social Security applications, census records, cemetery records, church records, newspaper announcements, and Bible records. Other than Bible records, which have been discussed previously, you will find out more about these types of documents later.

Death Records

A death record, at a minimum, will tell you the name of the deceased and the cause of death. As with birth records, twentieth and twenty-first-century death records will be found in each state's department of health. The state generally began keeping these records at the same time as birth records for that locale. These death records will be provided in the form of a certificate—an official document issued by a government entity that declares the date, location, and cause of a person's death. On one side of the certificate is information provided by the attending physician. The other side contains information provided by an informant. The informant can be anyone—parent, child, sibling, or even the landlady—who was present at the time of death who could provide information about the decedent. The document contains the complete name of the deceased, the date of death, the cause of death, and his or her age at the time of death. You may also discover the person's place of birth, occupation, name of spouse, and names of parents, including the mother's maiden name, and their places of birth. Look at all the information with a critical eye. It may be correct, but it could also be wrong. My grandmother was the informant for her father's death certificate, but she did not state the correct names of his parents. She wasn't even close to being correct. I don't know why, but I have a plausible reason: my great-grandfather was born in Norway. He immigrated to the United States in approximately 1863, but his parents never left Norway. My grandmother never traveled to Norway and never met her grandparents. Either she did not know their correct names, or in the moment of grief she did not remember their correct names. I discovered the true names of his parents by obtaining the information from a relative still living in Norway who was intimate with the facts.

Figure 3.3 is a copy of the death certificate of Israel Israelson purchased by the author from the State of Michigan Vital Records Department. The place of death is Houghton County, Franklin Township, Ripley Village. The personal and statistical particulars are sex, male; color or race, white; marital status, widower; his [deceased] wife's name, Mary Israelson; date of birth, November 9; age 68 years and 4 months; occupation, retired; birthplace, Norway; name of father, John Israelson; birthplace of father, Norway; maiden name of mother,

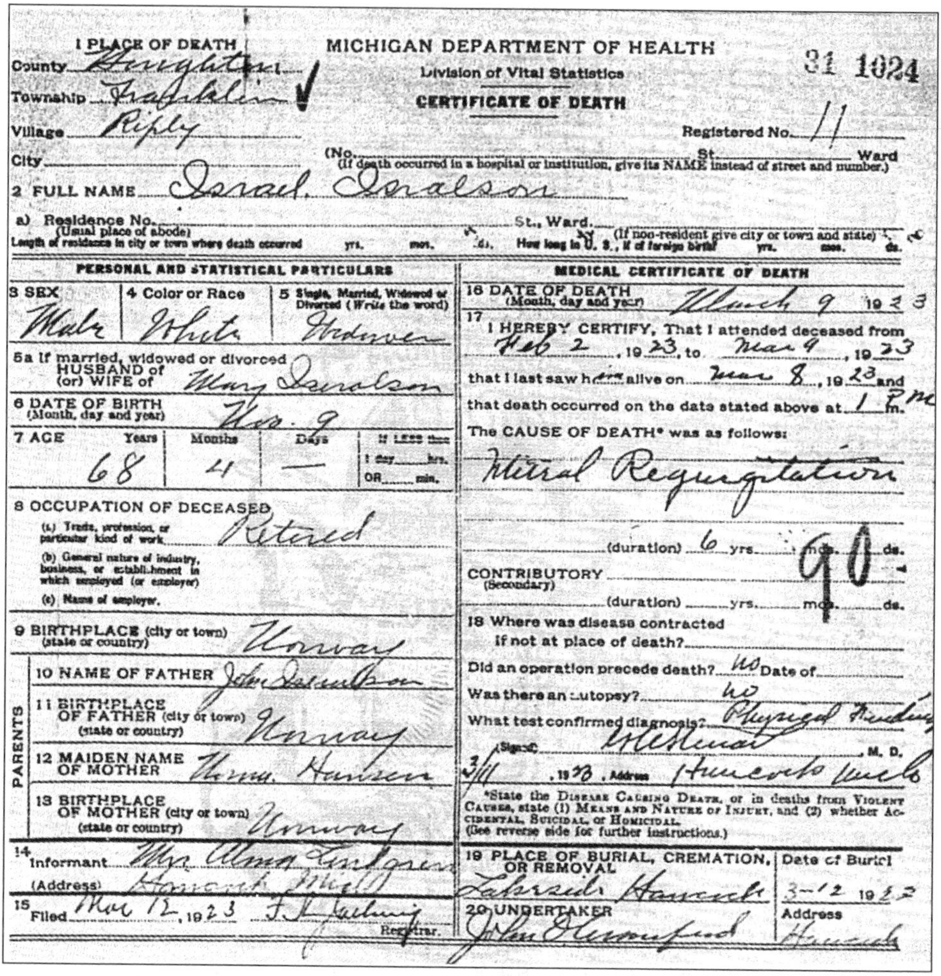

1 PLACE OF DEATH
County Houghton
Township Franklin
Village Ripley
City .... (No. .... St. .... Ward) (If death occurred in a hospital or institution, give its NAME instead of street and number.)

MICHIGAN DEPARTMENT OF HEALTH
Division of Vital Statistics
CERTIFICATE OF DEATH

31 1024

Registered No. 11

2 FULL NAME Israel Isralson

a) Residence No. .... St., Ward. .... (If non-resident give city or town and state)
(Usual place of abode)
Length of residence in city or town where death occurred ... yrs. ... mos. ... ds. How long in U. S., if of foreign birth? ... yrs. ... mos. ... ds.

PERSONAL AND STATISTICAL PARTICULARS

3 SEX Male
4 Color or Race White
5 Single, Married, Widowed or Divorced (Write the word) Widower
5a If married, widowed or divorced HUSBAND of (or) WIFE of Mary Isralson
6 DATE OF BIRTH (Month, day and year) Nov. 9
7 AGE Years 68 Months 4 Days — If LESS than 1 day ... hrs. OR ... min.
8 OCCUPATION OF DECEASED
(a) Trade, profession, or particular kind of work Retired
(b) General nature of industry, business, or establishment in which employed (or employer)
(c) Name of employer.
9 BIRTHPLACE (city or town) (state or country) Norway

PARENTS
10 NAME OF FATHER John Isralson
11 BIRTHPLACE OF FATHER (city or town) (state or country) Norway
12 MAIDEN NAME OF MOTHER Norma Hansen
13 BIRTHPLACE OF MOTHER (city or town) (state or country) Norway

14 Informant Mrs Alma Lindgren
(Address) Hancock Mich
15 Filed Mar 12, 1923 F. H. Jaeling Registrar.

MEDICAL CERTIFICATE OF DEATH

16 DATE OF DEATH (Month, day and year) March 9 1923
17 I HEREBY CERTIFY, That I attended deceased from Feb 2, 1923, to Mar 9, 1923
that I last saw h... alive on Mar 8, 1923 and
that death occurred on the date stated above at 1 P.M.
The CAUSE OF DEATH* was as follows:
Mitral Regurgitation
(duration) 6 yrs. ... mos. ... ds.
CONTRIBUTORY (Secondary)
(duration) ... yrs. ... mos. ... ds.
18 Where was disease contracted if not at place of death?
Did an operation precede death? no Date of
Was there an autopsy? no
What test confirmed diagnosis? Physical Finding
(Signed) W. H. Menard M. D.
3/11, 1923. Address Hancock Mich

*State the Disease Causing Death, or in deaths from Violent Causes, state (1) Means and Nature of Injury, and (2) whether Accidental, Suicidal, or Homicidal.
(See reverse side for further instructions.)

19 PLACE OF BURIAL, CREMATION, OR REMOVAL Lakeside Hancock
Date of Burial 3-12 1923
20 UNDERTAKER John Olson ...
Address Hancock

FIGURE 3.3

A copy of the death certificate of Israel Israelson purchased by the author from the State of Michigan Vital Record Department

Norma Hansen; birthplace of mother, Norway; informant, Mrs. Alma Lindgren; address, Hancock, Michigan. Other than the name of the informant, the personal information comes from the informant's knowledge of the deceased and is subject to further investigation by the genealogist. The certificate also indicates the date and cause of death, place of burial, and the burial date. This information is probably accurate.

Nowadays most states automate their records. The electronic records are usually abbreviated death certificates giving the name of the deceased, the cause of death, and the place of burial. The other information found on the original, long form of the death certificate is absent on the electronic record. If the state will provide one, ask for a copy of the long form of the death certificate. Some states offer local access to some of their vital records at county health departments. If the state has determined these are public records, you may find copies of them on the Internet. Online, you might find an index to death certificates, transcriptions, or copies of the original records. If you are looking for death records online, a good place to start is the website Online Searchable Death Indexes and Records at www.deathindexes .com. The site has links to each U.S. state. Once in the site for a state, you will find numerous links to death records and indexes. The site will indicate if there is a fee to obtain copies of death records.

Nineteenth-century and prior death records will be found in death record books in county courthouses, with one line per person and many recordings on each page. The main reason counties kept these records was to have readily available information for causes of death in the area. You will only find the name of the deceased, his or her age, and the cause of death in these files. Only attending physicians reported deaths to the county officials. If there was no attending physician, there will be no death record. At that time, the family did not have to provide proof of a death as we do today. If a man died while plowing his field, the family was unlikely to call a physician to state the obvious, that he was dead. They simply buried him in the family plot on the farm. Now we provide a copy to the Social Security Administration, insurance companies, banks, and all other interested parties. Many of these older death records can be found on the Internet in one form or another in indexes, transcriptions, or digitized copies.

Other places to find information about deaths of individuals may be found on census mortality schedules, newspaper obituaries, pension records, tombstones, the Social Security Death Index (SSDI), and church records. The SSDI is a searchable name index of deaths reported to the Social Security Administration (SSA), beginning in 1962. Deaths were reported to the SSA to stop Social Security payments to the decedent. If the decedent was not collecting Social Security at the time of death, there will be no record of death in the SSDI. The SSDI can be found on most commercial genealogy databases.

Marriage Records

When searching for a female ancestor, one must know her maiden name to be able to search for her forebears. A marriage record is the best source to determine the maiden name of a woman. Marriage records tell us the names of the bride and groom and prove that a marriage took place. They are seldom held as state government records, but are usually a county or town record, with local holdings beginning from the date of formation of the county. The place of marriage is generally the home county of one, or both, of the bridal couple unless they eloped. There are several types of records you could encounter: marriage records, certificates, applications, returns, and bonds.

Early marriage records are found in bound volumes in the courthouse in the county where the marriage occurred. They show the name of the groom, the maiden name of the bride, the name of the officiating minister or the person who presided over the marriage, and perhaps the church and/or the names of the witnesses. You might find letters after the name of the person presiding over the ceremony. "JP" indicates that the person was a justice of the peace. "MG" stands for "minister of the gospel."

Figure 3.4 shows a page of marriages from the marriage book in Jackson County, Missouri, from 1918 to 1922. The fifth marriage on the page is that of Harry Truman and Elizabeth Wallace, who were married on June 28, 1919. They were married at Trinity Church in Independence, Missouri.[4]

You are probably most familiar with a document called a marriage certificate. It is the official record of marriage given to the bride and groom which can be used as proof of marriage. The individual presiding at the ceremony is obligated to file a copy at the county courthouse. This ensures that the marriage is recorded. If you have recently applied for a driver's license in a new state and have had a change of name since your birth, a marriage certificate is a trusted legal document that signifies the name change. Marriage certificates are generally a later type of document; one usually found after 1900. You will usually find the full name of the bride and groom, the date of application, the date of marriage, the name of the minister or the justice of the peace, and the religious affiliation of the minister. You may also discover the names of the witnesses. Take special note of those names; they are often siblings of one, or both, of the parties.

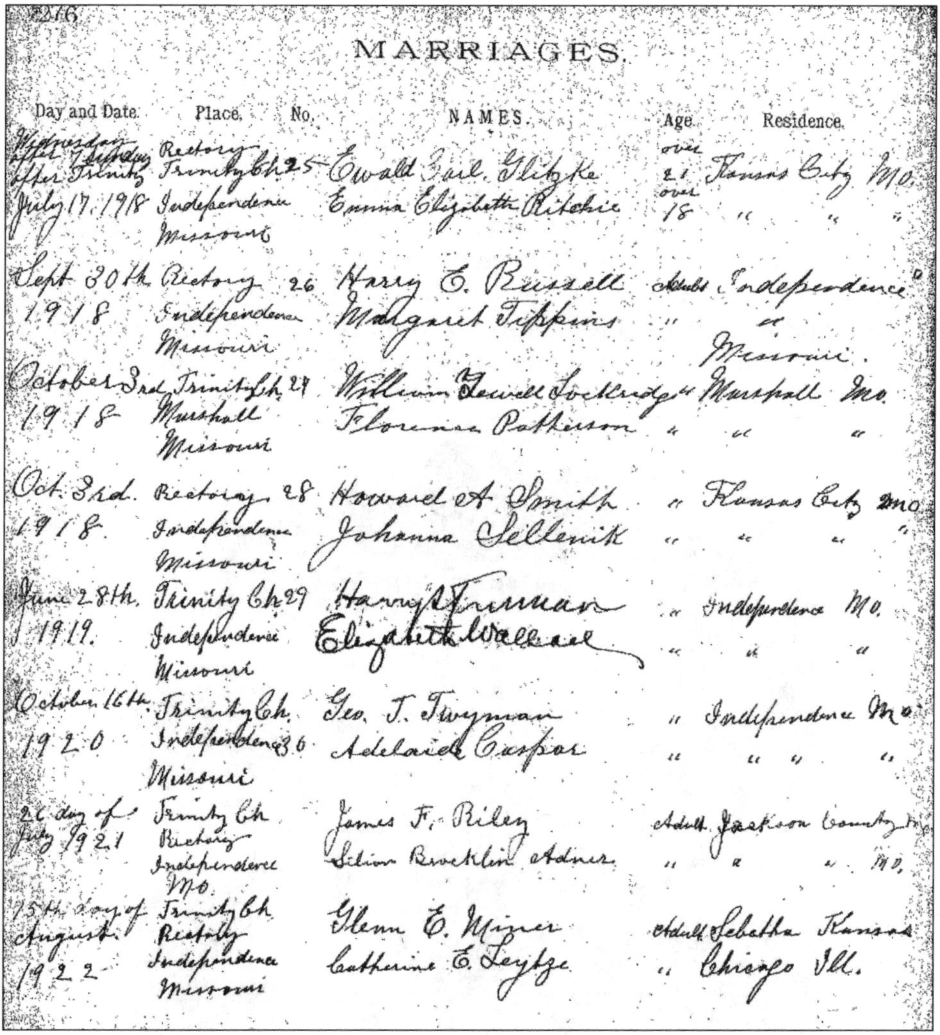

276

MARRIAGES.

Day and Date.	Place.	No.	NAMES.	Age.	Residence.
Wednesday after 7 Sunday after Trinity July 17, 1918	Rectory Trinity Ch. Independence Missouri	25	Ewald Earl Glitzke Emma Elizabeth Ritchie	over 21 over 18	Kansas City Mo. " " "
Sept 30th 1918	Rectory Independence Missouri	26	Harry E. Russell Margaret Tippins	Adult "	Independence " Missouri.
October 3rd 1918	Trinity Ch. Marshall Missouri	27	William Lowell Lockridge Florence Patterson	" "	Marshall Mo. " "
Oct. 3rd 1918	Rectory Independence Missouri	28	Howard A. Smith Johanna Sellenik	" "	Kansas City Mo " " "
June 28th 1919	Trinity Ch. Independence Missouri	29	Harry S. Truman Elizabeth Wallace	" "	Independence Mo. " "
October 16th 1920	Trinity Ch. Independence Missouri	30	Geo. T. Twyman Adelaide Casper	" "	Independence Mo. " " "
2[illegible] day of July 1921	Trinity Ch Rectory Independence Mo.		James F. Riley Lilian Brocklin Adner	Adult "	Jackson County Mo. " " Mo.
15th day of August 1922	Trinity Ch Rectory Independence Missouri		Glenn E. Miner Catherine E. Leytze	Adult "	Sabetha Kansas Chicago Ill.

FIGURE 3.4

A page of marriages from the marriage book in Jackson County, Missouri, from 1918 to 1922

A different type of marriage certificate or document might also have been given the bride and groom by the church in which they were married. This is usually a fancier type of document than that given by the local governmental jurisdiction. You may run across one of these as you search through family papers in your attic.

Figure 3.5 shows a marriage certificate given to my grandparents, John Emil Lindgren and Alma Nelsina Israelson, by the minister of the church in which they were married.

Marriage applications are the documents created when the bride and groom apply for a marriage license. The information required will vary from state to state. It will show the names of the bride and groom and their ages, although they were not required to show proof of age. If they were over 21 they may have been allowed to avow "over 21," and if they were underage, a parent's signature was required. You will also find their place of residence. Some states even ask for the names of the parents of each party, including the maiden name of the mother,

FIGURE 3.5
Marriage certificate of the author's grandparents,
John Emil Lindgren and Alma Nelsina Israelson

place of birth of the bride and groom, place of birth of mother and father, number of times married, and occupation. Will the information be correct? It will be as correct as the bride and groom desire it to be. Many a young person has lied about his or her age when applying for a marriage certificate. My great-grandmother, by family tradition, was fourteen years old when she was married. The marriage record states that she was sixteen, however. No birth record can be found to verify her age, but she often testified to her granddaughters that she was fourteen when she married.

Figure 3.6 is a marriage application for Harry S Truman of Grandview, Missouri, and Bess Wallace of Independence, Missouri.[5] Marriage

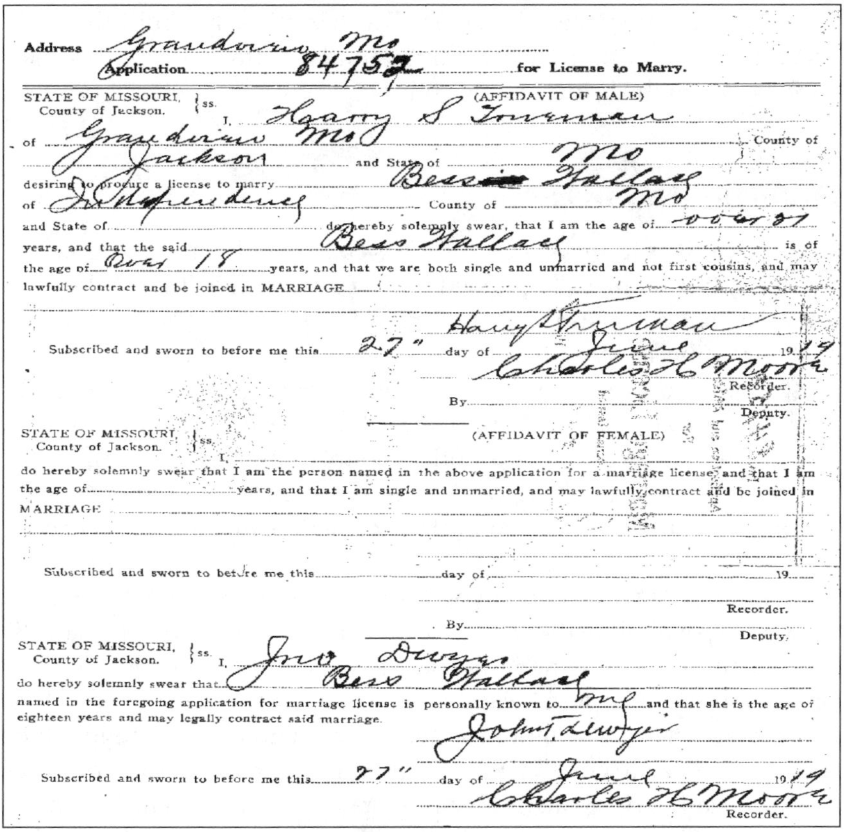

Address Grandview Mo
Application 84752 for License to Marry.

STATE OF MISSOURI, } ss.
County of Jackson. }
(AFFIDAVIT OF MALE)
I, Harry S Truman
of Grandview Mo County of Jackson and State of Mo
desiring to procure a license to marry Bess Wallace
of Independence County of Mo
and State of do hereby solemnly swear, that I am the age of over 21
years, and that the said Bess Wallace is of
the age of Over 18 years, and that we are both single and unmarried and not first cousins, and may lawfully contract and be joined in MARRIAGE

Harry S Truman

Subscribed and sworn to before me this 27" day of June 1919
Charles H Moore
Recorder.
By Deputy.

STATE OF MISSOURI, } ss.
County of Jackson. }
(AFFIDAVIT OF FEMALE)
I,
do hereby solemnly swear that I am the person named in the above application for a marriage license, and that I am the age of years, and that I am single and unmarried, and may lawfully contract and be joined in MARRIAGE

Subscribed and sworn to before me this day of 19
Recorder.
By Deputy.

STATE OF MISSOURI, } ss.
County of Jackson. }
I, Jno Dwyer
do hereby solemnly swear that Bess Wallace
named in the foregoing application for marriage license is personally known to me and that she is the age of eighteen years and may legally contract said marriage.

John Dwyer

Subscribed and sworn to before me this 27" day of June 1919
Charles H Moore
Recorder.

FIGURE 3.6

Marriage application for Harry S Truman of Grandview, Missouri, and Bess Wallace of Independence, Missouri

returns are records of marriages performed and "returned" by the minister to the courthouse. The returns will generally not be in date order in the record books. A minister often waited until he had several marriages to report before he sent the returns to the county. The benefit of finding a marriage return is the knowledge that the marriage definitely occurred. Not all courthouses have books containing marriage returns.

You may also find another type of record, marriage bonds, in courthouses in Southern states. A marriage bond was a legal document which required a posted monetary bond that ensured there was no legal reason that the marriage could not occur. The pledged money would defray the cost of litigation should the marriage be nullified. The groom and a bondsman, who was often a near relative such as his father or brother, posted the bond. This signified that both the bride and groom promised they were not bound to someone else. Look for these bonds in the bride's home county.

Divorce Records

None of us likes to think about the possibility of divorce in our ancestral lines, but divorces happened in all families. Don't be fooled into thinking that divorces did not happen in our ancestors' days. It is a misconception to think that divorces were historically rare. Divorces did happen to our ancestors as they happen today. Unfortunately, they are the part of a family history that most people don't like to talk about. Divorce records are found in county courthouses. Few of the records exist online. When looking for divorces prior to the twentieth century, you might find them in state legislative documents as private acts of the state legislature.

Figure 3.7 shows two divorce records granted by the Missouri General Assembly in 1841.[6] Divorce records contain the names of the minor children and sometimes the age of the husband and wife, the cause of the divorce, and the date of the marriage. When looking at the cause cited for the disunion, we need to remember the time in which these records were created. Before no-fault divorces became common, someone had to be blamed. Therefore, personality flaws may be over-exaggerated and not totally reflective of your ancestors' behavior, but they were stated in such a way to ensure that the judge would grant the divorce.

DIVORCE.

AN ACT for the relief of Jane Richards and Polly Jane Botts.

SECTION	SECTION
Jane Richards authorised to sue for a divorce, without being required to wait two years after the absconing of her husband. - - 1	The same right granted to Polly Jane Botts, on the ground of abandonment. - - - 2

Be it enacted by the General Assembly of the State of Missouri, as follows :

§ 1. That Jane Richards, of the county of Cape Girardeau, be permitted to sue in the circuit court of the county of Cape Girardeau, at the next term thereof, or as soon thereafter as convenient, to be divorced from the bonds of matrimony by her contracted with John Richards, of the county and State aforesaid; and that the law concerning divorce and alimony, approved January 24th, 1835, requiring that the absconding party shall have been absent two years before the party aggrieved shall have a right to sue, shall not operate as a bar to action in this particular case.

§ 2. Polly Jane Botts, of Macon county, shall be at liberty to institute a suit for a divorce against her husband, Seth Botts, on the ground of abandonment or the commission of felony, and, if it shall appear on trial that she has been wilfully abandoned by her husband, without just cause, she shall be at liberty to maintain her suit, and the circuit court shall be competent to render a decree of divorce in her favor, even if the abandonment complained of shall not have been continued for the space of two years at the time of bringing her suit, or at the time of the trial thereof.

This act to take effect from its passage.

APPROVED Feb. 16, 1841.

FIGURE 3.7
Two divorce records granted by the Missouri
General Assembly in 1841

Vital records are important documents to locate as one delves into genealogical research. When available, they uniquely identify an individual and provide the clues to the names, dates, and locations of significant events. Uniformity in records prior to current times was slow to take hold, so the information will be varied. It is important to remember that the data found, even though it is on an official document, can be wrong; sometimes by transcription error or ignorance, and sometimes by a desire by the informant to hide the true information. The documents should be analyzed carefully.

Knowing if the record could possibly exist is equally imperative. I have seen many patrons scouring genealogy websites looking for a vital record, not realizing that the state or county was not keeping records for the time needed. As an information specialist, you can assist your patron in the discovery of the availability of records. A possible response to the harried genealogist could be, "Let's see when the county began keeping records." What other records can be used to find the information someone is seeking? We will explore that question as we continue to look at the types of written documents that inform us about our ancestors' lives.

LESSON FOUR

1. Investigate the availability of vital records for one set of your grandparents.

   ■ Were vital records being kept?

   ■ If so, who is the record-keeper?

   ■ What is the cost of purchasing a death certificate?

2. When did your state begin keeping vital records?

3. When did your county begin recording vital records?

Census Records

Any record that tells us about our ancestors is an important record, but I consider census records, or population schedules, to be second in importance only to vital records. You may never find your ancestor's name written in a book. You might not find that important vital record that gives the birth, death, or marriage dates you seek. You might not find the elusive relative who has the missing piece of information that is so vital to your research. But federal census records will relate information about your ancestors every ten years. The records are useful for learning about one's family and the environment in which they lived. While some may view these documents as hearsay evidence, they are still valuable records, though like any other document, they must be evaluated for errors.

The United States began enumerating, or counting, its citizens in 1790 to determine congressional representation. The *Merriam-Webster Unabridged Dictionary* defines "census" as "an official enumeration of the population of a country, city, or other administrative district generally including vital statistics and other classified information relating to the social and economic conditions." This enumeration has been taken every ten years since its initiation in 1790 and lists varying degrees of information, depending on the data Congress wanted collected in each census year. Census records are kept private for seventy-two years after the census by an act of Congress. When genealogists wanted access to the 1910 census, a law was enacted, a privacy act, to allow limited access to it (Title 44, U.S. Code). The law states that census records will be released seventy-two years after the official census date. That was the projected life expectancy at the time the law was enacted. This privacy allows individuals to freely give their personal information to census takers without concern that others would immediately see the data and pass judgment or levy fines on those individuals. In taking a census, the enumerator, the person collecting the data, went from door to door (though this has changed with more recent censuses) in the district assigned to him, which was called an enumeration district. If the enumerator was in a large metropolitan area with city blocks, he would go around the block, staying on the same side of the street. When he was back at his starting point he would go across the street and again go around the block. In a rural community he would travel up one side of the road and then down the other. Every family on a census page is a neighbor to the family listed above or below them on the census form. However, if the neighbor lived across the street, the information might be several pages away.

The data collected in each enumeration year reflected information about each person listed, or their family unit if the entire population was not surveyed. One might find the names of everyone in the household and their ages. Children born between the time of the effective date of the census and the date when the enumerator came to the door, which could be several days or a month after the initial date, were not to be counted, though the enumerator did not always follow the instructions explicitly. The effective census dates were:

August 2, 1790

August 4, 1800

August 6, 1810

August 7, 1820

June 1, 1830, 1840, 1850, 1860, 1870, 1880, 1890, and 1900

April 15, 1910

January 1, 1920

April 1, 1930 and 1940

Why is it important to note the onset date of the census? It is important in order to determine if your ancestor could have been on the schedule or not. My mother was born in March 1920. The effective date of the census that year was January 1, so she was not recorded on a census schedule until 1930.

It is important to know the questions asked in each census year to anticipate the information a census will contain. You can find the questions asked for the years 1850 through 2010 on the website for the Minnesota Population Center at the University of Minnesota (http://usa.ipums.org/usa/voliii/tEnumForm.shtml). You can also find a PDF of an older, priceless U.S. Government Printing Office publication entitled *Twenty Censuses: Population and Housing Questions, 1790–1980* at https://www.census.gov/history/pdf/20censuses.pdf. It contains the questions and the instructions given to the enumerators. The more recent the census, the more information you will find, and the older the census, the less information you will find.

When helping patrons with their genealogy, look at their pedigree chart, determine the ancestor they are seeking, and look at all available census records on which they should be recorded. If I am looking for census information for Sylvester McGeorge, I will consult the timeline I created. He was born in 1826 in Ohio, so he should be a statistic on the 1830 federal census for Ohio. He died in 1907 in Solano County, California, therefore the last census on which he will recorded should be the 1900 federal census for California. Note that I used the word "should" when I referred to the census location. An individual is not always where you think he or she might be. It was the 1900 federal census which directed me to look for Sylvester's death in California. I always thought he died in Michigan and had focused my examination of the census there, but a search on Ancestry.com for all states brought his location to light and redirected my focus to a new location for his death and burial. Other censuses on which I should find Sylvester and the locations are 1850 Michigan, 1860 Michigan or Iowa, 1870 Iowa, 1880 Michigan, and 1890 (not extant). Common Internet locations for locating census records are Ancestry.com or AncestryLibraryEdition, Heritage Quest Online, Findmypast, and FamilySearch.

Since our genealogy research goes from the current back to the past generations, the discussion of the federal population schedules will begin with the most recently available census.

1940 Federal Population Schedule

Like all population schedules before it, the 1940 census was created on paper. Unlike prior censuses, it was not microfilmed by the National Archives prior to becoming digital. Other census years were microfilmed, but the original schedules were not retained. Once the Internet became a genealogy tool, those earlier microfilmed records were digitized. The 1940 census schedules were the first to be released digitally. The date of release is always seventy-two years from the effective census date which, in this case, was April 1, 2012. However, April 1 fell on a Sunday, and the National Archives delayed its release by one day to Monday, April 2. It was an exciting time with the population schedules due to go live at 8:00 a.m. eastern time. My library had a census watch party. We opened the doors to our facility early and had classes and a continental breakfast for those genealogists who were super-excited to be a part of the historic occasion. My library director was in attendance and compared it to the release of a new Harry Potter novel. The only Internet location for viewing the newly released data was the National Archives website. Unfortunately, all did not go well, and the NARA website was deluged with users. It was nearly impossible to view that data during those morning hours.

The questions that were asked on the 1940 census are as follows: address (if they lived in a city), whether their home was owned or rented, value of the home if owned or the monthly rental amount if rented, an indication if the family lived on a farm, name of each person in residence on April 1, 1940, and their relationship to the head of the house, sex, color or race, age at their last birthday, marital status, education (highest grade of school attended), place of birth of each person and if foreign-born, the country in which their birthplace was situated on January 1, 1937 (due to European boundary changes), and the citizenship status of the foreign-born person. Each person's residence on April 1, 1935, was sought—whether city, town, or village, which county, state (or territory or foreign country), and whether on a farm. For persons fourteen years and older there was an interest in their employment. Congress desired to know whether they were working, and if they were working, whether it was for pay, profit, or government-support work (such as the WPA and CCC); if they were seeking work, they indicated the number of hours they were employed or the

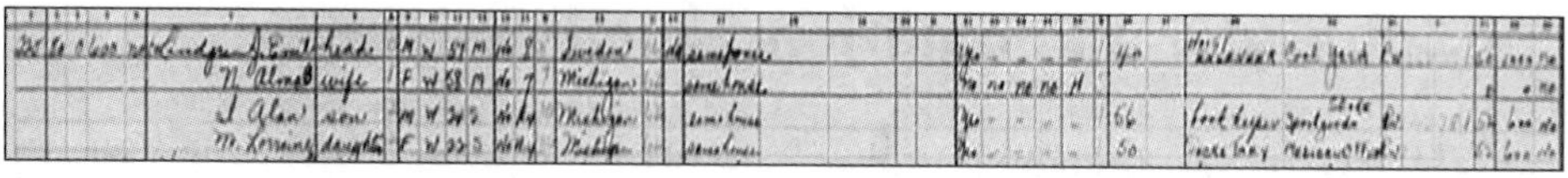

FIGURE 3.8

Copy of the 1940 schedule for Ripley, Houghton County, Michigan

duration of their unemployment, their occupation, if they had their own business, and if the person received an income of fifty dollars or more from sources other than wages or salary.

Figure 3.8 is a copy of the 1940 schedule for Ripley, Houghton County, Michigan, which shows the family of J. Emil Lindgren in 1940.[7] Since Emil used his middle name as his commonly used name, his name was recorded with an initial and then his middle name. The enumerator then used a similar format for the rest of the family members, but put the middle initial first and then the first name. So instead of Alma N. we have N. Alma, I. Alan instead of Alan I., and M. Lorraine instead of Lorraine M. We can see without a doubt that Emil was the head of the household, Alma was his wife, Alan was his son, and Lorraine was his daughter. They lived in the same house in 1935 and except for Alma, all were employed outside the home.

1930 Population Schedule

The 1930 census relates information about everyone in each household in the 48 U.S. states plus Alaska, Hawaii, American Samoa, Guam, Consular Services, Panama Canal Zone, Puerto Rico, and the U.S. Virgin Islands. If a family was living in a city, the street and house number are given. Each person is named with his or her relationship to the head of the household, his or her age, sex, marital status, and his or her age at their first marriage. If there had been more than one marriage, you should find that indicated by a M2 or M3 (or more) indicating if that person was in his or her second or third (or more) marriage, but the age given is the age at his or her first marriage. The birthplace of every individual plus the birthplace of his or her parents is shown on the schedule. If your ancestor was an immigrant, you will find his or her citizenship status and the year of immigration. Under citizenship status you will find the abbreviations "al" which stands for "alien," meaning no effort has been made toward citizenship, "pa" which stands for

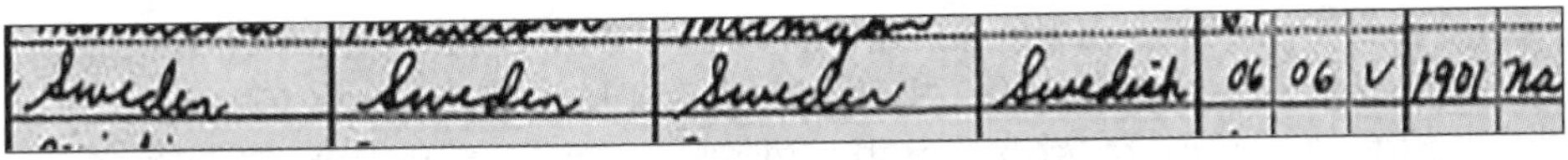

FIGURE 3.9
Copy of an extract from a 1930 census of Ripley, Houghton County, Michigan

"papers" (the first step toward naturalization has begun), and "na" for a naturalized citizen. What did they do for a living? The occupation is shown, as well. This census also gives the value of the person's home and if a veteran, what years he served. The war service is indicated by the following abbreviations: WW = World War, Sp = Spanish American, Civ = Civil War, Phil = Philippine Insurrection, Box = Boxer Rebellion, and Mex = Mexican Expedition. A supplemental schedule has an enumeration of Indians both on and off the reservation.

Figure 3.9 shows an individual who was born in Sweden and whose father and mother were born in Sweden. The language spoken was Swedish and the year of immigration was 1901. This person was a naturalized citizen as indicated by the "na."[8]

1910 and 1920 Population Schedules

The 1910 and 1920 census schedules were very similar. In addition to the names and ages of every individual in the household, you will find the number of years each person was married, the number of children each woman birthed, and how many were still living. The state or country in which each person was born plus the language spoken is given, along with the year of immigration and citizenship status for immigrants. For occupation, each person was asked his or her trade or occupation, nature of industry or business, whether he or she is an employee, employer, or self-employed (shown as "OA," which means "own account"). If they were an employee, it indicates whether they were out of work during the year. You will find whether they could read or write, if they had attended school within the year, and whether their home was owned or rented and, if owned, whether it was mortgaged and if it was a farm or a house. The schedule also asks if they were blind or deaf and dumb. On the 1910 schedule, they were asked if they were a survivor of the (Civil War) Union or Confederate Army or Navy. The 1910 census also had a special enumeration of Indians that included the tribe of the Indian, tribe of father, tribe of mother, blood quantum (the degree of Native American blood), and marriage information, but only for those living on reservations or in tribal relations and in certain counties containing a significant number of Indians.

1900 Population Schedule

The 1900 census records the name of every person and his or her relationship to the head of the household. The unique element of this census is that the month and year of birth of everyone are recorded along with their ages. This is the only census that did so. As with the 1920 and 1930 schedules, you will find the sex and marital status of each person as well as his or her place of birth, the place of birth of their father and mother, his or her year of immigration, his or her citizenship status, and his or her occupation. Also recorded is ownership of the home (owned or rented), whether it was a house or a farm, and if it was free or mortgaged.

1890 Population Schedule

If you find an ancestor on the 1890 census, consider yourself very fortunate. Only about 1 percent of the enumerations for this census schedule are extant. This is because a fire in Washington, DC, in 1921 in the Commerce Department building that housed the schedules damaged the originals. Some were partially destroyed by fire, while others had smoke and water damage. They were ordered to be destroyed about ten years later by Congress due to damage by mold. You will find no complete extant counties. This is sad news for those who suddenly find a twenty-year gap (1880 to 1900) between available census information. This was the first and only census that had each family listed on a separate census sheet, like a family group sheet.

Figure 3.10 shows an entry from the 1890 census, giving information on the Harrison L. Smith family of Perry County, Alabama.[9] In addition to Harrison Smith, we see his wife, Mary E., sons Henry W. and Jasper, and Harrison's sixty-year-old mother, Martha. The schedule indicates Martha is a widow. All were born in Alabama and each person's parents were born in Alabama, excepting Martha's parents, who were born in South Carolina. Harrison was unable to read and write.

FAMILY SCHEDULE—1 TO 10 PERSONS.

[7-556 a.]

Eleventh Census of the United States.

SCHEDULE No. 1.

POPULATION AND SOCIAL STATISTICS.

Supervisor's District No. 3
Enumeration District No. 78

Name of city, town, township, precinct, district, beat, or other minor civil division: Severe Beat No 8 ; County: Perry ; State: Alabama ;

Street and No.: X ; Ward: X ; Name of Institution: X

Enumerated by me on the 26ᵈ day of June, 1890. LeRoy E Davis

Enumerator.

A—Number of Dwelling-house in the order of visitation: 424
B—Number of families in this dwelling-house: 1
C—Number of persons in this dwelling-house: 5
D—Number of Family in the order of visitation: 424
E—No. of Persons in this family: 5

INQUIRIES.	2 15%	6 0 2	1 3	2 4	3 5
1 Christian name in full, and initial of middle name.	Harrison L	Mary E	Henry W	Jasper	Martha
Surname.	Smith	Smith	Smith	Smith	Smith
2 Whether a soldier, sailor, or marine during the civil war (U.S. or Conf.), or widow of such person.	Sv	X	X	X	X
3 Relationship to head of family.	Head	Wife	Son	Son	Mother
4 Whether white, black, mulatto, quadroon, octoroon, Chinese, Japanese, or Indian.	White	White	White	White	White
5 Sex.	Male	Female	Male	Male	Female
6 Age at nearest birthday. If under one year, give age in months.	38	23	4	2	60
7 Whether single, married, widowed, or divorced.	Married	Married	Single	Single	Widow
8 Whether married during the census year (June 1, 1889, to May 31, 1890).	Sv	Sv	X	X	X
9 Mother of how many children, and number of those children living.	X	2	X	X	2-1
10 Place of birth.	Alabama	Alabama	Alabama	Alabama	Alabama
11 Place of birth of Father.	Alabama	Alabama	Alabama	Alabama	South Carolina
12 Place of birth of Mother.	Alabama	Alabama	Alabama	Alabama	South Carolina
13 Number of years in the United States.	X	X	X	X	X
14 Whether naturalized.	X	X	X	X	X
15 Whether naturalization papers have been taken out.	X	X	X	X	X
16 Profession, trade, or occupation.	Farmer	Housewife	at Home	at Home	Housekeeper
17 Months unemployed during the census year (June 1, 1889, to May 31, 1890).	0	0	0	0	0
18 Attendance at school (in months) during the census year (June 1, 1889, to May 31, 1890).	X	X	X	X	0
19 Able to Read.	Sv	Yes	X	X	Yes
20 Able to Write.	Sv	Yes	X	X	Yes
21 Able to speak English. If not, the language or dialect spoken.	English	English	X	X	English
22 Whether suffering from acute or chronic disease, with name of disease and length of time afflicted.	X	X	X	X	X
23 Whether defective in mind, sight, hearing, or speech, or whether crippled, maimed, or deformed, with name of defect.	X	X	X	X	X
24 Whether a prisoner, convict, homeless child, or pauper.	X	X	X	X	X
25 Supplemental schedule and page.					

TO ENUMERATORS.—See inquiries numbered 26 to 30, inclusive, on the second page of this schedule. These inquiries must be made concerning each family and each farm visited.

FIGURE 3.10

1890 census, Severe, Perry County, Alabama; entry for the Harrison L. Smith family

1880 Population Schedule

The 1880 census was the first time individuals' relationships to the head of the household were given. In prior years, household units listed everyone in the home but did not indicate if there were any familial relationships. As you have gone backward into the census schedules, you will have already seen the relationships given to individuals in the household. Those relationships you might have seen are wife, son, daughter, adopted son/daughter, stepson/daughter, mother/father/brother/sister-in-law, boarder, servant, and inmate. Other more obscure relationships are also possible such as cousin, niece/nephew, farm hand, and laborer. As with the 1900 through 1940 schedules, the 1880 census shows the name of the street and house number (in cities), color, sex, age, marital status, and occupation. This schedule also shows the number of months unemployed during the census year, health (blind, deaf and dumb, insane, etc.), whether they attended school during the census year, whether they were able to read and write, and the place of birth of each person and their parents.

The 1880 census schedule in figure 3.11 shows Charles Lux, who is the only person in his household. Note the numbers to the left of his name, in this case 851. Each family unit was numbered to indicate a household. Lux was a white male, thirty years old, and single. His

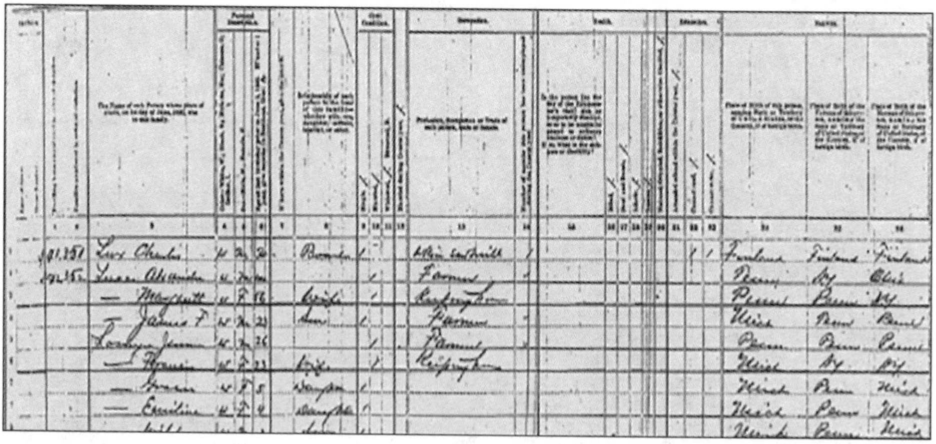

FIGURE 3.11
1880 census schedule showing Charles Lux, who is the only person in his household

relationship is "boarder," which is unusual in a single-family household. He may have been a boarder to family number 850 on the previous page, Mr. and Mrs. Joseph Lucas. Mr. Lux worked in a sawmill, was born in Finland, and his parents were born in Finland. The family below him has two family units within the household. This is evident because Alexander Lucas, the head of his household, has no relationship given (indicating he is the head). Below him are his wife and son. Below them, within the same numbered household, is James Losmyer, who has no relationship given. Below him are a wife, two daughters, and a son.[10]

1850, 1860, and 1870 Population Schedules

The 1850, 1860, and 1870 census schedules contain similar information. The 1850 schedule was the first time all people were listed by name, but their relationships were not given. We might assume that everyone within a household is related to each other, but that might not be the case. Everyone might have the same surname, but we cannot assume that the next person is the wife and the others listed are the children. If someone had a different surname, there might have been a familial relationship or the person might have been a boarder or hired hand. In figure 3.12 we see Josiah Finley, age 46. Julia Ann, listed under him, is 26 years old. Is Julia Ann his wife or a daughter? If she is Josiah's wife, is she his first or second wife? Judson F. was 14 years old and there were two younger children, William, age 6 and Harriet H., age 9

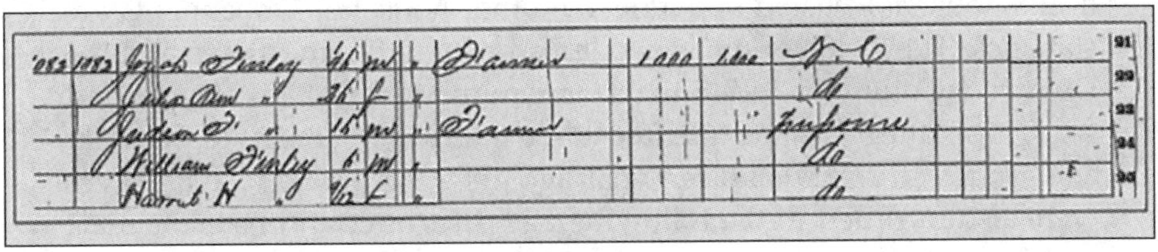

FIGURE 3.12
1860 census schedule showing household of Josiah Finley,
who was born in "N.C.," meaning North Carolina;
Julia Ann's place of birth was "do," meaning ditto

months (9/12 = 9 months). We could possibly conclude that Judson is the product of a first marriage, considering that Julia would have been only 12 years old at the time of Judson's birth, and William and Harriet are the children of Josiah and Julia Ann. But one should not be too hasty with conclusions. More research should be done to determine the relationships here. In addition to each person's name, there is entered their age, sex, color, occupation, value of real estate (1860 and 1870 also show the value of personal property), place of birth, and whether each person could read and write. Health information was also given if an individual was deaf and dumb, blind, insane, or idiotic. Supplemental slave schedules were also taken on separate schedules. The names of the slave owners were shown on the slave schedules, but the names of the slaves were not given. We only see information about each slave's age, sex, and color (Black or Mulatto), and if they were a fugitive from the state, number manumitted, and whether deaf, dumb, or idiotic.

Figure 3.12 shows, in a flourishing hand, in the column showing the place of birth, that Josiah was born in "N.C," meaning North Carolina. Julia Ann's place of birth was "do," meaning ditto. She was also born in North Carolina. Judson's place of birth is Missouri.[11] How can I tell that? It comes with lots of practice. In nineteenth-century writing, look for the long S especially when it occurs as a double S. It will look like an "fs." Reading old handwriting can take time to decipher, but it is worth the effort to learn.

1840 Population Schedule

From 1840 and back to the 1790 census you will only find the head of the household listed by name. All other household inhabitants are statistics. The 1840 census is available for twenty-nine states and the District of Columbia. Individuals were numbered by age category and sex. Those categories include free white males and females in five-year age groups to age 20 and ten-year age groups from 20 to 100. Slaves were also recorded in the following age categories and listed as male and female: Under 10, 10 to under 24, 24 to under 36, 36 to under 55, 55 to under 100, and over 100 years of age. Free "colored" persons are recorded in the same age categories as slaves, both male and female. On this census schedule you will also find the numbers of persons involved in mining, agriculture, commerce, manufacture and trade, navigation of the ocean, navigation of canals, lakes, and rivers, and learned professional engineers. Additionally, you will also find the names and ages of military pension

FIGURE 3.13
1840 census entry
for Joseph Hatch, age 82

holders from the Revolutionary War or other military service. Information about schools was also recorded, indicating universities or colleges, academies and grammar schools, primary and common schools with their numbers of students at public charge. Finally, the numbers of those deaf and dumb, blind, and insane were given. Figure 3.13 shows an entry from the 1840 census taken in Barnstable County, Massachusetts, giving the name of the pensioner Joseph Hatch, age 82.[12]

1830 Population Schedule

The 1830 was the first census that uniformly used a preprinted form. Prior to 1830, the census forms contained hand-drawn columns. Twenty-eight states plus the District of Columbia are extant. The age categories indicated free white males and females in five-year age groups to age 20 and ten-year age groups from 20 to 100. Slaves were recorded in the following male and female age categories: under 10, 10 to under 24, 24 to under 36, 36 to under 55, 55 to under 100, and over 100 years of age. Free "colored" persons are recorded in the same age categories as slaves, both male and female. Numbers of aliens/foreigners not naturalized, deaf and dumb (in age categories), and the number of blind people are also recorded.

Figure 3.14 shows Jesse Noland on the first line. In his household are one male who is age 15 to 20, two males who are ages 20 to 30, one male who is age 50 to 60, one female age 15 to 20, one female age 20 to 30, and one female age 50 to 60.[13] We can assume that Jesse Noland was the male who is age 50 to 60 years old, as was his wife. There were either older children who were unmarried or there was a son age 20 to 30 who is married to the female age 20 to 30. As you can see, we can make speculations, but we cannot know for certain who might be in the household.

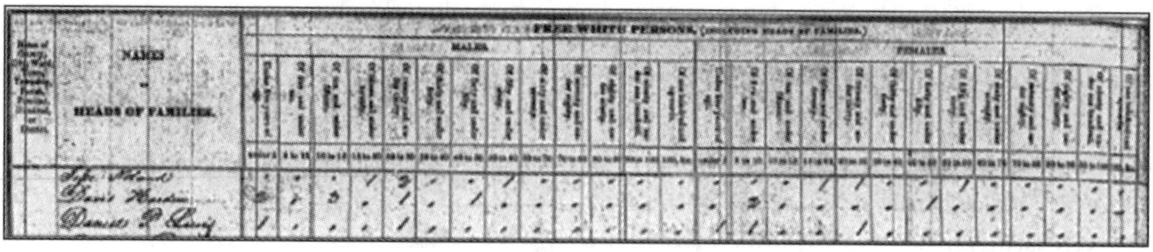

FIGURE 3.14

1830 census, Jackson County, Missouri, showing household of Jesse Noland

1820 Population Schedule

The 1820 census is available for twenty-two states and the District of Columbia. Those states are Connecticut, Delaware, Georgia, Illinois, Indiana, Kentucky, Louisiana, Maine, Maryland, Massachusetts, Michigan, Mississippi, New Hampshire, New York, North Carolina, Ohio, Pennsylvania, Rhode Island, South Carolina, Tennessee, Vermont, and Virginia. Again, only the names of the heads of the households are listed. The numbers of free white males and females are listed in the following age categories: 0 to 10, 10 and under 16, 16 and under 26, 26 and under 45, and 45 years and older. Slaves are shown, male and female, in almost the same age categories. In addition, the numbers of free white males between the ages of 16 and 18 are also shown. Beware that males in this age category are listed twice, once as 16 to 18 and again in the 16- to 26-year-old age category. The purpose of the extra enumeration of young men was to indicate how many were available for military duty. We also find data on the number of foreigners who were not naturalized, persons engaged in agriculture, persons engaged in manufacturing, and all other persons except Indians who were not taxed.

Figure 3.15 shows Samuel Brooks on the first line.[14] In his household are one male child under the age of 10, one male between the ages of 16 and 26 (but he is not between the ages of 16 and 18), one male age 45 or older, two females under the age of 10, five females ages 10 to 16, three females ages 16 to 26, and one female age 45 or older. On the right-

FIGURE 3.15

1820 census entry for Samuel Brooks' household

hand side of the schedule we see the number of slaves. There appear to be two male slaves between the ages of 14 and 26.

1810 Population Schedule

The 1810 census is extant for sixteen states: Connecticut, Delaware, Kentucky, Louisiana, Maine, Maryland, Massachusetts, New Hampshire, New York, North Carolina, Pennsylvania, Rhode Island, South Carolina, Tennessee (Rutherford County only), Vermont, and Virginia. As in the previous census, only the name of the head of the household was listed, and there was no preprinted form for the enumerator to use. The numbers of free white males and females are listed in the following age categories: 0 to 10, 10 and under 16, 16 and under 26, 26 and under 45, and 45 years and older.

1800 Population Schedule

The 1800 census is extant for twelve states and the District of Columbia. The states are Connecticut, Delaware, Maine, Maryland, Massachusetts, New Hampshire, New York, North Carolina, Pennsylvania, Rhode Island, South Carolina, and Vermont. This very simple hand-drawn census form shows only the names of the heads of households. The numbers of free white males and females are listed in the following age categories: 0 to 10, 10 and under 16, 16 and under 26, 26 and under 45, and 45 years and older. Also included were the numbers of other free persons other than Indians not taxed, and the number of slaves.

The first individual listed on enumeration in figure 3.16 is David Anthony. In his household are one male under the age of 10, one male between the ages of 16 and 26, one male between the ages of 26 and 45, three females under the age of 10, one female between the ages of 10 and 16, and one female between the ages of 26 and 45.[15]

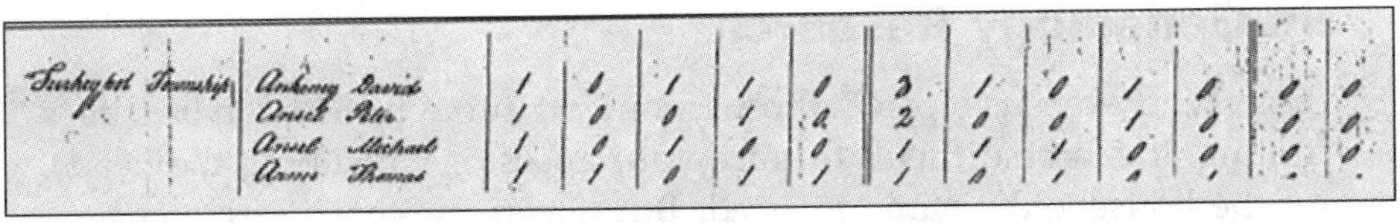

FIGURE 3.16
An enumeration from the 1800 census

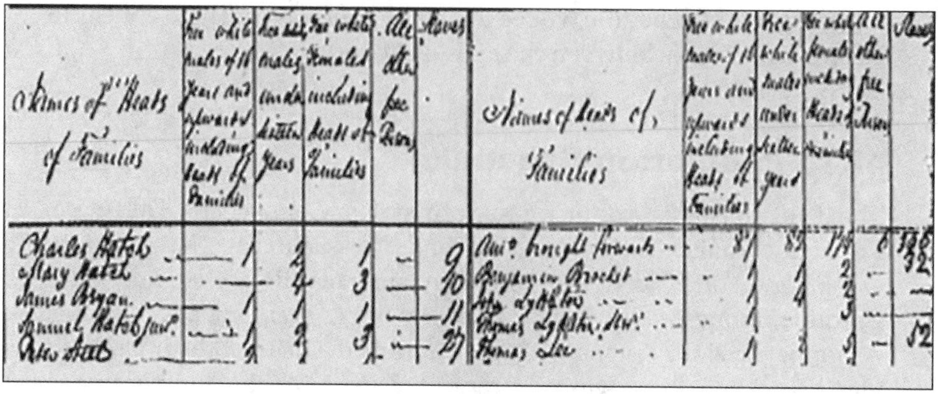

FIGURE 3.17
1790 census, Jones County, North Carolina, showing
the entry for the household of Charles Hatch

1790 Population Schedule

The first census taken in the United States was the 1790 census. It was a basic enumeration of the taxpayers residing in the country, by state. The enumeration of eleven states is extant: Connecticut, Maine, Maryland, Massachusetts, New Hampshire, New York, North Carolina, Pennsylvania, Rhode Island, South Carolina, and Vermont. This census took the form of a rudimentary enumeration on a hand-drawn chart and, as in the previous census, the only names recorded were those of the heads of each household. Following each person's name were the numbers of free white males 16 years and older, free white males under the age of 16, free white females (with no age categories), slaves, and other persons residing in that house. Figure 3.17 shows Charles Hatch on the first line. In his household is one male over the age of 16, two males under 16, one female, and nine slaves.[16]

Using Early Census Records in Genealogy Research

Using early census records, those from 1790 through 1840, can be frustrating. It can be difficult to trace your ancestor when only the head of the household's name is listed. But if you use these early census enumerations as clues, they can help narrow your search when trying to determine the parents of an ancestor. Note the 1830 Jackson County, Missouri, census sample (figure 3.14). Let's use this as an example. The Jesse Noland household has four males between the ages of 15 and 60 and three females between the ages of 15 and 60. If you knew from previous research that your Noland ancestor was born in Missouri in 1812, you should look for every head of household in Missouri with the surname Noland who had at least one male in the 15- to 20-year-old age category. Jesse Noland's household would be one of those. Rule out any household that did not have a male in that age category. Those who remain will be those for whom you will want to do further research and find other documents that might list the names of children, such as a will or church record. This gives you the first and last names of possible fathers and possible counties in which to do further research.

States themselves often enumerated residents in off-census years. Some, like the state of Kansas, were very regular. They took a census once every five years between federal censuses, beginning with the territorial census in 1855 and every ten years after that. Other states did state enumerations more sporadically. Those that took a census between the years 1880 and 1900 help to bridge the twenty-year gap caused by the destruction of the 1890 census, a gap that would otherwise be a long span between enumerations. Excellent coverage of this topic is found in *State Census Records* by Ann Lainhart.[17] Many state census records are found on Ancestry.com and FamilySearch. Let's take an example from my own genealogy. There is no federal census in which my grandfather and his father were together in the same household. Finding the two of them on a census schedule would help prove a relationship I did not otherwise have. A state census gave me that option. They lived in Michigan, which had 1884 and 1894 state censuses. My grandfather and his father were shown together on the 1894 state census, which helped me cement that relationship.

Non-Population Schedules

We have been looking at population schedules, which named individuals in specific locations at specific periods in time. In addition to the population schedules, the enumerators recorded non-population schedules that are extant for the years 1850 through 1880. Statistics were gathered from the schedules. Those schedules created after 1880 were destroyed after the statistics were gathered. The non-population schedules are mortality (numbering those who were deceased), agricultural (gathering statistics from those involved in farming), manufacturing (gathering statistics from those involved in industry), and social statistics.

Mortality schedules give the names of persons who died in the twelve months prior to the census date. For instance, the 1860 mortality schedule included persons who died from June 1, 1859, to May 31, 1860. It would be wonderful if they showed everyone who died within the ten years since the previous census, but alas, they do not. But since many states or counties were not keeping a record of deaths during those years, these mortality schedules may be the only records of death for many individuals. For each listed person, the following information is found: name, age, sex, marital status, state or country of birth, month of death, occupation, cause of death, and the length of the final illness. The top line of figure 3.18 shows Ross K. Daling, age 6 months who died in December (1859). He was born in Missouri and died of pneumonia.[18]

Many of our ancestors were involved in farming. Agricultural schedules recorded the following information for each farm: name of the owner or manager, number of improved and unimproved acres, and the cash value of the farm, farming machinery, livestock, animals slaughtered during the past year, and "homemade manufactures." The schedules also indicated the number of animals owned by the farmer

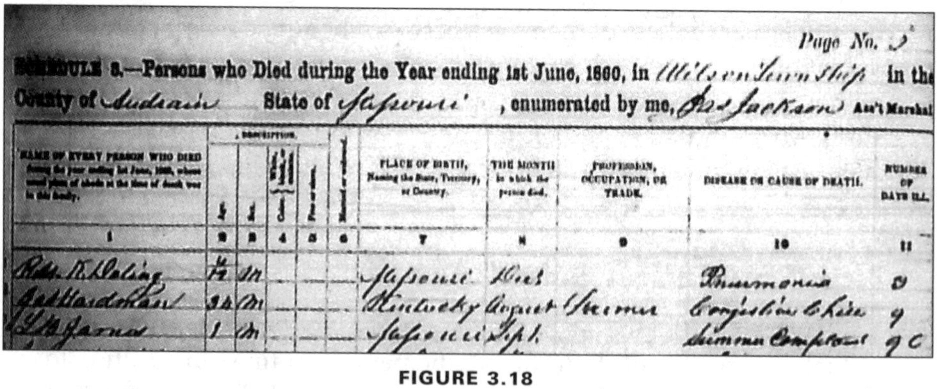
Page No.
SCHEDULE 3.—Persons who Died during the Year ending 1st June, 1860, in
County of
State of
, enumerated by me,
Ass't Marshal
PLACE OF BIRTH, Naming the State, Territory, or Country.
THE MONTH in which the person died.
PROFESSION, OCCUPATION, OR TRADE.
DISEASE OR CAUSE OF DEATH.
NUMBER OF DAYS ILL.

FIGURE 3.18
Entry from Missouri mortality schedule, Adair County, 1860

and the amounts of crops grown during the preceding year. The 1880 schedules provided additional details, such as the amount of acreage used for each kind of crop, the number of poultry, and the number of eggs produced. Not every farm was included in these schedules. Some census years required a minimum-sized farm to be reported. If your ancestor was on a census with the occupation of "farmer" and significant real estate value is shown, then you will want to look at the agricultural schedules for that county. You will not find a lot of personal information, but these schedules will give you a unique glimpse into your forebear's life as a farmer.

On the 1870 agricultural schedule shown in figure 3.19, we see Reuben Allen on line one.[19] He had 16 acres of improved land with a cash value of $350. He owned three horses, one "milch" (milk) cow, one "other cattle," twelve sheep, and twelve swine. During the year ending June 1, he produced 130 bushels of winter wheat and 200 bushels of Indian corn.

Manufacturing/industry schedules are available for the census years 1810, 1820, and 1850 through 1880. The 1810 data was not shown

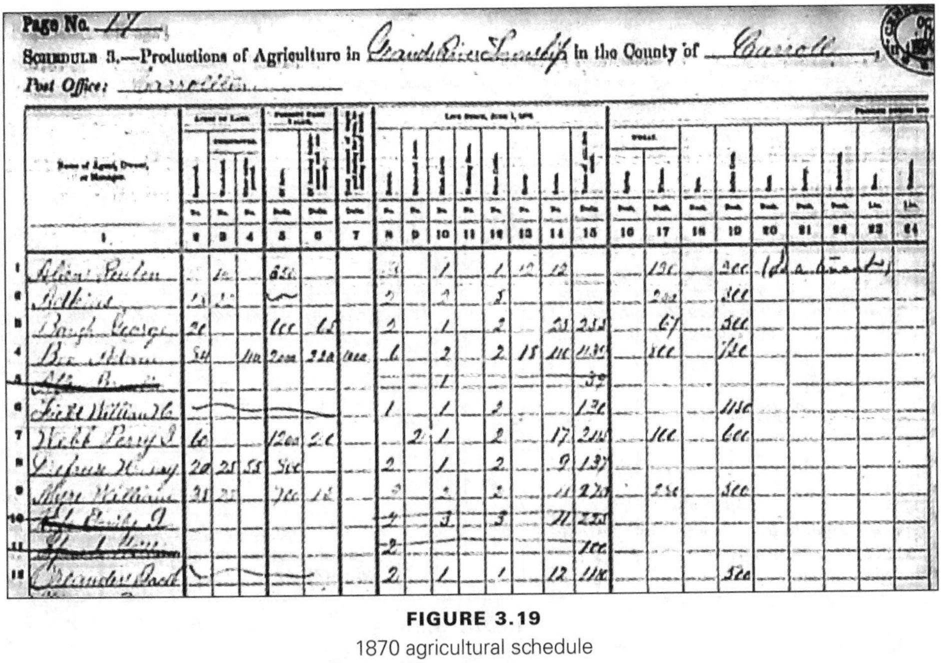

FIGURE 3.19
1870 agricultural schedule

on separate schedules. You will find annotations on the population schedules, but since Congress had not specified the information to be collected, the results vary within the schedules. In 1820, 1850, 1860, 1870, and 1880 you will find the name of the manufacturer doing business over $500, the type of business or product, the amount of capital invested, the quantities and types of products, and the number of men and women employed. Even though you may not find your ancestor's name on these schedules, you will be able to identify the businesses in your ancestor's community. If the census shows your ancestor's occupation as a worker in a linen mill, the manufacturing schedule could help you identify the place of his or her employment.

Line one of the 1870 industry schedule in figure 3.20 shows Louis Hoevner, who owned a malt house.[20] The columns ask for the following: the name of the corporation or individual producing to the value of $500 annually, the name of the business, manufacture, or product, the amount of capital (real and personal) invested, the type of power used and if steam or water, the number of horsepower, the name or description of machines, and the number of machines. Information extends

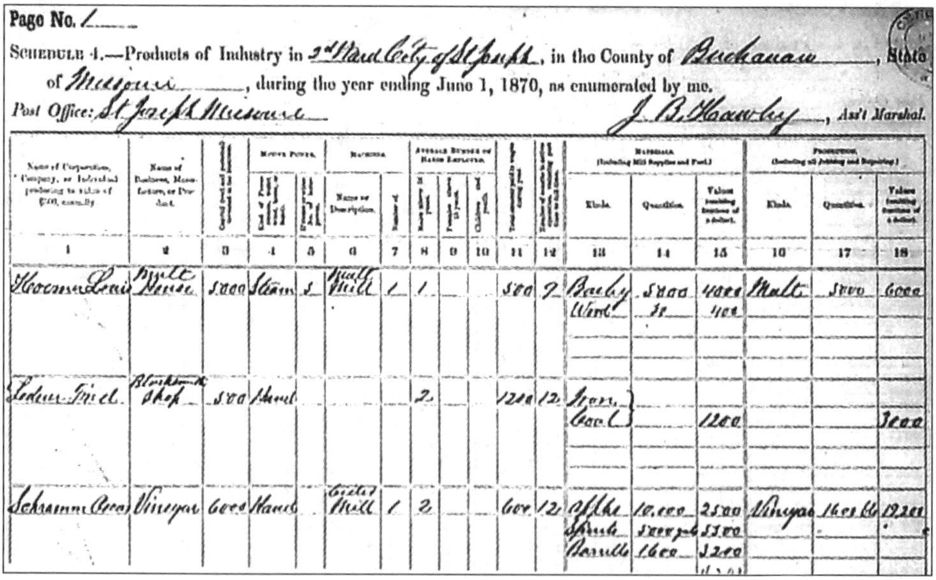

Page No. 1

SCHEDULE 4.—Products of Industry in 2d Ward City of St Joseph, in the County of Buchanan, State of Missouri, during the year ending June 1, 1870, as enumerated by me.

Post Office: St Joseph Missouri

J. B. Hawley, Ass't Marshal.

FIGURE 3.20
1870 manufacturing/industry schedule

to the next page, asking for the average number of hands by age category, the total dollar amount of wages paid, the number of months in operation, the kinds, quantities, and values of materials used, and the kinds, quantities, and value of production. Louis Hoevner had $5,000 invested in the business, both real and capital. He used steam with five horsepower. He used one malt mill and employed one male over the age of sixteen. This person was paid $500 during the year and the malt house was in business for nine months of the year. Hoevner used 5,000 units of barley, valued at $4,000, and 30 units of wood, valued at $400. The malt house produced 5,000 units of malt, valued at $6,000.

Social statistics schedules provide information about your ancestor's community. In 1850 through 1880, these schedules indicate the total value of real estate, the annual taxes paid, the number of schools, teachers, and pupils, the number and types of libraries with the number of volumes they contained, the names of newspapers with type and circulation, church denominations, the number of people each church could seat and the value of the property, the number of paupers and the cost of supporting them, the number of criminals convicted and in prison, and the average wages paid to farmhands, day laborers, carpenters, and female domestics. The information on these schedules is statistical only. You will not find your ancestor's name. But the economic and social life in your ancestor's community, again, gives you a unique glimpse into the community. In 1880, you will also find the DDD schedules (Delinquent, Defective, and Dependent). These schedules record the names of delinquent, defective, and dependent (deaf and dumb, blind, criminals, indigent, etc.) individuals in the community. This is indeed a unique source.

The 1880 DDD schedule in figure 3.21 shows those who were blind in Polk County, Missouri.[21] The columns indicate the name of the blind person, his or her city or town, county, and whether he or she is self-supporting (yes/no). The schedule indicated the form of blindness, its cause, whether totally blind or semi-blind, if he or she has ever been in an institution for the blind, and if individual is also insane, idiotic, or deaf mute.

Excluding the mortality schedules, the non-population schedules are difficult to find online. Look for these gems in larger research libraries or in the records repository of the state, such as the state historical society or archives.

Population and non-population census schedules are some of the best sources of information for genealogists. They were not intended

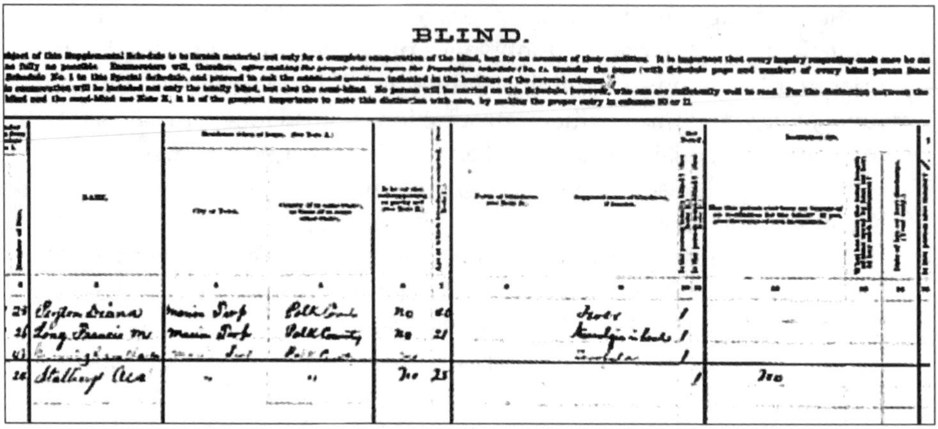

BLIND.

FIGURE 3.21
1880 DDD schedule

to be a significant genealogical source when they were originally created, but with the limited availability of vital records before 1900, they are a gold mine of information for family historians. William Dollarhide gives an excellent overview of all census years in his aptly named book, *The Census Book.*[22] For most researchers who are just getting started, census records can jump-start their research and take them back to unknown ancestors quite rapidly.

Federal, State, and Local Government Records

Courts played an important part in the lives of our forebears. They were established to keep the law, hear cases, and conduct the day-to-day business of the government. Our ancestors often had transactions with courts during their lifetimes and often visited the county courthouse. To find court documents which may contain your ancestor's name, examine the area when and where he or she lived. A timeline is a great help in this regard. If an ancestor lived in an area long enough to conduct business, such as pay taxes, buy property, record a marriage, or apply for a business license, then you may find information in the local jurisdiction.

Sometimes we don't find a trace of an ancestor within the community's records. Those are usually the folks who were "passing through."

LESSON FIVE

As a librarian working with genealogists, it is important to be knowledgeable about census records. They are an often-used source.

- Examine your pedigree chart. Select one ancestor who was born before 1900.

- Find all available census records for that person. You can make a copy of the record or transcribe it. Extraction forms can be found at www.ancestry.com/charts/census.aspx and at https://wiki.familysearch.org/en/United_States_Census_Forms.

- Compare the data found. You might find one census record which states your great-grandfather was born in New York, while another indicates the birthplace was Pennsylvania. Perhaps your ancestor was listed as 26 years old on an enumeration but ten years later was recorded as 34. Comparing every census year allows you to come to a better conclusion concerning the facts.

They lived in a community for such a short amount of time that they left no imprint in the area. But what if your ancestor was in an area for a long time and still left no record in the courthouse? Courthouse fires are responsible for the loss of many important documents. They could have occurred from a lightning strike, faulty wiring, or intentional burning during the Civil War. Counties with a loss of records due to fire are called "burned counties." Check nearby jurisdictions for copies or similar records on file. There may have been county boundary changes over time from the county's formation to the current day. As the state grew, counties were formed out of other counties. For example, if county "A" exists today but an ancestor lived in a part of the county that was county "B" at the time of a marriage, look for the marriage record in the courthouse of county "B." Let's look at Cumberland County, Pennsylvania, in 1810 as a specific example. At that time, the county encompassed current-day Perry County as well as Cumberland County. The record holdings for each county can only be found from its earliest existence. Perry County was formed in 1820, therefore, you will not find any records in the county before that year. The *Handy Book* or *Ancestry's Red Book* can help you determine when a county was formed and from what parent county it came. A good visual illustration of the evolution of county boundary changes can be found in the *Map Guide to the U.S. Federal Censuses, 1790–1920.*[23] It is no longer in publication but may be purchased from a used book dealer. The maps for each state are by census year (or years if there were no further boundary changes). The current-day county names and boundaries are in white lettering. The boundaries of the year in question are in black. The maps from the publication can also be found on Heritage Quest Online. From its home page, look for the header that says "Maps." You will be able to select a state and a year to visualize the geography of that year. There is also a series of books which were published by Charles Scribner's Sons/Simon & Schuster entitled *Atlas of Historical County Boundaries.* They were published one book per state. These may also be purchased through used book dealers.

Courthouse fires and county boundary changes are not the only reason for a loss or lack of records in a courthouse. First, there had to be a law that required the information to be collected. For instance, if there was no law for births and deaths to be recorded in 1850, you will not find those records today. Sometimes the county clerk did not comply with the law and neglected to record the information. Improper storage or archiving of documents is yet another reason for a lack of records. The records may have been stored in an attic where mice or climate conditions caused their demise. Security has not always been as stringent as it is today, and records have been known to have "walked away."

There are several types of government jurisdictions: federal, state, county, and municipal. Each branch of government conducts business appropriate to its parameters and each has a physical location where that business is conducted. The country is divided into federal court districts, and each state is also divided into districts. Counties usually have one jurisdiction in the city or town where the courthouse is located, called the county seat. Municipal governments deal with the administration of a city or town. The important thing to remember when looking for government records, in whatever jurisdiction or level, is that each is responsible for its own unique records. You will sometimes hear of a court being referred to as a "court of record." This refers to a court that is required by law to keep a record of its proceedings.

There are many types of courts within the courts system, each playing a part in record-keeping for its own legal parameters: appellate courts, courts of appeals, circuit courts, district courts, inferior courts, criminal courts, family or juvenile courts, municipal courts, and probate courts.[24] Appellate courts exist on both the federal and state levels. These courts listen to appeals from lower courts. They are also called courts of appeals. Circuit courts are movable courts. The judge can and does move his or her court from place to place for a specific time to conduct official business. In a sense the judge is "riding the circuit." A family court is one which handles domestic disputes, especially those regarding children, while a juvenile court deals specifically in juvenile cases, such as adoption. Municipal courts manage misdemeanors and civil lawsuits involving less money than higher courts. In some states, municipal courts only handle disputes and violations dealing with the city or local municipality, such as traffic citations. Probate courts have jurisdiction over wills and the administration of estates, including guardianships.

Cases filed at the jurisdictional level are divided into two categories—civil and criminal. Civil cases exist where there is an offense between two or more parties, people, legal entities, or corporations and may involve property damage, libel, divorce, personal injury, or breach of contract; these cases often end in a monetary judgment. Criminal cases exist where crimes or offenses were committed against the state. These offenses can include murder, theft, arson, or treason. Serious crimes are called felonies and minor crimes are called misdemeanors.

The types of records found in the courthouse are often bound in books. These may be bond books, court dockets, court calendars, order books, minute books, fee books, packets, loose papers, and miscellaneous papers. Bond books are used by sheriffs and justices of the peace. They contain bail bonds and executor bonds. Docket books can be thought of as a table of contents to the proceedings of the court, while court calendars are chronological listings of those proceedings in date order. The dockets and calendars contain lists of names of the plaintiffs (those who file a complaint) and defendants (those required to answer the complaint), the case file numbers, brief descriptions of the actions, lists of documents brought to the court, and the date of the hearing. They may be found as order books. There are often separate dockets for civil versus criminal cases. Minute books are the recordings or notes taken by the clerk of the court; in other words, the daily record of the court. Listed in minute books are an account of the proceedings including a brief description of all actions, the names of the plaintiffs and defendants, brief reports of each case, and summaries of actions taken. These also are in chronological order and part of the court record. Fee books contain lists of fines and fees ordered and subsequently collected.

An official court record includes the minutes, pleadings (the cause for action by the plaintiff), documents filed (which can include evidence, correspondence, and petitions), orders (requiring a person to do or cease doing an act), and rulings (decisions by the court). There are often too many documents filed to be kept in a court record. This necessitates the creation of packets, folders, or bundles that contain all the pertinent documents. The packets are given the same number as the court record and are usually put into storage, whether it be within the courthouse or in a separate off-site facility. The packets and such can be difficult to find unless you find a friendly clerk or paralegal to tell you where their location is. There can also be documents and papers in storage that were not filed, called miscellaneous or loose papers, which are related to a case but are not deemed necessary to include in the packets. The authors Bill Gann and Gary Toms used loose papers in researching their book *Widows Dowers of Washington County, Tennessee, 1803–1899*.[25] They found rich documentation in the papers found housed at the Archives of Appalachia which had never been used by researchers before then. They "recognized that the detailed information contained in these accounts did not occur in the recorded volumes in the courthouse volumes in the facility at the county seat in Jonesborough. These volumes ordinarily contain only a brief, abstracted entry for dowers."[26] Going beyond the easily found documents in a courthouse or archive is often needed to find records related to one's ancestors.

Wills and Probate

Imagine a document that can relate to you the wealth your ancestor accumulated during his or her lifetime, the name of that person's spouse and the names of their children, the names of other family members, and perhaps the charities he or she favored. This information can be found in a will. A will can be a treasure trove of information. But a will does not stand alone and has no legal effect until it is probated.

Probate is the legal method of administering an individual's property or estate after his or her death. The *Merriam-Webster Unabridged Dictionary* says that probate is "the action or process of proving before a competent judicial officer or tribunal that a document offered for official recognition and registration as the last will and testament of a deceased person is genuine."[27] The last will and testament is the documentation of a person's wishes as to the dispersal of his or her estate. The probate record, the entire group of papers generated in the probate process, can be found in a county courthouse. When one dies with a will, the estate is "testate." Think of this as someone leaving a testament or statement prior to his death. There are several types of wills. Attested wills are those which are prepared in writing and witnessed; holographic wills are written in one's own hand; and nuncupative wills are given orally to witnesses. It is standard procedure to name an executor in a will. This is the individual who will carry out the wishes stated in the document. If the deceased does not leave a will, the estate is "intestate," which means there is no document that dictates the dispersal of the property. Intestate estates require steps to be taken in the court system and a ruling to determine the division of the estate. An administrator is appointed by the court to carry out the proceedings in the case.

The probate process, settling the estate, has many steps during which probate packets are created. After documents are recorded in court, they are placed in a folder or folders if the papers become too numerous. The folders are called packets. Notes are placed on the outside of the packet to indicated items as they are placed inside. The paperwork inside the packets are the original documents. The onset of handling probate begins when the principal heir or executor petitions the court for authority to begin the probate process. The executor is then formally approved by the court. In an intestate proceeding the court appoints the administrator, who is often a relative. Bonds are posted as a binding agreement to protect the heirs in ensuring that the terms of the will are followed. The amount posted is equal to the assets of the estate. The bondsmen are usually relatives and friends and can also be heirs. An inventory is always taken in an intestate estate, but is only required in a testate estate if the will does not say that "all" or "the remainder of my estate" is going to one specified individual. A disinterested party, not an heir, conducts the inventory, which is filed within ninety days. The inventory is often recorded in the will book.

The will is then "proven." This means testimony is given by those who witnessed the signing of the will, and these individuals swear that they saw the individual sign it, he was in sound mental condition to do so, and he did it of his own free will. The document is then recorded in the will book and the proceedings are recorded in the court minute books, all heirs are notified of the reading of the will, and the administrator or executor petitions the court to sell the property as listed in the inventory. If minor children are involved, the petition could include an order to pay for their care while the estate is being settled. Guardianship is appointed to provide legal assistance to any minor children or those incapacitated or of low mental acumen. A guardian may be appointed even if one of the parents was still living. Property could also be petitioned to be sold if the heirs need money to pay expenses while the estate is being settled. If inventory is to be sold, the estate is advertised for sale, usually in the local newspaper. A record of the sale will be recorded in the court minute book, with the list of buyers recorded in the probate packet or will book. Always look at the names of those purchasing items from the estate. Low sale prices may indicate a family relationship.

When the settlement is near, a notice of the pending probate is publicized for three weeks in a local newspaper or is posted in a public area. If there is real estate to be divided, a plat or drawing of the land is submitted to the court. If the property was to be sold and the money divided among the heirs, the final sale is presented. A final accounting is rendered by the executor or administrator, and all other property is divided and the case closed. Each heir signs a receipt for the property or cash received. Finally, the judge releases the executor or administrator from their obligations. Guardians are only released from their obligations after minor children have reached the age of maturity.[28]

Figure 3.22 is a copy of notice of pending probate for the estate of Israel Israelson that was most likely published in the (Houghton, Michigan) *Daily Mining Gazette* in June 1923. The named administrator was his son-in-law. Those related to the deceased are often executors or have other duties in the administration of the estate. The clipping was found in papers belonging to the author's aunt.

When looking for probate records, check in the docket books, minute books, will books, newspapers, and probate packets. You will find the will to be the most interesting document. Often information about

family members and their relationships will be found in it. The
most interesting will I found in
my research was for William
E. Schultz.[29] William had been
married two times and had children from both marriages. The
first marriage resulted in the
birth of two sons. When William's first marriage dissolved,
one son continued to live with
him and the other went to live
with the mother. William's second marriage resulted in one
daughter. His will record (see
figure 3.23) divided his property equally among his current
wife, his daughter, and the son
that had lived with him. The son
who had lived with William's
ex-wife was given only five dollars. There is no indication why
this was so, but I believe William did not intend his second
son to inherit a portion of the
estate. He was given a negligi-
ble amount in the will to show
that he was not forgotten, and
thus reduce the possibility that
he might contest the will.

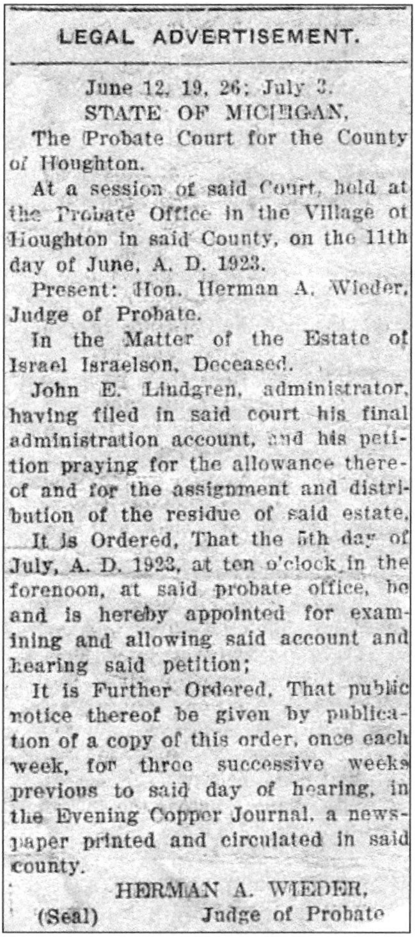

LEGAL ADVERTISEMENT.

June 12, 19, 26; July 3.
STATE OF MICHIGAN,
The Probate Court for the County
of Houghton.
At a session of said Court, held at
the Probate Office in the Village of
Houghton in said County, on the 11th
day of June, A. D. 1923.
Present: Hon. Herman A. Wieder,
Judge of Probate.
In the Matter of the Estate of
Israel Israelson, Deceased.
John E. Lindgren, administrator,
having filed in said court his final
administration account, and his petition praying for the allowance thereof and for the assignment and distribution of the residue of said estate,
It is Ordered, That the 5th day of
July, A. D. 1923, at ten o'clock in the
forenoon, at said probate office, be
and is hereby appointed for examining and allowing said account and
hearing said petition;
It is Further Ordered, That public
notice thereof be given by publication of a copy of this order, once each
week, for three successive weeks
previous to said day of hearing, in
the Evening Copper Journal, a newspaper printed and circulated in said
county.
HERMAN A. WIEDER,
(Seal)   Judge of Probate

FIGURE 3.22
A copy of notice of pending probate
for the estate of Israel Israelson

Land and Deed Records

Our ancestors often came to this country to acquire land for themselves.
In many European countries, most of the arable land was owned by
aristocrats or landed gentry, and so farm laborers and other ordinary
people were starved for land of their own. Our ancestors often left

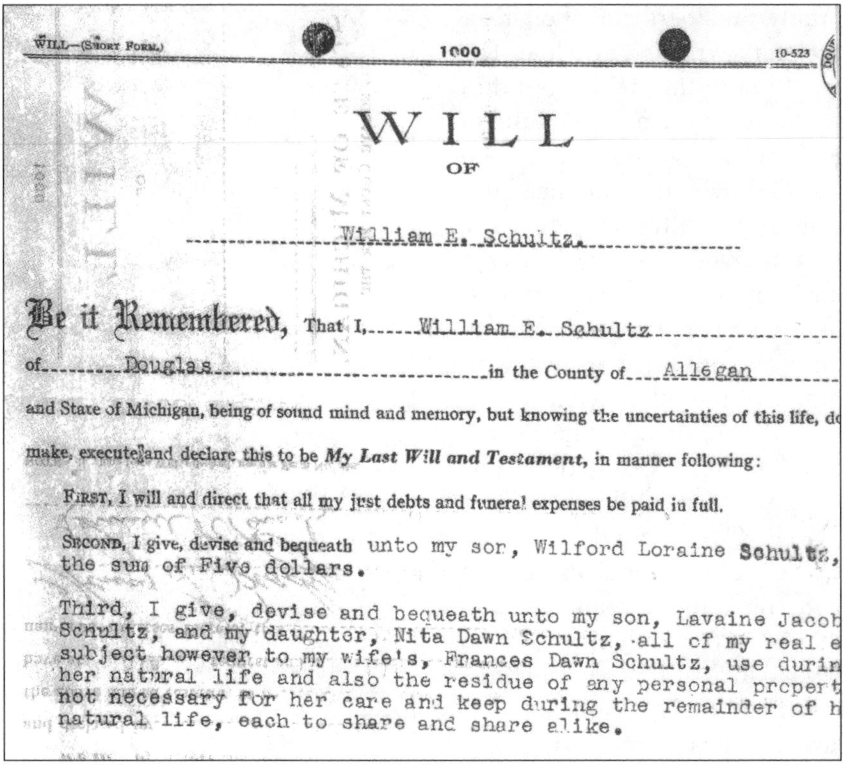

FIGURE 3.23
William E. Schultz's will record

the eastern seaboard of the United States for the same reason: there was often not enough land to be divided up among all the children in a family when the parents died. Individuals had several options for obtaining land; they could buy land from another individual, they could homestead (i.e., live on and cultivate the land), or they could receive the land as military bounty land.

The United States is divided into two types of land record-keeping. Most, but not all, of the states east of the Mississippi River are called *state land* states. These states had landholdings when they were colonies, or else they were formed from existing colonies and possession of those lands was given to them after the Revolutionary War. These states are Connecticut, Delaware, Georgia, Kentucky, Maine, Maryland, Massachusetts, New Hampshire, New Jersey, New York, North Carolina, Pennsylvania, Rhode Island, South Carolina, Tennessee,

Vermont, Virginia, and West Virginia. Hawaii and Texas are also state-land states. In these twenty states, land is measured by metes and bounds. Metes means to "assign by measure."[30] Bounds is defined as "the external or limiting line of an object, space, or area . . . usually used in plural."[31] The land was measured first by the degrees in distance using a compass and then in distance by using various units. The distance could be in chains ("a measuring instrument that consists of 100 links joined together by rings and is used in surveying"),[32] which would be the measure between two points. You probably have seen the use of chains in measuring football yardage. It is the same concept. Another measurement unit was a rod. A rod is "a unit of length equal to 5½ yards or 16½ feet."[33] "Poles" was another measuring term, and meant "a unit of length varying from one locality to another; especially: one measuring 16½ feet."[34] Another term, which was used by the British, was "perch," meaning "any of various units of measure (as 24¾ cubic feet representing a pile 1 rod long by 1 foot by 1½ feet, or 16½ cubic feet, or 25 cubic feet) for stonework"[35] The measurement would therefore give the number of degrees in a direction (north, south, east, west, northeast, southeast, northwest, or southwest) and the number of chains, rods, poles, or perches. Land measurements would often include a physical landmark such as a tree, watercourse, or fence. Because it usually included these physical attributes, a plat of land was seldom square.

Figure 3.24 shows a metes and bounds plat which has been drawn over a 1973 topographical map as found in *First Families of Cumberland County*.[36] You will observe that the individual plats are not square. They are oriented in varying degrees north, south, east, and west. The map accompanies a book containing the names and dates of the first surveys. Tract SH161 was surveyed in 1775 "on warrant to David Porter dated 18 Feb 1775."[37] The surrounding land was owned by James Dunn (SH162), David Foglesanger (SH175), John Maclay (SH173), and Benjamin Blyth (SH167).

When the colonies were first established, there were no boundaries on their western edges. Land ownership went west without an end, except perhaps to the Pacific Ocean. By 1802, land owned by state-land states that lay west of their current borders had been given to the United States government. This was the basis for *federal land* states. The remaining thirty states are federal land states. Those states are, in alphabetical order: Alabama, Alaska, Arizona, Arkansas, California,

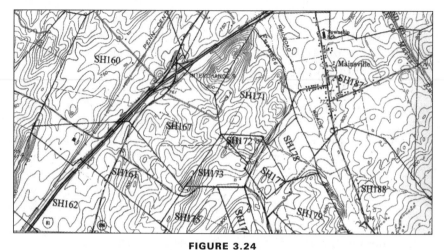

FIGURE 3.24

A metes and bounds plat which has been drawn over a 1973 topographical map

Colorado, Florida, Idaho, Illinois, Indiana, Iowa, Kansas, Louisiana, Michigan, Minnesota, Mississippi, Missouri, Montana, Nebraska, Nevada, New Mexico, North Dakota, Ohio, Oklahoma, Oregon, South Dakota, Utah, Washington, Wisconsin, and Wyoming. When the United States government was newly established, these unsettled areas were land-rich and cash-poor. Land, known as bounty land, was given to veterans of the Revolutionary War for compensation of service, in lieu of a cash payment. It was not unusual for the land to be immediately sold for cash and the bounty holder never actually lived on the land. Other land was given later as bounty land for military service in the War of 1812 and as homestead land for those wishing to settle in the western lands. As more land was acquired, those lands were considered part of federal land.

Federal land states are divided, not by metes and bounds, but by meridians, townships, ranges, and sections. A meridian is "a representation of such a circle or half circle on a map or globe [or] any of a series of lines drawn at intervals due north and south or in the direction of the poles and numbered according to the degrees of longitude (the 90th *meridian* east of Greenwich [England])."[38] Once the meridians had been established, a grid system was formed with vertical lines (ranges) set six miles apart and horizontal lines (townships) also set six miles apart. The townships are numbered and labeled north or south. The ranges are numbered and labeled east or west. Where each township and range intersected, a Congressional township was formed. Each township is 36 square miles. Within each township are 36 sections of one-mile square each. The sections are numbered one through 36 beginning in the northeast corner, numbering 6 across to the west, south one square and numbering 6 across (7 through 12) to the east, and so forth, until ending with section 36 in the southeast corner of the township.

6	5	4	3	2	1
7	8	9	10	11	12
18	17	16	15	14	13
19	20	21	22	23	24
30	29	28	27	26	25
31	32	33	34	35	36

FIGURE 3.25

The sequence of numbering in a Congressional township

Figure 3.25 shows the sequence of numbering in a Congressional township. Each section of one square mile can be divided in numerous ways. It can be quartered, and each quarter can be quartered, and then quartered again—as many times as is needed. If a section is divided into quarters, you would see something like what is shown in figure 3.26, which is a one-square-mile section divided into four quarter sections. Each quarter section would be one-fourth of a mile square.

Northwest Quarter	Northeast Quarter
Southwest Quarter	Southeast Quarter

FIGURE 3.26

Example of a one-square-mile section divided into four quarter sections

If we were to divide up the northeast quarter section into quarters, you would see something like what is shown in figure 3.27.

Quarters can continue to be divided into quarters. Sometimes sections are divided into halves, or into quarters and halves. This can get very complicated, but it allows us to create a legal description of the land. A legal land description

NW ¼ of the NE ¼	NE ¼ of the NE ¼
SW ¼ of the NE ¼	SE ¼ of the NE ¼

FIGURE 3.27

The northeast quarter section in figure 3.26 divided up into quarters

starts with the smallest entity and works up to the largest (the meridian). For example, the section of land belonging to Linville Hays in Jackson County, Missouri, shown in figure 3.28, would be described as such: *Southeast half of the northeast quarter, section 5, township 48 north, range 33 west, 5th principal meridian.*[39]

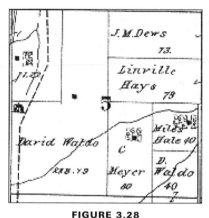

FIGURE 3.28

The section of land belonging to Linville Hays in Jackson County, Missouri

Bottom of Form. When land is surveyed, it is called a cadastral survey. "A cadastral survey is a survey which creates, marks, defines, retraces or re-establishes the boundaries and subdivisions of Federal Lands of the United States."[40] A survey plat, a drawing of the boundaries, is a part of a survey. Field notes are also a part of a cadastral survey. They are the narrative of the survey and contain a detailed description of the survey procedure and process, including a list of the individuals who participated in the survey.

Land Entry Case Files

Public domain lands, those owned by the federal government, were either given away or sold at various times and in diverse ways in the early history of our country. The largest distributions took place under the Cash Sale Act of 1820, the Preemption Act of 1841, and the Homestead Act of 1862 (and acts subsequent to 1862 are also known as Homestead Acts). To determine if land was granted or purchased from the federal government, use the Bureau of Land Management (BLM) website to search for land patents at www.glorecords.blm.gov. A land patent is a legal document transferring the ownership of land from the federal government to an individual. Receiving the patent generally required a set duration of homesteading the land and making improvements to it.

Figure 3.29 is a land patent for land in Michigan received by Edmund Harvey. This copy was obtained from the Bureau of Land Management, but copies may now be printed from the BLM website.

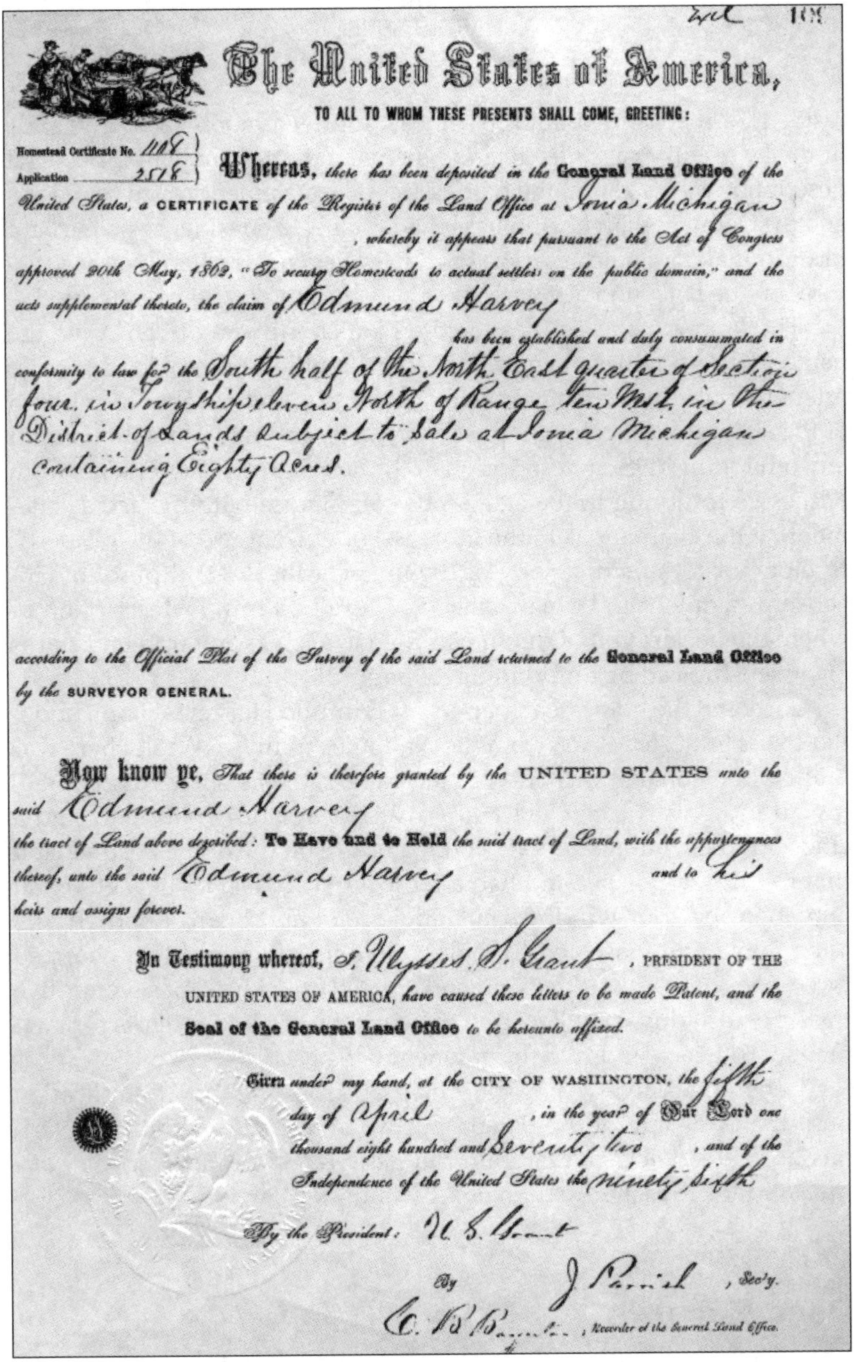

The United States of America,

TO ALL TO WHOM THESE PRESENTS SHALL COME, GREETING:

Homestead Certificate No. *1108*

Application _____ *2518*

Whereas, there has been deposited in the **General Land Office** of the United States, a CERTIFICATE of the Register of the Land Office at *Ionia Michigan* , whereby it appears that pursuant to the Act of Congress approved 20th May, 1862, "To secure Homesteads to actual settlers on the public domain," and the acts supplemental thereto, the claim of *Edmund Harvey* has been established and duly consummated in conformity to law for the *South half of the North East quarter of Section four, in Township eleven North of Range Ten West, in the District of Lands subject to Sale at Ionia Michigan Containing Eighty Acres.*

according to the Official Plat of the Survey of the said Land returned to the **General Land Office** by the SURVEYOR GENERAL.

Now know ye, That there is therefore granted by the UNITED STATES unto the said *Edmund Harvey* the tract of Land above described: **To Have and to Hold** the said tract of Land, with the appurtenances thereof, unto the said *Edmund Harvey* and to *his* heirs and assigns forever.

In Testimony whereof, I, *Ulysses S. Grant* , PRESIDENT OF THE UNITED STATES OF AMERICA, have caused these letters to be made Patent, and the **Seal of the General Land Office** to be hereunto affixed.

Given under my hand, at the CITY OF WASHINGTON, the *fifth* day of *April* , in the year of Our Lord one thousand eight hundred and *Seventy two* , and of the Independence of the United States the *ninety sixth* .

By the President: *U. S. Grant*

By *J. Parrish* , Sec'y.

C. B. B_____ , Recorder of the General Land Office.

FIGURE 3.29

A land patent for land in Michigan received by Edmund Harvey

resident of the claimed land for at least fourteen months.[41] The records in the land entry case files include the name of the purchaser, the legal description of the claim, the date of the sale, statements from witnesses and the claimant that the purchaser had established residence on the land prior to making an application for purchase, a description of any structures on the land, and a statement of how the land was currently used.

The land entry case files for the Homestead Act of 1862 give the name of the purchaser, the application for the homestead, notice of intent to make the purchase, the marital status and number of children of the claimant, the relevant post office, a description of the house and any other buildings, a description of the crops grown, statements from witnesses testifying to the claimant's compliance with the act, a statement by the claimant as to the intended or current use of the property, receipts for fees paid, a copy of the final certificate, and proof of citizenship or intent to be naturalized, if foreign-born. A description of where the declaration of intent was filed as well as any updated status of citizenship can be found in the papers.

I ordered the homestead papers for Edmund Harvey's claim, under the 1862 Homestead Act, from the National Archives. While there was minimal personal information in the papers, this is what I discovered: my ancestor was a married man, over the age of twenty-one, and a citizen of the United States. He built a house on the homesteaded land that was 1½ stories tall and had a footprint of 14 feet by 32 feet. It had one door and four windows, a shingle roof, and board floors. It was a log home and was "comfortable to live in." Edmund had chopped three acres of wood off the land and created an orchard of seventy-five trees. He also dug a well. Within the packet were two receipts for payment of $14 each and two for payment of $4 each.

Generally, a five-year period elapsed from the initial application until the awarding of the patent. Further information about the various homestead acts can be found in *Basic Researcher's Guide to Homesteads & Other Federal Land Records* by James C. Barsi.[42]

Deed Records

Buying land from another person requires a transfer of the property deed. A property deed is the legal instrument in the transfer of real property. Records of these deeds can be found in a county courthouse.

There are often two indexes to the deed records. One is an index of sellers. This will be identified as the grantor index or direct index. The other is an index of purchasers. It will be identified as a grantee index or indirect index. If you are tracing the ownership of a piece of land, or what is called the "chain of title," indexes are very important because they will allow you to search by the names of either the buyer or the seller. You should work backward from one deed to the next to determine who conveyed the right of possession to whom. This is called a "title search." You may find the grantor and grantee indexes online and, perhaps, digitized copies of deeds.

In each deed record will be the names of the buyers and sellers, the relationships of individuals, the value of the land, the description of the property, and the date of the transaction. Early deeds were handwritten. Today, you will find them typed and easily read. The first words in the deed will say "this indenture," meaning a legal contract. When people look at deeds for the first time, they are often confused when they see the term "indenture." They may think that someone is offering himself (or herself) as an indentured servant, but this is not the case. The date of the sale is given next. Later the deed would be sent to the court to "prove" the sale. The parties involved are then named. It may say, "John and Jane Doe, husband and wife" or "John Doe and his wife Jane." The name(s) of the buyer and seller(s) are listed. The amount paid for the property involved is listed, the seller acknowledges he has been paid, and the basic property description (the legal description) is given. It was important to identify the property with as much detail as necessary to ensure the sale of the correct tract of land. You may see the term "heirs and assigns." This is attributed to the buyer: "To John Smith and his heirs and assigns." This means that the property can be inherited or sold at a future date. The seller then claims that he holds a valid title and the deed is dated again. Each party signs the agreement. You may find a release of spousal rights. A "dower release" means the wife has agreed to the sale of the property. A "release of courtesy rights" means the husband has agreed to the sale. There is an excellent form on the Internet you can use when transcribing deeds. It can be found at http://dohistory.org/on_your_own/toolkit/deeds_form.html.

There are two major types of deeds: warranty and quit claim. Warranty deeds assure that the seller holds the title and can legally sell the property. Quit claim deeds relinquish all rights held by the grantor to the grantee. There is no guarantee that the grantor is the sole owner, therefore, the grantor is only relinquishing rights to what is his or hers at the time of the sale. A quit claim deed does not promise title, and thus offers no warranty. These deeds are often used to transfer property between family members as a gift, or to transfer property from one spouse to another in the case of divorce. In the event of the latter, the spouse who receives the marital home in the divorce settlement is given a quit claim deed by the other spouse, who is relinquishing his or her rights to the property. You will very seldom see a quit claim deed between non-related buyers and sellers.

"Deeds of trust" are also recorded in the county courthouse. They convey property to a trustee and are often used to secure a promissory note or mortgage. A deed of trust specifies the collateral for the loan and gives the lender the right to seize and sell the collateral should the borrower fail to repay. In some localities, you will also find deeds of adoption mingled among the land deeds. Figure 3.30 shows a warranty deed recorded in Houghton County, Michigan, in 1922.[43]

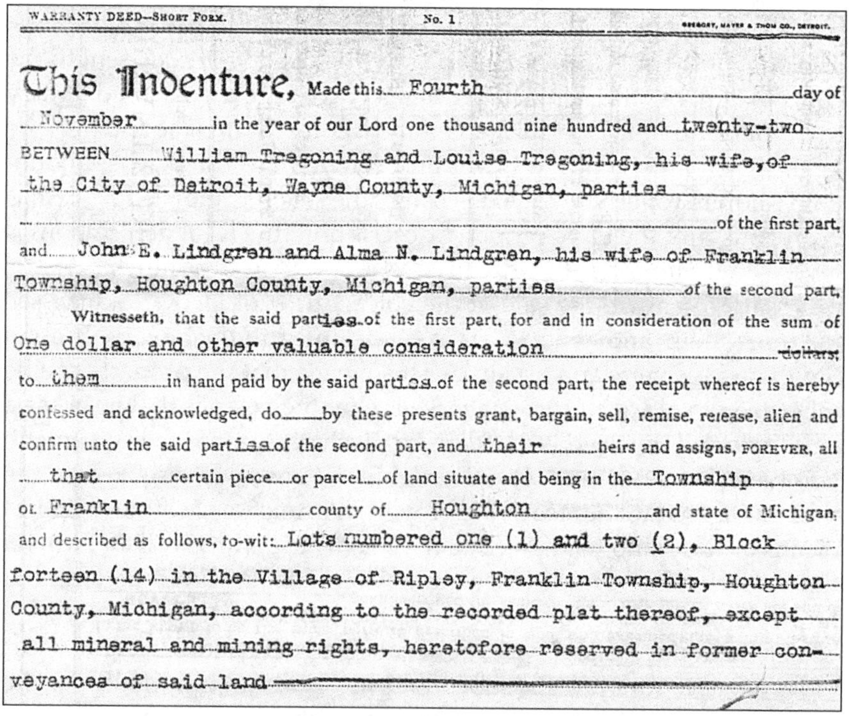

WARRANTY DEED—SHORT FORM. No. 1 GREGORY, MAYER & THOM CO., DETROIT.

This Indenture, Made this Fourth day of November in the year of our Lord one thousand nine hundred and twenty-two BETWEEN William Tregoning and Louise Tregoning, his wife, of the City of Detroit, Wayne County, Michigan, parties of the first part, and John E. Lindgren and Alma N. Lindgren, his wife of Franklin Township, Houghton County, Michigan, parties of the second part,

Witnesseth, that the said parties of the first part, for and in consideration of the sum of One dollar and other valuable consideration ~~dollars,~~ to them in hand paid by the said parties of the second part, the receipt whereof is hereby confessed and acknowledged, do by these presents grant, bargain, sell, remise, release, alien and confirm unto the said parties of the second part, and their heirs and assigns, FOREVER, all that certain piece or parcel of land situate and being in the Township of Franklin county of Houghton and state of Michigan, and described as follows, to-wit: Lots numbered one (1) and two (2), Block forteen (14) in the Village of Ripley, Franklin Township, Houghton County, Michigan, according to the recorded plat thereof, except all mineral and mining rights, heretofore reserved in former conveyances of said land

FIGURE 3.30

A warranty deed recorded in Houghton County, Michigan, in 1922

Tax Records

You may be thinking, "Tax records!?" Yes, they can be used in genealogical research. Your ancestors paid taxes, and the records of these payments can give a glimpse of life in their day. Some early tax records still exist, but their availability varies by state and county. Many of them have been filmed by the Family History Library. In colonial records, you might find the word "tithable" in records. Tithables are akin to tax records, but the monies collected were levied to help pay for the parish minister, not to run the government, and were levied on all adult males.

Yearly tax assessments can help determine the age of your ancestor. Poll taxes were levied on all adult males in a household beginning at age 16 or 18 or 21 (voting age), depending on the locality. You may have to do a little research of the laws of the area in which your ancestor lived, but once you know the age of majority in that locality, you can determine someone's approximate birth year by when he first appeared on the poll tax records. For example, if a man first shows up on a poll tax record in 1821 and the age of majority is sixteen, you can assume he was born about 1805.

Property or real estate taxes and personal property taxes were (and are) levied on owners of real estate or personal property. Tax records can be used in place of missing land or census records. You can trace a man (and therefore his family) in a county year by year. In figure 3.31, we see a property tax record for Calloway County, Kentucky, taken in the year 1831.[44] Everyone on the list were property owners or owners

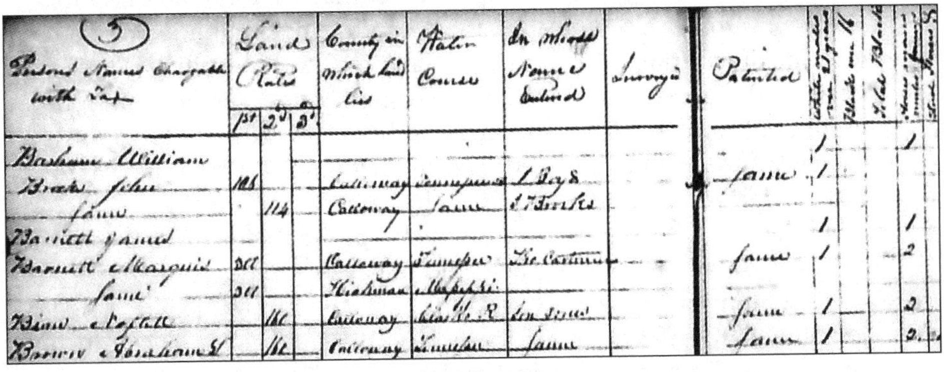

FIGURE 3.31

A property tax record for Calloway County, Kentucky, in 1831 of personal property. The locality recorded was a farming community. The right-hand page shows the crops and livestock that are subject to taxes. Only a portion of that page is shown in the image.

Our ancestors also paid income taxes, at least temporarily. The first income tax law was passed in 1862. The U.S. Congress established an income tax to help pay for the Civil War and the law remained in force for about ten years. Persons and businesses were taxed, and the records have been microfilmed by the National Archives. In the winter 1986 issue (vol. 18, no. 4) of *Prologue Magazine,* a periodical published by NARA, there is an article explaining this rather unpopular tax. It is entitled "Income Tax Records of the Civil War Years" by Cynthia G. Fox and can be read in its entirety at www.archives.gov/publications/prologue/1986/winter/civil-war-tax-records.html.

Naturalization Records

Naturalization is "the legal procedure by which an alien becomes a citizen of a state or country—the process by which a person acquires nationality after birth."[45]

Naturalization records are the papers created when an alien pursues citizenship in the United States. The process has changed over time, so one must know the laws that were in place when our ancestors sought citizenship. The records one might find are declarations of intent, petitions for citizenship, and certificates of naturalization. A declaration of intent is often the first paper filed. It states that the person has the intention of seeking citizenship. The petition is a formal request for citizenship. It may also be called the second or final papers. The final certificate of naturalization is a document given the new citizen stating that he or she is indeed a citizen of the United States. The final naturalization is recorded in the naturalization books in the court of record. The declaration of intent of Frederick Schultz is shown in figure 3.32.[46]

During colonial times, people on this continent were either British citizens or aliens born outside the British Empire. Most aliens in colonial America were German. Each colony had its own laws regarding naturalization for those who were non-British citizens. This allowed aliens the rights of British citizenship within the colony. The British government also had naturalization laws in effect. In 1740, the British Parliament passed a general naturalization law which granted British

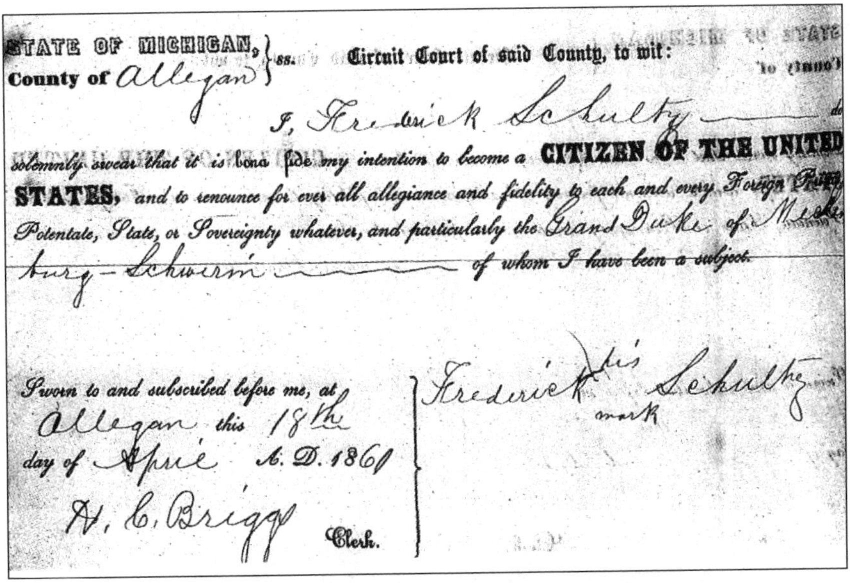
STATE OF MICHIGAN, } ss. Circuit Court of said County, to wit:
County of Allegan }

I, Frederick Schultz — do solemnly swear that it is bona fide my intention to become a CITIZEN OF THE UNITED STATES, and to renounce for ever all allegiance and fidelity to each and every Foreign Prince, Potentate, State, or Sovereignty whatever, and particularly the Grand Duke of Mecklenburg-Schwerin — of whom I have been a subject.

Sworn to and subscribed before me, at Allegan this 18th day of April A.D. 1860

H. C. Briggs Clerk.

Frederick his mark Schultz

FIGURE 3.32
The Declaration of Intent of Frederick Schultz, April 18, 1860

citizenship to an alien after seven years of residence in a colony, proof that he had taken the sacraments of the Church of England, and an oath of allegiance to the Crown. Most extant records for pre-1790 naturalizations have been published. A good bibliography of naturalization records, before and after 1790, is *Passenger and Immigration Lists Bibliography, 1538–1900.*[47] Along with books and printed matter that list the names of individuals naturalized, this bibliography cites the titles of printed matter that list the names of arrivals into the colonies, and subsequently, into the United States and Canada. Rather than have researchers begin a tedious search through each book, the editor realized that an index to the books would benefit its users. This resulted in the publication of the *Passenger and Immigration Lists Index.*[48] This idea promoted an extended project of indexing books and publishing lists of names that are found in the various works recorded in the bibliography and created a work with many supplements. The indexes can be found on Ancestry.com.

In 1776, the Continental Congress in the newly formed United States of America stated that all persons abiding within the American Colonies and giving allegiance to the same were citizens of such.

Each resident had to decide if his loyalty was to the British Crown or the new American government. No oath of allegiance was required for officers in Continental service and for all those holding civil office. This law was rescinded in 1790.

The first naturalization law in the United States was passed in 1790. It allowed citizenship for free-white persons who had lived in the United States for two years and the state in which they applied for one year. Such persons were to be of good moral character and swear an oath to support the Constitution. Subsequent naturalization laws changed the number of years of residency. One law required fourteen years of residency, but that was short-lived. Until the late twentieth century, one could be naturalized in any court of record, creating a myriad of possibilities when looking for an ancestor's naturalization papers. In 1906, the Bureau of Immigration and Naturalization (INS) was formed to supervise the process of immigration. Beginning at that time, a copy of all final papers was sent to the INS.

There are some facets of the naturalization laws with which you should become familiar. Prior to 1922, the wife and children of a man applying for citizenship became citizens upon his naturalization; this is called derivative citizenship. Therefore, you will not find a married woman's name in naturalization records before 1922, nor will you find the names of minor children whose father applied for citizenship. Women were naturalized, in their own right, starting in 1922. Between 1907 and 1922, an American woman acquired her foreign-born husband's nationality upon marrying, if she was a citizen, losing her U.S. citizenship. Some laws shortened the waiting period to those aliens who served in a branch of the U.S. military, allowing a petition of naturalization without first filing a declaration of intent. Many persons were granted citizenship outside the normal process and given U.S. citizenship *en masse*. Those living in territories acquired via purchase or treaty by the United States were granted a blanket American citizenship when the land was obtained, such as: Louisiana (1803), Florida, Mississippi, and Alabama (1819), Alaska (1867), Hawaii (1900), Puerto Rico (1917), and the U.S. Virgin Islands (1927). *En masse* naturalizations also applied to former slaves (via the Fourteenth Amendment of the Constitution in 1868) and Native Americans (in 1887 for all who would renounce allegiance to the tribe, and in 1924 to all those born within the United States). You will not find the names of those given blanket citizenship within naturalization papers because citizenship was acquired by law or act rather than personal application (see figure 3.33).

As stated previously, in the past an alien seeking citizenship could be naturalized in any court of record. When looking for your ancestor's naturalization papers, look at the locality in which he settled. Which courthouse would have been the easiest physical location in which to complete the task? Often the most convenient location was the county courthouse. But a federal courthouse might also be a possibility. In Kansas City, Missouri, for example, there is a federal courthouse and a county courthouse in close proximity to each other. But most of our ancestors did not live near a federal facility. So, start with the county courthouse. Naturalizations could be recorded in any book within the walls of the building: court dockets, court minutes, court orders, case files, judgments, and so on. Some courts had separate volumes labeled "naturalization" and "citizenship."

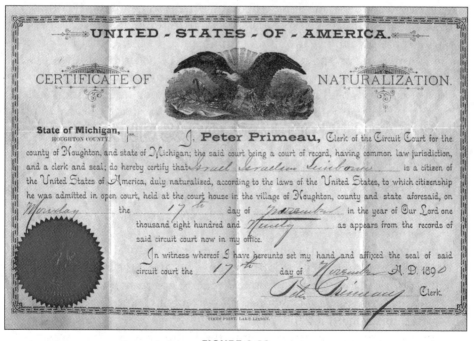

FIGURE 3.33

A Certificate of Naturalization for Israel Israelson Lonbom, from the author's personal collection

Federal naturalization records can be obtained from the United States Citizenship and Naturalization Service. Genealogists may request post-1892 immigration records and naturalization records between 1906 and 1956. The website is www.uscis.gov/hisoryandgenealogy. When you enter the site, look for the sidebar, click on "genealogy," and select the option in the dropdown menu that meets your needs. You may ask a question, seek help, request records, or request an index search. The records searched are the "C files," which are naturalization certificates from 1906 to 1956; alien registration forms (Form AR-2) from 1940 to 1944 and A files from 1944 to 1951; visa files from 1924 to 1944 and visa records from 1944 to 1951 as found in the A files; registry files from 1929 to 1944; and registry records from 1944 to 1951. C files contain at least one application form (a declaration of intent and/or petition for naturalization) and a duplicate certificate of naturalization or certificate of citizenship. The AR-2 files were completed by all aliens age fourteen and older.

How can you determine when and where someone was naturalized? Begin with census records. The 1900, 1910, 1920, and 1930 census records give the year of immigration and citizenship status. If the person had begun the process but was not yet naturalized, the indication will be "pa" (for "papers") on the census form. If the person had gone through all the steps and was naturalized, the indication will be "na," for "naturalized citizen." The indication of "al" means your ancestor was still an alien resident at the time the census was taken. Use your ancestor's location on all census records to begin your search of naturalization records. Search the courthouses in those areas that could be easily reached by your ancestor with the mode of transportation available at the time. If you find your ancestor in several different counties and/or states on census records, search all those locations.

Family histories, county histories, family records, and family tradition are other good sources in discovering naturalization status, location, and date. Federal land records can also give clues to naturalization. To purchase land from the federal government, your immigrant ancestor must have obtained his citizenship before the end of the process to receive the land patent. He could start the naturalization process at any time after arriving in the United States. There was no set time to begin or end the process, and no requirement that he obtain citizenship if he did not want to buy land.

If you are going to visit a courthouse to look for any type of records, make sure you call ahead or check their website for their open hours and for days on which they are closed. Courthouses and other government records facilities are not just closed for federal holidays alone. States and municipalities may have special holidays relevant only to their area. Ask about ease of parking, the cost of making copies, and whether there are particular days that are specific research days for genealogists. I made the mistake of not calling ahead when I went to visit a courthouse to look for marriage records. In my defense, I did not think I would have the time to visit the courthouse during a family vacation, but when the opportunity arose I eagerly seized it. On the Friday that I arrived at the courthouse, the clerk kindly told me that Tuesdays, Wednesdays, and Thursdays were days on which genealogists were welcome. Mondays and Fridays were particularly busy days for the office staff, and they didn't have time to help genealogists on those days. It would have been an opportunity lost, but the clerk took pity on me and allowed me into the vault to look at the marriage records. What a break for me! Don't expect all visits to turn out so well. Another unfortunate experience occurred when my husband and I were looking for probate records in a courthouse. We drove to the courthouse and discovered there was no free parking. After digging in my husband's pockets and my purse, we found enough coins to last us for an hour's visit on the parking meter. We went through security and found the appropriate office only to be told that the older probate records had been moved to an off-site location "last week." We had to retrace our steps back to our car and drive three miles to the off-site location where, luckily, there was free parking. Be wise and call ahead before you visit any records facility.

■ ■ ■

You will be able to find some of the records discussed in this chapter on Ancestry.com, Fold3, FamilySearch, and America's Genealogy Bank.

Visiting a courthouse can be a rewarding experience. Looking for your ancestors in books or finding information about them on the Internet is great, but holding an original document in your hands is an exciting moment. Knowing your ancestor was in that building and walked those halls can make him or her seem more real. Don't limit your research to secondary experiences. Spend some time traveling

LESSON SIX

- Review your pedigree and family unit charts. Create a timeline by year for your ancestor, indicating every location of residence.

- What courthouses were within a reasonable travel distance of your ancestor? Depending on the era, consider the time it would take via horseback or horse and carriage or by car.

- Where was your ancestor living when he or she died? Check the indexes for wills or probate records. You may find these on microfilm, online, transcribed in a book or periodical, or in the courthouse.

- Review census records. Did your ancestor own land? (Look for the value of real estate on the 1850–1870 census schedules, and note if the home was rented or owned on the 1900–1930 schedules to determine if there was land ownership.) Check the Bureau of Land Management website, noted previously, and the grantor/grantee indexes at the courthouse.

and creating a visual picture of the area in which the ancestor lived. You won't be sorry.

NOTES

1. Alice Eichholz, *Ancestry's Red Book: American State, County & Town Sources,* 3rd ed. (Salt Lake City, UT: Ancestry, 2004).

2. *Handybook for Genealogists,* 11th ed. (Baltimore, MD: Genealogical Publishing Co., 2006).

3. From http://familysearch.org, digital image from microfilm 2320575, digital folder number 4207019, image number 156.

4. Jackson County (MO) Recorder of Deeds Web Access, www.jacksongov.org/295/Marriage-License-Search/.

5. Ibid.

6. Missouri 11th General Assembly, Laws, 1st Session 1841.

7. "United States Census, 1940," database with images, *FamilySearch,* https://familysearch.org/ark:/61903/3:1:3QS7-L9M1-J97B?cc=2000219&wc=QZX1

–75L%3A790103601%2C794201501%2C790163701%2C951803501, Michigan > Houghton > Franklin Township > image 8 of 50; citing Sixteenth Census of the United States, 1940, NARA digital publication T627; Records of the Bureau of the Census, 1790–2007, RG 29 (Washington, DC: National Archives and Records Administration, 2012).

8. "United States Census, 1930," database with images, *FamilySearch*, https:// familysearch.org/ark:/61903/3:1:33SQ-GR46–6CD?cc=1810731&wc=QZF9 –5S3%3A648805801%2C650241201%2C648861001%2C1589282324, Michigan > Houghton > Franklin > image 34 of 42; citing NARA microfilm publication T626 (Washington, DC: National Archives and Records Administration, 2002).

9. 1890 U.S. Census, Severe, Perry County, Alabama, roll: M407_1, page: 436, E.D. 78, Family History Library Film: 0926497; Ancestry.com and The Church of Jesus Christ of Latter Day Saints, *1890 United States Federal Census Fragment* (database online) (Provo, UT: Ancestry.com Operations, 2009).

10. 1880 U.S. Census, Montcalm County, Michigan, p. 327, NARA microfilm publication T9, roll 327.

11. Josiah Finley family, 1860 U.S. Census, Clay County, Missouri, p. 993, NARA microfilm publication M653, roll 614.

12. 1840 U.S. Census, Barnstable County, Massachusetts, p. 90, NARA microfilm publication M704, roll 173.

13. 1830 U.S. Census, Jackson, County, Missouri, p. 301, NARA microfilm publication M19, roll 73.

14. 1820 U.S. Census, Fauquier County, Virginia, p. 130, NARA microfilm publication M33, roll 136.

15. 1800 U.S. Census, Somerset County, Pennsylvania, p. 538, NARA microfilm publication M32, roll 43.

16. 1790 U.S. Census, Jones County, North Carolina, p. 424, NARA microfilm publication M637, roll 7.

17. Ann S. Lainhart, *State Census Records* (Baltimore, MD: Genealogical Publishing Co., 1992).

18. From Missouri Mortality Schedule, 1860, Adair County, p. 3, photographed by American Micro Corp. for the State Historical Society of Missouri.

19. 1870 Agriculture Census, Carroll County, Missouri, filmed by the State Historical Society of Missouri.

20. 1870 Industry Census, Buchanan County, Missouri, filmed by the State Historical Society of Missouri.

21. Missouri Historical Society, *Census Books of St. Louis, Mo.*, filmed by Central Microfilm Service Corp., St. Louis, MO.

22. William Dollarhide, *The Census Book: A Genealogist's Guide to Federal Census Facts, Schedules and Indexes: With Master Extraction Forms for Federal Census Schedules, 1790–1930* (Bountiful, UT: Heritage Quest, 1999).

23. William Thorndale and William Dollarhide, *Map Guide to the U.S. Federal Censuses, 1790–1920* (Baltimore, MD: Genealogical Publishing Co., 1987).

24. Bryan A. Garner, ed., *Black's Law Dictionary*, 7th ed. (St. Paul, MN: West Group, 1999), 356–60.

25. Gary R. Toms and William R. Gann, *Widows Dowers of Washington County, Tennessee, 1803–1899* (Milford, OH: Little Miami, 2004).

26. Ibid., preface.

27. "Probate," in *Webster's Third New International Dictionary, Unabridged* (Merriam-Webster, 2002), http://unabridged.merriam-webster.com.proxy.mcpl.lib.mo.us.

28. "Probate," in *Gale Encyclopedia of American Law*, 3rd ed., ed. Donna Batten (Detroit, MI: Gale, 2010), 8:133–37, Gale Virtual Reference Library, http://go.galegroup.com/ps/i.do?p=GVRL&sw=w&u=inde80299&v=2.1&id=GALE%7CCCX1337703494&i t=r&asid=4f8562ca625682d88795a9ecf24a681f.

29. Found in the Allegan County (Michigan) Probate Court, Allegan, Michigan.

30. "Mete," in *Webster's Third New International Dictionary, Unabridged* (Merriam-Webster, 2002), http://unabridged.merriam-webster.com.proxy.mcpl.lib.mo.us.

31. "Bound," in *Webster's Third New International Dictionary, Unabridged* (Merriam-Webster, 2002), http://unabridged.merriam-webster.com.proxy.mcpl.lib.mo.us.

32. "Chain," in *Webster's Third New International Dictionary, Unabridged* (Merriam-Webster, 2002), http://unabridged.merriam-webster.com.proxy.mcpl.lib.mo.us.

33. "Rod," in *Webster's Third New International Dictionary, Unabridged* (Merriam-Webster, 2002), http://unabridged.merriam-webster.com.proxy.mcpl.lib.mo.us.

34. "Pole," in *Webster's Third New International Dictionary, Unabridged* (Merriam-Webster, 2002), http://unabridged.merriam-webster.com.proxy.mcpl.lib.mo.us.

35. "Perch," in *Webster's Third New International Dictionary, Unabridged* (Merriam-Webster, 2002), http://unabridged.merriam-webster.com.proxy.mcpl.lib.mo.us.

36. Hayes R. Eschenmann, *First Families of Cumberland County*, Vol. I, Shippensburg (with accompanying map) (Carlisle, PA: Cumberland County Historical Society, 2005).

37. Ibid., p. 32.

38. "Meridian," in *Webster's Third New International Dictionary, Unabridged* (Merriam-Webster, 2002), http://unabridged.merriam-webster.com.proxy.mcpl.lib.mo.us.

39. Jackson County Missouri Historical Society, *An Illustrated Historical Atlas Map, Jackson County, Mo.: Carefully Compiled from Personal Examinations and Surveys* (Independence, MO: Produced for Jackson County Historical Society by Graham Graphics, 1976, reprint; originally published Philadelphia, PA: Brink, McDonough, 1877).

40. U.S. Department of the Interior: Bureau of Land Management, https://glorecords.blm.gov/default.aspx.

41. The Minnesota Legal History Project, www.minnesotalegalhistoryproject.org/assets/Microsoft%20Word%20-%20Preemption%20Act%200f%201841.pdf.

42. James C. Barsi, *Basic Researcher's Guide to Homesteads & Other Federal Land Records* (Colorado Springs, CO: Nuthatch Grove, 1994).

43. From the author's personal collection.

44. Kentucky Tax Books, Calloway County, 1831, reel 54.

45. Loretto Dennis Szucs, *They Became Americans: Finding Naturalization Records and Ethnic Origins* (Salt Lake City, UT: Ancestry, 1998), 3.

46. Michigan, Circuit Court (Allegan Co.), *Index to Naturalizations 1850–1955, Declarations*, v. 1–4, no. 1–100, 9346 1850–1914 (Salt Lake City, UT: filmed by the Genealogical Society of Utah, 1955), film #1994145.

47. P. William Filby, *Passenger and Immigrations Lists Bibliography, 1538–1900: Being a Guide to Published Lists of Arrivals in the United States and Canada* (Detroit, MI: Gale Research, 1988).

48. P. William Filby, *Passenger and Immigration Lists Index: A Guide to Published Arrival Records of About 500,000 Passengers Who Came to the United States and Canada in the Seventeenth, Eighteenth, and Nineteenth Centuries* (Detroit, MI: Gale Research, 1981–).

CHAPTER FOUR

Continuing the Search

Military Records

Many of our ancestors served in the military at some point in their lifetime, whether this was during peacetime, in conflicts with Native Americans, or in full-fledged wars with other countries. Our nation has been involved in warfare throughout its existence, and even before we were an established country. A knowledge of history, military history, and military operations is essential to effectively use military records. Knowing the military conflicts that occurred during our ancestors' lifetimes will facilitate finding their military records, should they exist. To understand the conflicts, a short U.S. history lesson is needed, and will be given in this chapter. The Internet Archive has digitized an *Alphabetical List of Battles: 1754–1900.*[1] It can be viewed free online at www.archive.org/details/alphabeticallist00stra. It can also be viewed on Heritage Quest and FamilySearch in their digitized book collections.

Many of our conflicts when we were still British colonies involved Native American tribes. Early settlers desired to take up residence in land on which Indian tribes were well established, on land the tribes considered theirs alone. Indian wars occurred in the colonies of Virginia, Connecticut, Massachusetts, Rhode Island, New York, the Carolinas, Florida, and Georgia, and in territorial lands now known as Michigan and Ohio. The longest and best-known of these conflicts was the French and Indian War, also known as the Seven Years' War, which lasted from 1754 to 1763. It took place in the northern colonies and Canada and was a result of border conflicts between British troops and American colonists on one side, and French colonists and their Indian allies on the other. The war ended in a British-American victory.

The Revolutionary War, also known as the American Revolution or the U.S. War of Independence, lasted from 1775 to 1783. It was a long war that resulted in America winning its independence from Great Britain. On the American side, counties and towns maintained local militias to defend themselves against Indian attacks, and these militias eventually made up the bulk of the Continental Army. Some units only fought within the borders of their own colonies, while others fought under the overall command of General George Washington. Each colony was requested to provide a given number of men for the Continental Army. A navy was also formed at the beginning of the war. Many American men fought for the right to become a country. Many others gave patriotic service by providing hay for horses and food for the troops, and by manufacturing bullets and cannonballs. Each man provided his own uniform and musket.

The next major war was the War of 1812. This is not as famous or as popular a war as the Revolutionary War, and many Americans know little about it. There are fewer records available for this conflict and less written material. The origins of the War of 1812 lay in the British Navy's practice of seizing American ships and impounding their crews to supplement the British need for additional naval personnel in Britain's wars against Napoleon. The War of 1812 was not America's finest hour. Our young nation's capital, Washington, DC, was captured by British forces and burned. A planned American invasion of Canada failed. And America's biggest success in the war, the Battle of New Orleans, was actually fought after the peace treaty between Britain and the United States had already been signed.

After the War of 1812, Indian wars continued until 1858. One prominent trend during this time was the forced removal of the remaining Native American tribes east of the Mississippi River in the 1830s to lands in the west using military personnel. The War of Texas Independence from Mexico was fought in 1836, with the Mexican War following a decade later, from 1846 to 1848. The United States' victory over Mexico in the latter war resulted in the U.S. acquisition of what are now the states of California, Nevada, and Utah and most of what are now the states of New Mexico, Arizona, and Colorado. The war also established a permanent, well-defined border between the United States and Mexico along the Rio Grande River.

The bloodiest war in our history was the American Civil War, which lasted from 1861 to 1865. The war was sparked by the secession of the Southern states from the Union in 1861 in order to preserve their institution of slavery. In the war, the Northern states eventually overcame the Southern Confederacy in a series of battles and reestablished the unity of the United States. (Slavery was also abolished as a result of the war.) Early in the war, the Confederate Congress had enacted a conscription law in 1862 when it became apparent that volunteer forces alone would not fill its need for soldiers. The United States (i.e., the North) passed a similar law in March 1863. However, if a man paid $300, he could become exempt from military service or he could directly pay someone to fulfill his duty for him. The Civil War was a complicated war and often pitted brother against brother. Record access is good due to the varied records kept by both sides, though more records have survived for the North than the South.

After the Civil War, there were more and continued Indian wars. These were fought in areas that are now the states of North and South Dakota, Montana, New Mexico, California, and Idaho. In 1898 there was the very short Spanish-American War. The war was fought in Cuba and the Philippines. America's victory over Spain in this war gave Cuba its independence from Spain, and the United States acquired Puerto Rico and Guam as territories and bought the Philippines for $20 million. The Philippine Insurrection followed the Spanish-American War and lasted from 1899 to 1902, though the fighting was sporadic. The United States had supported the Filipinos in fighting the Spanish during the Spanish-American War, but when America did not give the Filipinos their independence after war's end, their government went to war against the United States. The war ended in an American victory, but the United States eventually committed itself to granting the Philippines their independence.

The Great War, now known as World War I, was fought from 1914 to 1918. An assassination in Serbia in 1914 began a ripple effect that resulted in Britain, France, and Russia going to war against Germany,

Austria-Hungary, and Turkey. Before the war's end, many other nations had been drawn into it. The United States did not enter the war until 1917, when it sided with Britain and France against Germany. The United States declared war on Germany on April 6, 1917. Many American troops lost their lives fighting the Germans in the trenches that ran through northern France. The U.S. forces gave a timely and needed boost to the Allied forces, however, allowing them to claim victory in November 1918. In May 1917 the U.S. Congress had created the Selective Service System, requiring eligible males to register for potential military service. The World War I draft registrations have been declassified and filmed by the National Archives. Digital images are available on Ancestry.com and Fold3. All draft boards closed following the war.

World War I was not "the war to end all wars," as people at the time had hoped. What followed was World War II, which lasted from 1939 to 1945, and in which the United States took part from 1941 to 1945. The United States sided with Britain and the Soviet Union in their struggle against Nazi Germany, Fascist Italy, and Japan. This war was followed by the Korean War, the Vietnam War, and today's many and continued conflicts. The records for conflicts after World War II are still largely classified documents, and these are unavailable for research by genealogists.

The Records and Where to Find Them

All U.S. military records are the property of, and are held by, the federal government. As they have become declassified the records have entered the possession of the National Archives and Records Administration. Some of the declassified records have been microfilmed, and some of those have been digitized. Others are still in the form of textual documents. You can find some of the digitized records on Ancestry.com and Fold3. Other extracted or indexed military records are on the National Archives' Access to Archival Databases (AAD) (http://aad.archives.gov/aad) or the National Archives' Online Public Access site (www.archives.gov/research/search). Nondigital records for wars prior to World War I can be viewed at the National Archives in Washington, DC, and all declassified records can be ordered from the archives at www.archives.gov/veterans. Records beginning with

World War I are at the National Personnel Records Center in St. Louis, Missouri. They can be ordered through the National Archives' eVet-Recs System at www.archives.gov/veterans/military-service-records. Declassified records are available for viewing at the St. Louis facility, but an appointment must be scheduled in advance. (See www.archives .gov/st-louis/military-personnel/visitors-and-researchers.html.)

Many types of military and related records have been created over time, some microfilmed and some not. They include service records, pension records, military histories, claims, letters and diaries, other miscellaneous government documents, and state adjutant general's reports. The principal types of records, and those used most frequently, are indexes to records, compiled service records, and pension and bounty land records. An excellent guide to these varied types of records is *U.S. Military Records* by James C. Neagles.[2] Consulting the National Archives catalog (http://catalog.archives.gov) is also a good way to discover the myriad of available records. Service records include muster rolls, enlistment records, rosters, discharges, prisoner lists, records of burial, oaths of allegiance, and payroll records. Pension records include records of payment, proof of military service, and, in the case of a widow, proof of marriage. Military histories are often regimental histories authored by someone within the regiment or a military historian. They may be privately printed or found within a county, state, or town history. Claim records are those exacted against the U.S. government for personal or property damage. Letters to and from a soldier and personal diaries are frequently found in repositories within records sets. Other government documents are those printed and published by the U.S. Government Publishing Office. State adjutant generals' records are those which were collected and compiled by the person holding that office within a state. Dated records are usually found in a state repository.

A description of the most frequently used records from our country's major military conflicts is discussed in the sections below.

Revolutionary War

Records for the Revolutionary War have been microfilmed by NARA, and many are available online. Many research libraries have copies of these microfilms, but they are seldom used now that the records have been converted to electronic form. Two of the best commercial sources for searching the compiled soldiers' records in digital form are Ancestry.com and Fold3. The first records to search are the compiled service records. These are records that have been gathered for each soldier in the Continental Army or for state troops. As various muster lists, rolls, and reports were searched, records relating to individual soldiers were written on separate abstract cards. The cards for each soldier were compiled in a packet, like a paper envelope, and were eventually microfilmed. Finding a soldier's compiled service record for Revolutionary War service means that he gave patriotic military service to the new nation. The service records will give very little, if any, personal data on the soldier. A service record will not give his age, nor will it state the names of members of his family. If there is more than one soldier with your ancestor's name, it may even be difficult to determine which one is your ancestor.

If your ancestor received a pension or bounty land, you may be able to find additional information about him and his family. He could have received a pension for a disability incurred during his service; this is called an invalid pension. Service pensions were also given. The longer the veteran lived after the war, the greater the possibility that he received a service pension. The earliest service pensions were given to officers who remained on active duty until the end of the war. By 1832, anyone having served two full years in the war could receive a pension. Widows, assuming they lived long enough, were also given pensions. The first widows' pensions were awarded to widows and orphans of officers in 1780. Eventually, as with service pensions, widows of all service personnel were offered pensions. The widows' pensions always give more information than other pensions. Not only did the widow need to prove that her husband had served, she also had to prove they had been married. That proof could have been a notarized statement of witnesses indicating knowledge of the marital union, or a page torn from the family Bible.

Bounty land was another option that soldiers and widows were allowed. The military bounty land was an option for free land in the official bounty-land area. It was an attractive offer to the veteran because he could sell the land for more money than he would have received had he chosen a pension. Some of these awards for land were given by states and others by the U.S. government. The Military District of Ohio, land now known as the state of Ohio, contained most of the land that was awarded as bounty land. To find records of pensions and bounty land, use Fold3 and Heritage Quest Online. For more information about Revolutionary War research and bounty land, see the following two works:

> Bockstruck, Lloyd DeWitt. *Revolutionary War Pensions: Awarded by State Governments, 1775–1874, the General and Federal Governments Prior to 1814, and by Private Acts of Congress to 1905.* Baltimore, MD: Genealogical Publishing Co., 2011.

> Bockstruck, Lloyd DeWitt. *Bounty and Donation Land Grants in British Colonial America.* Baltimore, MD: Genealogical Publishing Co., 2007.

War of 1812

Some records of the War of 1812 have been filmed, but there are no complete records of service for that war. An index to the compiled service records has been microfilmed by the National Archives and is also on Ancestry.com and Fold3. Compiled service records for all soldiers have not been microfilmed. This is a very difficult war to research due to the lack of complete microfilmed or digitized records. The practice of giving pensions and bounty land for military service continued with the War of 1812. The longer a soldier or his widow lived after the war, the more likely he was to have received remuneration. By 1814, however, bounty land was frequently promised immediately upon enlisting for military service because it was becoming more difficult to raise troops at that late stage of the war. Bounty land for War of 1812 service was available in Arkansas, Illinois, Louisiana, Michigan, and Missouri. Pension and bounty land acts were enacted at various times, and therefore not all soldiers who received payment or land are found on all microfilms or lists. For instance, the National Archives film series M858 contains War of 1812 Bounty Land Warrants for the years 1815–1858. Virgil White's *Index to War of 1812 Pension Files*[3] contains the names of the veterans or their widows receiving remuneration from the pension acts of 1871 and 1878. The textual records of the War of 1812 pension files have been digitized by Fold3 in conjunction with the Federation of Genealogical Societies (FGS) and Ancestry.com. More than $3 million was raised by genealogists, through the efforts of

FGS, and was matched dollar for dollar by Ancestry.com, in order to make these records freely available for searching on Fold3.

An invaluable but infrequently used source for finding information about Revolutionary War and War of 1812 soldiers, as well as those who fought in the Indian wars, is the Draper Papers. Additionally known as the Draper Manuscripts, they are a collection of papers written and gathered by Lyman Copeland Draper (1815–1891). Draper was a military historian who developed a great interest in the Revolutionary War during his childhood. His grandfather, along with his fellow Revolutionary War veterans, spent hours talking about their memories of the war and declared that it was through the sole efforts of the New England patriots that the war had been won. Draper spent most of his adult years traveling, corresponding with veterans and their families and acquaintances, and visiting courthouses to consult and copy documents, all in an effort to gain a fuller picture of those early military events and those involved in the conflicts. He soon developed an interest in the War of 1812 and the Indian wars. His original papers are housed at the Wisconsin Historical Society and they have been microfilmed. Many research libraries have copies of the films, including the Family History Library, which offers them available on loan for participating libraries. Unfortunately, the records have not been digitized.

The Draper Papers are difficult to use because there is no every-name index to them, but for the serious scholar they are a treasure trove. A *Guide to the Draper Manuscripts*[4] is most helpful when using the films. Very few of Draper's papers and documents are originals. You will find instead documents copied by Draper and many letters that were sent to him. The papers are divided into 491 volumes in 50 sections. One of these volumes contains copies of court documents that were used as sworn testimonies that a soldier had served in the Revolutionary War. For example, in 1832 in the Spartanburgh District of South Carolina, John Collins, at the age of seventy-eight, appeared before the judge of Common Pleas. His statement said, "I enlisted [in] the service of the United States as a volunteer and under Cpt. Berry and Col. Thomas, Col. Richardson having the chief command and served a six weeks campaign in 1775." He also served in 1778 and 1780.[5]

One can also find muster rolls interspersed within the Draper Papers, as shown in figure 4.1.[6] As you can see, the papers are difficult to read due to the handwriting and the poor microfilm quality. This muster roll is a "Return of the *officers of the Illinois regiment*" at Fort

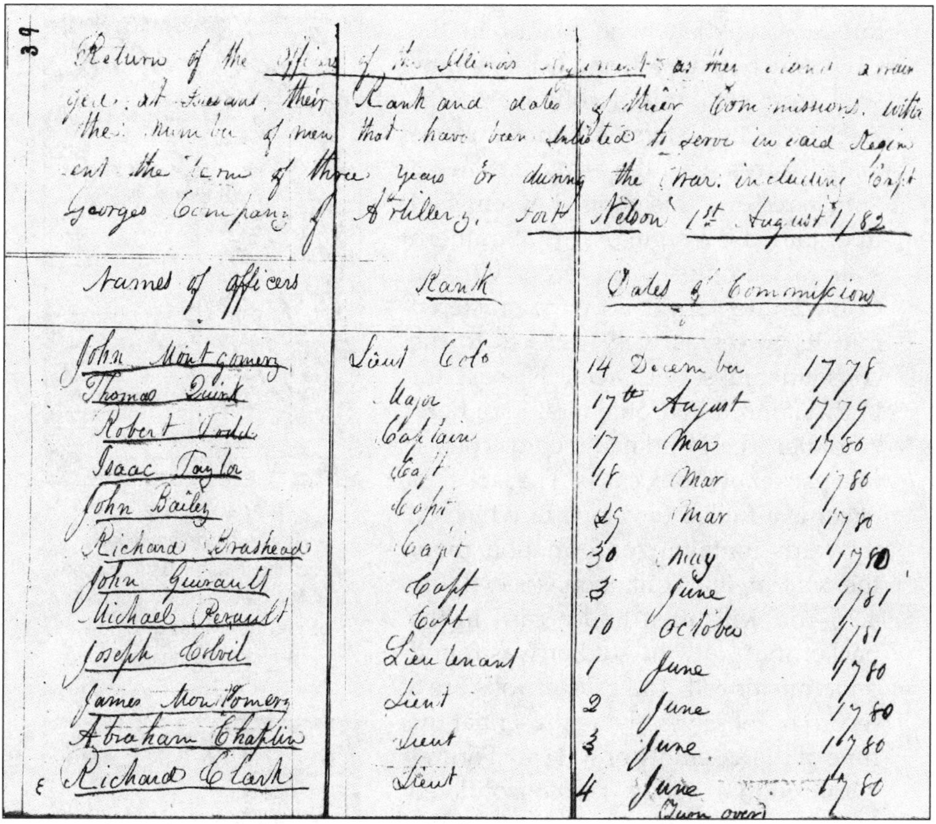

39

Return of the Officers of the Illinois Regiment as they stand at present, their Rank and dates of their Commissions, with the number of men that have been Inlisted to serve in said Regiment the term of three years or during the War, including Capt Georges Company of Artillery. Fort Nelson 1st August 1782

Names of officers	Rank	Dates of Commissions
John Montgomery	Lieut Colo	14 December 1778
Thomas Quirk	Major	17th August 1779
Robert Todd	Captain	17 Mar 1780
Isaac Taylor	Capt	18 Mar 1780
John Bailey	Capt	25 Mar 1780
Richard Brashead	Capt	30 May 1780
John Girault	Capt	3 June 1781
Michael Perault	Capt	10 October 1781
Joseph Calvit	Lieutenant	1 June 1780
James Montgomery	Lieut	2 June 1780
Abraham Chaplin	Lieut	3 June 1780
Richard Clark	Lieut	4 June 1780

(Turn over)

FIGURE 4.1
Muster roll from the Revolutionary War, in the Draper Papers

Nelson (Kentucky) and is dated 1st August 1782. In this roster, which was copied by Draper, some of the words are underlined. Draper frequently underlined words he wanted to stand out. The first name on the muster roll is Lieutenant Colonel John Montgomery, whose date of commission was 14 December 1778. None of the names of the men on this roll are indexed in the *Guide to the Draper Manuscripts.*

The Civil War

The American Civil War was the bloodiest conflict in U.S. history. Neighbor fought against neighbor and brother fought against brother. The United States had called a regular (official) army of enlisted men, but most soldiers who fought in the Civil War, both Union and Confederate, were from state-raised volunteer units. As the Northern states' volunteer troops joined forces with the army they were "mustered in," meaning they enlisted in or joined the regular army. Southern state-raised units joined forces with the Confederate Army and were mustered into its forces as well. Indexes to the consolidated service records exist for both Union and Confederate soldiers. A soldier's consolidated records consist of a packet of index cards. The jacket or cover is a folded envelope in which all the cards containing information about the soldier are contained. (See figure 4.2.) You will often find a card in the packet that says the soldier was found on a muster roll. The muster rolls are a record of those who were present at the time of the assembly or roll call. Figures 4.3 through 4.5 show the consolidated records of Private Abraham (Abram) Ebersole, who served in the 13th Missouri Cavalry (Union), Company C.[7] There are twelve cards in his consolidated record.

Many, but not all, of the service records have been microfilmed by the National Archives. They have been digitized and can be found on Fold3. Those that have not been filmed must be ordered online from the National Archives at www.archives.gov/veterans/military-service-records/pre-ww-1-records.html, or by using Form 86, which can be downloaded from the same site.

Co C, 13 Missouri Cav
Private | Private
CARD NUMBERS.

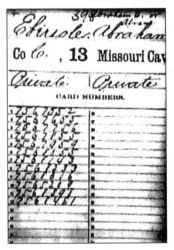

FIGURE 4.2
An image of the envelope in which index cards were placed for Abraham (Abram) Ebersole of the 13th Missouri Cavalry (Union), Company C

C | 13 Cav. | Mo.
Co. C, 13 Reg't Missouri Cavalry
Appears on
Company Muster Roll
for ...., 1864
Present or absent ....
Stoppage, $ ....100 for ....
Due Gov't, $ ....100 for ....

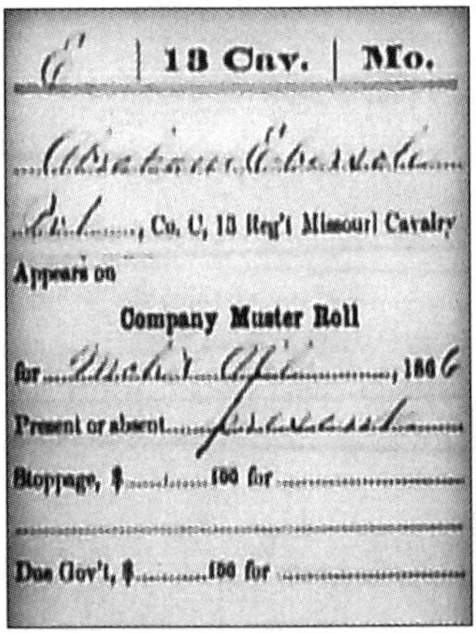

FIGURE 4.3
A portion of one of the cards in Abraham Ebersole's packet. It indicates he was a private. He appeared on a company muster roll during March and April 1864.

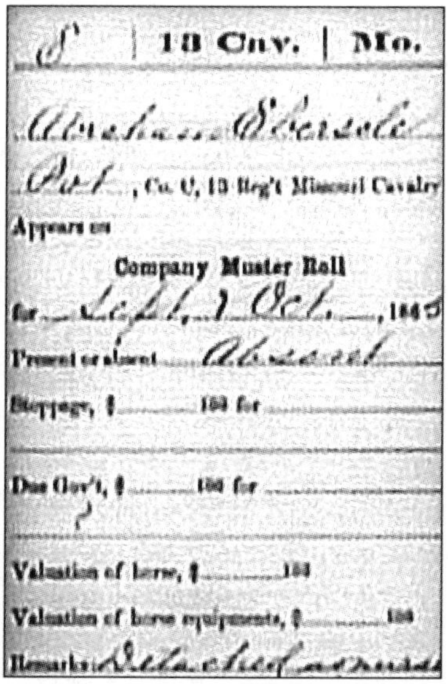

S | 18 Cav. | Mo.

Abraham Ebersole

Pvt, Co. C, 13 Reg't Missouri Cavalry

Appears on

Company Muster Roll

for Sept & Oct, 1865

Present or absent Absent

Stoppage, $ .... 100 for ....

Due Gov't, $ .... 100 for ....

Valuation of horse, $ 100

Valuation of horse equipments, $ 100

Remarks: Detached as nurse

FIGURE 4.4

A muster roll that indicates Private Ebersole was absent in September and October of 1865. He was "detached and nursed at Regtl Hospt Camp Wardnell C. T. [Colorado Territory] since Oct. 12, 1865."

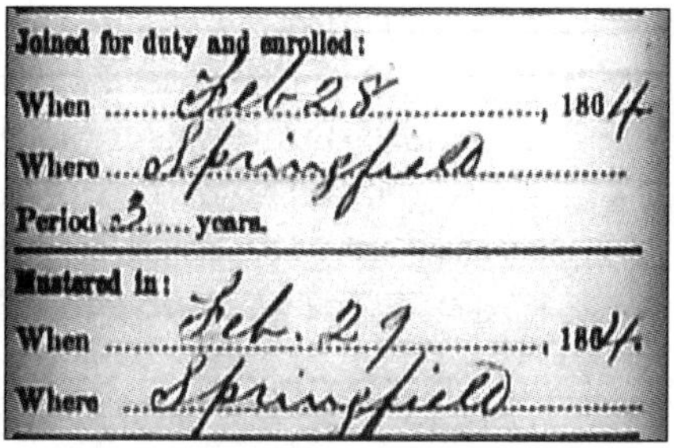

Joined for duty and enrolled:

When .... Feb 28 ...., 1864

Where .... Springfield ....

Period ..3.... years.

Mustered in:

When .... Feb. 29 ...., 1864

Where .... Springfield ....

FIGURE 4.5

Another card in Private Ebersole's packet indicating that he enrolled for duty on February 28, 1864, and mustered into the U.S. Army on February 29, 1864, in Springfield, Missouri

The microfilmed copies are available at major research libraries and at the Family History Library. The "Soldiers and Sailors System" made available through the National Parks Service (https://www.nps.gov/civilwar/search-soldiers.htm) has an index to all Union and Confederate soldiers and sailors who gave service during the war. This free website also gives information about regiments, battles, prisoners, cemeteries, and Medals of Honor. Many books have been compiled to give the same type of information. The following is a selected bibliography of Civil War print sources:

Dyer, Frederick H. *A Compendium of the War of Rebellion.* New York: T. Yoseloff, 1959. This three-volume set, later reprinted in two volumes, lists the names of Union units and gives brief regimental histories and lists battles. The names of individual soldiers are not given.

Hewett, Janet, ed. *The Roster of Confederate Soldiers, 1861–1865.* Wilmington, NC: Broadfoot, 1995– . This ten-volume set lists the names of Confederate soldiers and the state, rank, and unit to which they belonged.

————. *The Roster of Union Soldiers, 1861–1865.* Wilmington, NC: Broadfoot, 1997– . This series of volumes contains multivolume sets for each state that had Union soldiers. The name of each soldier plus his rank, state, and unit are given.

Morebeck, Nancy Justus. *Locating Union & Confederate Records: A Guide to the Most Commonly Used Civil War Records at the National Archives and Family History Library.* North Salt Lake, UT: HeritageQuest, 2001.

United States War Dept. *The War of the Rebellion: A Compilation of the Official Records of the Union and Confederate Armies.* Harrisburg, PA: National Historical Society, 1971. This multivolume set is often referred to as the "ORs." It contains no personal information on soldiers, but one will find accounts of battles and correspondence between units.

To find information for soldiers in the regular U.S. Army, look in the microfilmed records of *Registers of Enlistments in the U.S. Army, 1798–1914* (National Archives Series M233). They are in chronological order, then in loose alphabetical order (only alphabetical by the first letter of the last name), and then by date of enlistment. The digital images can be found on Ancestry.com and Fold3.

Pension records were available for Union veterans or their widows and can be found as textual records in the National Archives. They have not been microfilmed, but the index can be found on Fold3. Federal pension records were available for the veteran, if he qualified, or his widow. If a veteran fought for the South, applications for pensions were accepted by states in the former Confederate States of America but were not always granted. Don't look for Confederate pension applications at the National Archives because the federal government did not offer pensions to veterans who had not been Union soldiers. A Confederate veteran was eligible to apply for a pension to the state in which he lived at the time of the application, and if a pension was granted you will find the pension application in that state, most likely in its official records repository. If the Confederate veteran was living in a Northern state after the war you will not find a pension application. More information about Confederate pension records can be found on the National Archives website, https://www.archives.gov/research/military/civil-war/confederate/pension.html.

Another place to look for information about a Union Civil War veteran is the special 1890 census schedule of Union Civil War veterans or their widows. This separate enumeration was taken in conjunction with the 1890 population schedules. When a Union veteran was found in the household, the additional schedule was completed. It contains the name of the soldier (or his widow), his unit of service, and his rank. Additionally, information is found regarding any disability incurred because of the war. Occasionally one can find the names of Confederate veterans on the pages of the special schedule, but their names will be marked through. The names are usually readable through the markings.

Should you wish to find the burial place of a Union Civil War soldier, there are a couple of sources available. Shortly after the Civil War, the families of deceased Union veterans could request a tombstone for their loved one. As families applied for the headstones, index card files were created. Each card contains the name of the soldier or veteran, his unit and state, and the place of burial. Some of the cemeteries named on the cards are national cemeteries and some are not. The applications were amassed from about 1879 to about 1903. Figure 4.6 is an image from microfilm showing an application for a headstone for John W. Colyar, who served as a private in Company B, 9th Regiment, Pennsylvania Cavalry. He died on May 5, 1883, and is buried at Oak Hill Cemetery in Millersburg, Dauphin County, Pennsylvania.[8] The National Archives filmed the card files, and they can be found online at Ancestry.com.

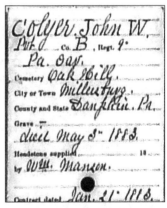

FIGURE 4.6

An image from microfilm showing an application for a headstone for John W. Colyar, who served as a private in Company B, 9th Regiment, Pennsylvania Cavalry

To find soldiers buried at national cemeteries, you can find the location of burials, which include Civil War soldiers, and those who were in other conflicts, online at the Nationwide Gravesite Locator, http://gravelocator

.cem.va.gov/j2ee/servlet/NGL_v1. You can search for names in specific cemeteries or in all cemeteries. The only required field in which to enter information is the last name. The site will search for veterans in national and state veterans' cemeteries as well as private cemeteries when the grave has a government grave marker. The results will show the name of the soldier, his rank and unit, the war in which he served, the date of death, the name and address of the cemetery, and possibly, the location of the grave within the cemetery. If a cemetery map is available, a link will bring up that image.

Civil War records can also be found in state repositories. Muster-out records containing the names of soldiers for a given state were placed in charge of the adjutant general of that state. He published the names either annually or compiled into a multiyear volume. These books of names can be found in research libraries and archives under the title *Report of the Adjutant General of the State of [name of state], [year or years encompassed]*. Figure 4.7 shows a page of the *Report of the Adjutant General of the State of Kansas 1861–'65*, vol. 1.[9]

Periodicals, newspapers, and county histories are additional sources for finding information about your Civil War ancestor. Look for a periodical entitled *The Confederate Veteran* for more information about Southern veterans. It was published between 1893 and 1932 and can be found in research libraries, historical societies, and on digital book sites such as *The Internet Archive,* http://archive.org. Veterans of the Union Army often joined with other veterans in a fraternal organization called the Grand Army of the Republic (GAR). Rosters of some of the state organizations of the GAR can be found in research libraries, historical societies, and digital book sites. The books may be entitled *Complete Roster . . .* or *Official Roster . . .* or *History and Roster . . .*, but the constant in the titles will be *Grand Army of the Republic.*

Spanish-American War

The muster rolls and general index cards to the compiled service records for the Spanish-American War are available as textual records at the National Archives and can be ordered using NATF Form 86. The index to the service records can be found on Fold3. Rosters and unit histories can be found on the Spanish American War Centennial Website,

FIRST REGIMENT KANSAS VOLUNTEERS—INFANTRY—*Continued.* COMPANY G—*Continued.*				
Names and rank.	Residence.	Date of enlistment.	Date of muster.	Remarks.
PRIVATES. Cole, Joseph.........	Leavenworth,	May 29, '61	May 29, '61	Shot for murder of Michael Stein, July 14, 1861, by order of Gen. Lyon.
Conley, George F.....	"	"	"	Des. Chillicothe, Mo., Oct. 6,'61.
Caswell, Wm. H.....	"	"	"	Des. Trenton, Aug. 10, '62.
DeGraff, Wm. H......	"	"	"	Dis. by order Gen. Fremont, Nov. 10, '62, Tipton, Mo.
Evans, Jeremiah.....	"	"	"	Mus. out with reg. June 17, '64.
Funk, Abraham......	"	"	"	Pro. Serg. May 29, '61.
Ford, Wm. W.,......	"	"	"	Mus. out with reg. June 17, '64.
Friend, Asa.........	"	"	"	Des. Spr'gfield, Mo., Aug. 2, '62.
Frederick, Armil.....	"	"	"	Dishonorably dis. by sentence of court martial, Oct. 28, '62, Corinth, Miss.
Fisher, Charles M....	"	"	"	Transf'd to Co. K, Oct. 1, '61.
Fitzgerald, Michael.	"	"	"	Pro. Corp. Mar. 1, '62.
Folsom, George H....	"	"	"	Dis. for disability, June 7, '62, Leavenworth, Kan.
Green, George B.....	"	"	"	Pro. Serg. May 29, '61; des. Trenton, Tenn., Aug. 1, '62.
Gladden, Wm. R....	"	"	"	Transf'd to Co. B, July 1, '63; mus. out with Co. B, June 16, '64.
Gross, Christian W...	"	"	"	Died, Lake Providence, La., July 22, '63.
Hendelong, John,	"	"	"	Pro. Serg. May 29, '61.
Hepworth, Jeremiah,	"	"	"	Pro. Corp. May 29, '61; trans. Co. K, Nov. 1, '61.
Harrison, Chas. T....	"	"	"	Pro. Corp. May 29, '61.
Hinckley, Reuben....	"	"	"	Pro. Corp. Oct. 25, '61.
Hemerith, Gotlieb...	"	"	"	Died of congestive fever, Lake Providence, La., June 20, '63; wounded in action.
Henry, John A.......	"	"	"	Pro. Serg. Maj. May 1, '62.
Hart, Henry P.......	"	"	"	Des., Rolla, Mo., Aug. 23, '61.
Hicklin, John........	"	"	"	Died of typhoid fever, St. Louis, Mo., Jan. 30, '62.
Holbush, Wm. S.....	"	"	"	Des., Rolla, Mo., Aug. 19, '61.
Johnson, Edwin S....	"	"	"	Mus. out with reg. June 17, '64.
Kline, Christian.....	"	"	"	App. Musician May 29, '61.
Kirwin, Michael	"	"	"	Trans. to Co. K, Nov. 1, '61.
Lareaux, Henry......	"	"	"	Des. Leavenworth, May 30, '61.
Lowry, James M....	"	"	"	Des. Memphis, Tenn., June 20, '63; wounded in action.
Lantz, John........	"	"	"	Mus. out with reg. June 17, '64.
Linturn, Phil'nder E.	"	"	"	Pro. Corp. May 29, '61; mus. out with reg. June 17, '63.
Morton, Wm. A......	"	"	"	Dis. for disability Nov. 10, '61, by order Gen. Fremont.
Meyer, Christian.....	"	"	"	Died, St. Louis, Feb. 20, '62.
May, Pierce.........	"	"	"	Died, Lake Providence, La. July 15, '63.
Morrison, James.....	"	"	"	Re-enlisted vet.; was wounded in action.
Munroe, James......	"	"	"	Re-enlisted veteran.
Miller, Jacob........	"	"	"	Des. Gr. Riv., Mo., July 12, '61

FIGURE 4.7
A page of the adjutant general's report of Kansas
volunteers from 1861 to 1865

www.spanamwar.com/units.htm. If the veteran received a pension, it can also be ordered from NARA. My husband's great-grandfather received an invalid pension as a result of his service in the Spanish-American War.

Figure 4.8 shows a copy of the written testimony of the wife of Fred E. Williams requesting an increase of pension, and stating that she had always known him to be in poor health due to tuberculosis contracted during his military service. Figure 4.9 is a copy of the marriage license of Fred Williams and Ella Windt. This was needed to verify the

GENERAL AFFIDAVIT.—PENSION. FORM A F. A. Onderdonk, Grand Rapids, Mich.

GENERAL AFFIDAVIT.

State of Michigan, County of Kent, ss:

In the Matter of Fred E Willims Claim for increase of Pension of Co "G" 4th U.S. Infantry

Here state name of claimant and of soldier and his military service.

On this 9th day of January, A. D. 1906, personally appeared before me, a Notary Public in and for the aforesaid County and State, duly authorized to administer oaths, Mrs Ella Williams, aged 22 years, a resident of Grand Rapids in the County of Kent and State of Michigan whose Post Office address is 302 Watson St. Grand Rapids Mich well known to me to be reputable and entitled to credit, and who, being duly sworn, declared in relation to the aforesaid case as follows:

NOTE.—Affiants should state how long they have known soldier, how often they have seen him on an average during their acquaintance with him, and any other matters that would tend to show the basis of their knowledge of the facts to which they testify.

I have known Fred E Williams for about 3½ years and know him to have been in poor health ever since our acquaintance he has complained of his Lungs aching A great deal and more so when the weather was bad he had A sort of hacking cough which grew gradually worse and about 2 years ago was taken with Hemorhage of the Lungs since which time he has grown gradually worse He has been subject to Chills and fevers and has taken quinine and sweat him self with hot water bottles for he said they treated him that way in the army Hospital He has also been bothered with his

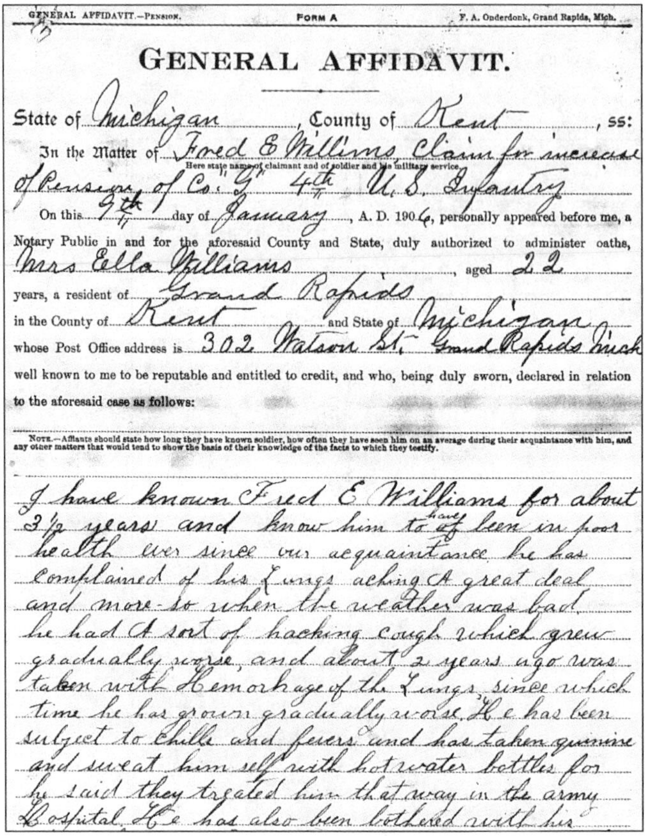

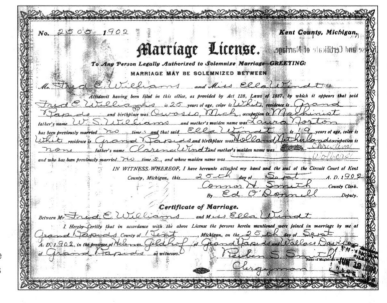

FIGURE 4.8
A copy of the written testimony of Fred E. Williams's wife regarding his poor health due to his war service

No. 2505 1902 Kent County, Michigan.

Marriage License.

To Any Person Legally Authorized to Solemnize Marriage—GREETING:

MARRIAGE MAY BE SOLEMNIZED BETWEEN

Mr. Fred E Williams and Miss Ella Windt

Affidavit having been filed in this office, as provided by Act 128, Laws of 1887, by which it appears that said Fred E Williams is 25 years of age, color is White, residence is Grand Rapids and birthplace was Owosso, Mich, occupation is Machinist father's name W. S. Williams and mother's maiden name was Laura Norton has been previously married no times and that said Ella Windt is 19 years of age, color is White residence is Grand Rapids and birthplace was Holland Netherlands occupation is none father's name Clarence Windt and mother's maiden name was Christine Wolbers and who has been previously married no times, and whose maiden name was

IN WITNESS WHEREOF, I have hereunto attached my hand and the seal of the Circuit Court of Kent County, Michigan, this 25th day of Sept A. D. 1902

Connor H. Smith County Clerk.

By Ed. O'Donnell Deputy.

Certificate of Marriage.

Between Mr. Fred E. Williams and Miss Ella Windt

I Hereby Certify that in accordance with the above License the persons herein mentioned were joined in marriage by me at Grand Rapids County of Kent, Michigan, on the 25th day of Sept A. D. 1902, in the presence of Helena Goldhof of Grand Rapids and Wallace Davis of Grand Rapids as witnesses.

Reuben S. Smith
Name of Magistrate or Clergyman
Clergyman

FIGURE 4.9
A copy of the marriage license of Fred Williams and Ella Windt

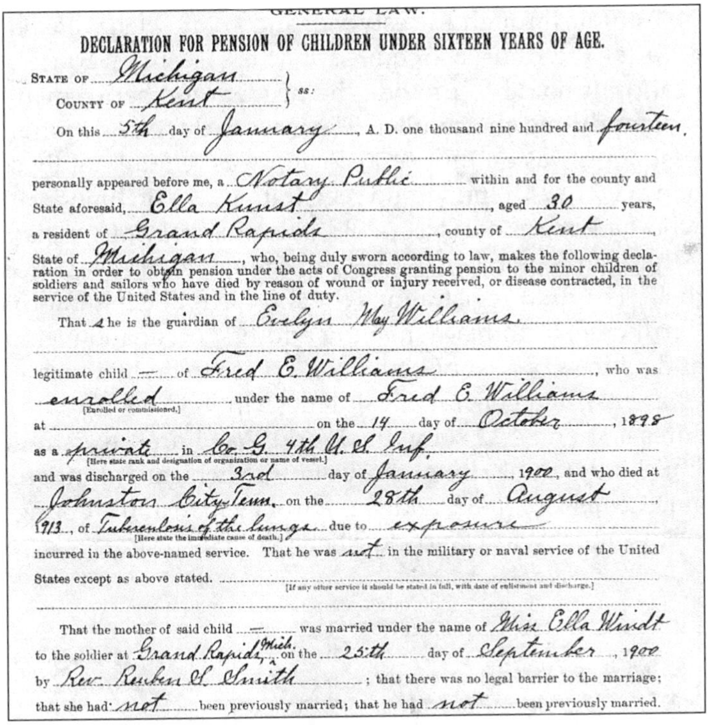

GENERAL LAW.

DECLARATION FOR PENSION OF CHILDREN UNDER SIXTEEN YEARS OF AGE.

STATE OF Michigan }
COUNTY OF Kent } ss:

On this 5th day of January, A. D. one thousand nine hundred and fourteen,

personally appeared before me, a Notary Public within and for the county and State aforesaid, Ella Kunst, aged 30 years, a resident of Grand Rapids, county of Kent, State of Michigan, who, being duly sworn according to law, makes the following declaration in order to obtain pension under the acts of Congress granting pension to the minor children of soldiers and sailors who have died by reason of wound or injury received, or disease contracted, in the service of the United States and in the line of duty.

That she is the guardian of Evelyn May Williams

legitimate child — of Fred E. Williams, who was enrolled [Enrolled or commissioned.] under the name of Fred E. Williams at on the 14 day of October, 1898 as a private in Co. G. 4th U. S. Inf. [Here state rank and designation of organization or name of vessel.] and was discharged on the 3rd day of January, 1900, and who died at Johnston City Tenn. on the 28th day of August, 1913, of Tuberculosis of the lungs [Here state the immediate cause of death.] due to exposure incurred in the above-named service. That he was not in the military or naval service of the United States except as above stated. [If any other service it should be stated in full, with date of enlistment and discharge.]

That the mother of said child — was married under the name of Miss Ella Windt to the soldier at Grand Rapids, Mich. on the 25th day of September, 1900 by Rev. Reuben S. Smith; that there was no legal barrier to the marriage; that she had not been previously married; that he had not been previously married.

FIGURE 4.10

A copy of the request for benefits for Evelyn Williams, minor child of Fred Williams

marriage and the subsequent legal birth of their daughter, Evelyn, for whom Ella was requesting benefits upon Fred's death. Ella was not eligible for benefits because she had remarried. (See figure 4.10.)

World War I

The service records for World War I have been declassified and are available at the National Personnel Records Center (NPRC) in St. Louis, Missouri. They can be viewed by appointment or by ordering online via https://vetrecs.archives.gov/VeteranRequest/home.html. These are considered archival records sixty-two years after an individual separated from the service. In addition to service records, the National Archives maintains the World War I draft registrations. They are searchable online through Ancesty.com and Fold3. Men were required to sign up for the draft, as required by the Selective Service Act, at their local draft board to provide the needed number of men in the armed forces during the conflict. There were three registrations: the first registration was on June 5, 1917, and was required of those men who were age 21 to 31; the second registration was on June 5, 1918, for those who had become 21 years old since the previous registration; and the third, on September 12, 1918, expanded the ages required to 18 through 45. The draft registrations contain the following information: name, birth date, birth place, mailing address, occupation, employer, name and address of next of kin (a great place to find the name of the wife or parents), and general physical description.

Figures 4.11 and 4.12 show the World War I draft registration for John Emil Lindgren of Houghton County, Michigan.[10] Lindgren was born on December 10, 1882, and was a trolley man at the Portage Coal and Dock Company in Hancock, Michigan. His nearest relative was

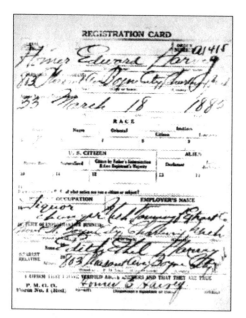

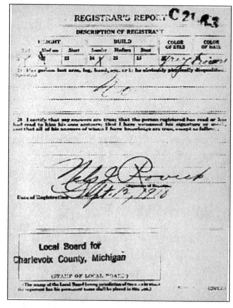

FIGURE 4.11

First part of the World War I draft registration for John Emil Lindgren of Houghton County, Michigan

FIGURE 4.12

Another part of the World War I draft registration for John Emil Lindgren of Houghton County, Michigan

his wife, Alma Lindgren. He was tall, of medium build, with blue eyes and light hair.

World War II

Service records from World War II are housed at the National Personnel Records Center (NPRC) in St. Louis but are not online. However, records of enlistments are available through NARA's Access to Archival Databases (AAD) website, Ancestry.com, and Fold3. The records do not include all U.S. Army enlistees and none of the Navy or Marine Corps enlisted personnel. They consist of punch-card data created during the war. This data now supplements the loss of records from a 1973 fire at the NPRC. The records for army personnel who separated from service between November 1, 1912, and January 1, 1960, were 80 percent destroyed. The records for Air Force personnel who separated from service between September 25, 1947, and January 1, 1964, (with names alphabetically after Hubbard, James E.) were 75 percent destroyed.[11] The enlistment records show the serial number, name, residence (state and county), place of enlistment, date of enlistment, rank upon enlistment, term of enlistment, place and year of birth, race and citizenship, education, civilian occupation, and marital status.

Figure 4.13 is a record showing the army enlistment record for my father. It was downloaded from Ancestry.com's database, but the information is from NARA's Access to Archival Databases website.[12]

World War II draft registrations for the fourth registration are available on Ancestry.com. It is the only regis-

Name:	**Alan I Lindgren**
Birth Year:	1917
Race:	White, Citizen *(White)*
Nativity State or Country:	Michigan
State of Residence:	Michigan
County or City:	Houghton
Enlistment Date:	11 Jul 1942
Enlistment State:	Michigan
Enlistment City:	Traverse City
Branch:	Branch Immaterial - Warrant Officers, USA
Branch Code:	Branch Immaterial - Warrant Officers, USA
Grade:	Private
Grade Code:	Private
Term of Enlistment:	Enlistment for the duration of the War or other emergency, plus six months, subject to the discretion of the President or otherwise according to law
Component:	Selectees (Enlisted Men)
Source:	Civil Life
Education:	1 year of college
Civil Occupation:	Bookkeepers and cashiers, except bank cashiers
Marital Status:	Single, without dependents
Height:	72
Weight:	143

FIGURE 4.13

A record showing the U.S. Army enlistment record for the author's father

tration open to the public due to privacy laws. The registration took place in 1942 for men born between the years 1877 and 1897. The information found on these records is like that found on the World War I draft registration cards. To find locations of the final resting places of those who were killed in action on foreign soil, see the American Battle Monuments (ABM) website, https://www.abmc.gov. You can search for World War I, World War II, and Korean War deaths for those interred in U.S. burying grounds on foreign soil. My uncle, Melvin Lindgren, is buried in the Philippines. The ABM website indicates he was a second lieutenant in the U.S. Army and his service number is given, along with his unit and regiment, and the date when he entered the service from Michigan. He died on May 12, 1945, and is buried at the American Cemetery in Manila, Philippines. The plot, row, and grave number are given. A photograph of the cemetery is also found on the website.

Finding our ancestors in military records helps us flesh out their life stories. Our country was founded on patriotism, and from the Revolutionary War to the current day our ancestors have put themselves in harm's way to protect our freedom. How exciting it is to find out that people from our own lineage were involved in those efforts! Finding military records can help place our ancestors in history, help us define their character, and give us a richer view of history.

LESSON SEVEN

- Look at the timeline of an ancestor's life. Compare the years he was of military age with the wars and conflicts taking place at that time. If you have family tradition or oral history that your ancestor was in the military, you can eliminate the creation of a timeline.

- What military records are available for that time? Use Fold3 or Ancestry.com to find the military records, if available to you, or order them from the National Archives.

- Explore NARA's overview of military records at https://www.archives.gov/research/military.

Church Records

Many of our ancestors came to America for religious freedom. Living in countries where an officially established church, called a state church, was the required religion caused those with a differing view to look for a home elsewhere. Freedom to worship as one saw fit was such an important concept that the First Amendment of the Constitution states, "Congress shall make no law respecting an establishment of religion, or prohibiting the free exercise thereof."[13] As churches in America grew and developed, records of important events in the lives of their members were made and preserved. Church records are an excellent genealogical resource for finding information about our families. In the United States, church records often preceded civil registrations and were often more complete. Documented church records are an excellent substitute for missing vital records.

The types of items found in church records will vary by religious denomination, but the most common types of records are baptisms and christenings, marriages, deaths and burials, memberships, church minutes, and ministers' records. To research the records, one must know the origin and traditions of record-keeping of each denomination. Substitutes for birth records as found in church records are christenings, births, and confirmations. A baptism is a sacred rite or ceremony proclaiming one to be a Christian, which involves the application of water either through sprinkling or immersion (immersing a person under the water). A christening is a form of baptism but is usually performed when the subject is an infant. The early term for christening meant "to give a name."[14] Both baptismal and christening records, at the very least, record the name of the individual and the date of the event. A baptismal record will sometimes give the age of the individual, while a christening often records the date of birth. A christening record will normally contain the names of the parents, sponsors or godparents, and residence. Confirmations can be a supplemental event that is a "rite of passage" for children of a set age who have prepared to receive their first communion. Knowing the age at which the first communion is normally taken can help determine the approximate year of birth of the child. Another rite of passage can be found in the Jewish faith. A bar mitzvah (for males) or bat mitzvah (for females) occurs about the age of twelve or thirteen and involves the young person reading the Torah or Haftarah portion, or both, of the Shabbat service. Again, knowing when this occurred can help determine the year of birth.

Marriage records found in church records can be banns, bonds, announcements, ceremonies, or blessings. Marriage banns are read or posted notices in the church of an upcoming wedding. Enough time is given to ensure that there is no known reason for the marriage not to occur. Not all religions required marriage banns. Marriage bonds were contracted by friends, relatives, or the groom to compensate the church if there were any reason the marriage could not occur, perhaps because of infidelity. Announcements of weddings can be found in church bulletins and publications, often inviting the congregation to the wedding. The marriage ceremony itself provided a written record that it had occurred. The minister recorded the event into the church record book. Marriage blessings are found when a civil ceremony is performed in a register office with a blessing in the church following.

Information about deaths may also be found in church records. Some denominations keep records of deceased members either as an official record or in a historian's report. If the denomination had a newspaper or periodical publication, you will often find obituaries in it. My great-grandfather made front-page news when he died. He was hit by a train, but while the newspaper account was very interesting, no obituary was printed. I found the obituary, which listed the names of his wife and children, in a church periodical. Now I have both a detailed account of his death and an obituary for my genealogy records. Ministers' records often record information about the funeral orations that were preached. Some churches have adjacent cemeteries, and records of those buried there can be found in the church records, as well as the names of the owners of the cemetery plots.

Records of church members are often kept at both the local and denominational level. Those who were admitted into membership, removals, dismissals, admonishments, trials, and letters of transfer are among the types of membership records kept. Some churches, usually on the local level, publish yearly membership directories. Often the directory will contain photographs of the parishioners, and many of those are pictures of family units.

As with any organization, church meetings are often held to determine the yearly budget, elect officers, and vote on a potential minister. The minutes of those meetings can be found locally and/or on the denominational level. In colonial America, the Protestant Episcopal Church, a part of the Church of England, kept vestry books. Vestry means "a body of persons entrusted with the administration of the temporal affairs of a parish in the Church of England or in the Protestant Episcopal Church."[15] These were records of a civil nature, such as the recording of the names of the poor who were helped and the taxes that were collected.

Many church records involving baptisms, christenings, and marriages have been filmed and can be found in the Family History Library or in digital form on its FamilySearch website. You might be able to find other church records online, though they are likely to be records from the nineteenth century or before. Others can only be found at the church itself or in a denominational repository. College and university libraries (especially those that are sponsored by a religious denomination) and historical societies may also have church records. I particularly like *A Survey of American Church Records*,[16] which lists denominations along with their repositories. Though the book is dated, I use the information as a guide. Once I know about the repository, I can do an online search for the current information. You might also want to look at the Periodical Source Index (PERSI), which can be found on the Findmypast website. Many church records have been transcribed in genealogy periodicals, and by searching PERSI you can find in which periodical the records were recorded. For more information about PERSI, see chapter 6.

When trying to locate your ancestors' church records, the most difficult task can be in determining the denomination. Family tradition may indicate the church to which your ancestors belonged. You should also look at the biographical sketches in county histories for clues. One of my ancestors began his life as a Quaker, but his biographical sketch in the county history states that he was a faithful member of the Baptist church. County histories often list the names of those who were charter members of the pioneer churches. For marriage records, look at the name of the person who performed your ancestor's marriage. If the record indicates the officiant was a "minister of the gospel" (MG), look for information about him in a county history or city directory. Family histories and genealogies will also give clues as to the denomination of the family. If the ancestor stayed true to his religion, the country of origin can give clues. In Scandinavian countries, the Lutheran Church was the state church. France was a Catholic country, but your French ancestor might also have been Protestant. The French Protestants were called Huguenots. Ancestors from England would be found worshipping in the Church of England, the Anglican state church of England. In Germany, an individual would have been either Lutheran or Catholic. This was largely determined by the parish or district in which he or she lived. A series of books to help you determine the type of German parish, should you know the locality, is the *Map Guide to German Parish Registers*.[17] There are currently fifty-six volumes in the series. A map for each parish is listed with an indication of the denomination. Be aware that your ancestors did not always stay true to the faith in which they started life. Sometimes they changed religions through conversion or convenience once they arrived in the United States.

Here is a short list of books to help you find out more information about church records:

> Betit, Kyle, and Beverly Whitaker. *Researching American Religious Records*. Toronto: Heritage Productions, 2002.
>
> Carter-Walker, Fran. *Searching American Church Records*. Bradenton, FL: published by author, 1995.
>
> Quillen, W. Daniel. *Mastering Family, Library, & Church Records*. Cold Spring Harbor, NY: Cold Spring, 2014.

Catholic Church Records

Before the Vatican II (1959) church council, Roman Catholic records were written in Latin. Records created after Vatican II are in the language of the country in which the rites were performed. The various records are kept at parishes or the dioceses. You can find the Diocesan Locator at www.usccb.org/about/bishops-and-dioceses/diocesan-locator .cfm. Baptism or christening records are a vital resource in the Catholic Church. You will find the christening date, the individual's given name, parents' names (and sometimes the maiden name of the mother), godparents' names, and the name of the officiating priest.

The first communion (Eucharist) records include the date of first communion, the individual's name, and the name of the officiating priest. They are found consistently after 1915. There are no registers of additional communions in a person's life. Matrimonial records are usually found in the bride's parish. You should find the marriage date, the given names and ages of the bride and groom, the parents' names and possibly the maiden name of the mothers, the names of witnesses, and the name of the officiating priest. Burial records, recordings of those buried by the church, are also available and proved that the surviving spouses were free to marry. They are usually found after 1915. The diocese may also have records of the cemeteries within its charge.

Lutheran Church

Lutheran church records in the United States can be found at two repositories: Missouri Synod records are held at the Concordia Historical Institute (www.lutheranhistory.org/ancestor.htm) and at the Evangelical Lutheran Church in America (www.elca.org/archives). The types of church records kept are baptisms, confirmations, marriages, member lists, and registers of families.

Jewish Records

Jewish synagogues did not usually keep vital records, unless required to do so by law. Those that were kept are not standard from place to place. But other records exist that can help with your search for ancestors. An excellent online source for basic guidance as well as for searching records is JewishGen at http://jewishgen.org. Some printed guides to research are:

> Kurzweil, Arthur. *From Generation to Generation: How to Trace Your Jewish Genealogy and Family History*. San Francisco: Jossey-Bass, 2011.
>
> Mokotoff, Gary. *Getting Started in Jewish Genealogy: 2016–2017 Edition*. New Haven, CT: Avotaynu, 2016.

Quaker Records

The Quaker Church, also known as the Religious Society of Friends, is a unique religious organization. They have no ministers, believing that everyone has an inner light allowing for direct communication with

God. Their records are well documented, and most of what you will find are those recording the happenings of their monthly meetings. The monthly meetings are named, such as the Contentnea Monthly Meeting. Swarthmore College is one of the repositories of Quaker records. Their website is www.swarthmore.edu/friends-historical -library/quaker-meeting-records. Though far from comprehensive, other repositories include Harvard University, the Nantucket Historical Association, and Guilford College. The Family History Library also has microfilmed records.

In Quaker monthly meeting records, one can find information about entire family units. William Wade Hinshaw transcribed many Quaker records in the *Encyclopedia of American Quaker Genealogy.*[18] Records from monthly meetings from the states of North Carolina, Pennsylvania, Ohio, New York, and New Jersey are included in the five-volume set. The Quakers do not believe in naming months, so dates will be numerical. Figure 4.14 is an example of Hinshaw's work. The image shows Dicene S. Pearson, the daughter of Joseph and Ruth

```
Page 103.
John T. Pearson, s. Lazarus & Sarah, b.  3-21-
                                           1837.
Dicene S. Pearson, dt. Joseph & Ruth Newlin,
             Alamance Co., b.  3-19-1836.
Ch: Joseph L.         b.  6- 2-1859.
    John N.            "  11- 8-1861.
    William E.         "   8-20-1863.
    Emily R.           "   9-29-1865.
    James R.           "   6- 8-1868.
    Minnie Whitaker    "   5- 5-1871. (d.  7- 3-
                                   1872, p. 119-D)
    Mary Achsah        "   4-10-1874.
    Thomas O.          "   3-16-1877.
Page 119-D.
John T. Pearson, s. Lazarus & Sarah, d. 10-29-
             1877, aged 40 yrs. 7 mos. 8 das.


Page 108.
Jonathan Pearson, s. Ichabod & Elizabeth, b.
                                  3-17-1823.
Sallie Pearson, dt. Warren & Sallie Woodard, b.
                                  1-22-1831.
```

FIGURE 4.14
Hinshaw's transcription of the Quaker Church
record of Dicene S. Pearson

Newlin, born in Alamance County [North Carolina], on 3 [March] 19, 1836. The children [Ch.] listed below Dicene's name are hers. Two of the daughters are listed with their married names.

Cemetery Records

Cemeteries are resting places of the dead and provide a unique genealogy research experience. Family members are often buried side by side, allowing you to re-create the family unit. The information contained on tombstones varies. Many provide only the birth year and death year. If you are fortunate, the full birth and death dates will be shown. Some tombstones have the names of both the husband and wife on the same stone. If the husband and wife have separate stones, there may be an indication of relationship such as "loving wife of" and then the husband's name. A child's stone may indicate "child of." Cemetery art can also yield facts about a person's life. Look for crosses, stars of David, and Masonic symbols. There are difficulties involved in cemetery research, however. Not every grave is marked, and even if there is a tombstone, it may be weathered and unreadable. An active cemetery will have an office allowing you to obtain the location of the grave. The office records may also indicate the interment date and the name of the person paying for the lot.

There are different types of cemeteries: religious-based, municipal, family, and private cemeteries. A religious-based or church cemetery will often be found next to the church to which the decedents belonged. The records will often be found there or in the church's archives. A municipal cemetery is owned by the city in which it resides, and the records might be found in the town or city clerk's office in the deed records. Private, or corporate, cemeteries are owned by an organization that usually operates many burying grounds. There will often be an office at each cemetery, assuming they are still selling lots, where you will find the deed and burial records. You may find cemetery readings (a transcription of the information found on the tombstones within the cemetery) of older cemeteries, those no longer active, in books, periodicals, microfilm, or online at various websites.

Family plots were established on land owned, at least at one time, by the family. Searching deed records for land ownership may help you locate the resting place of those ancestors. Some family burial plots no longer exist. As land changes hands from one family to another, burying grounds are susceptible to destruction either by vandalism or farming. But I know that there are many family plots which are well-cared for by the current owners. Most states have laws regarding the accessibility to burying grounds on private land, allowing descendants to visit the graves of their forebears.

You can also look for potter's fields, sanatorium cemeteries, and national cemeteries. Most large cities, at one time or another, have had a burial location for paupers and unknown or indigent persons. "Potter's field" is the term used for those types of burying grounds. Records of those interred can be extremely hard to locate, but check with the local historical society for availability. If an ancestor spent time in a sanatorium and died while there, he or she may be buried in the cemetery next to the medical facility. Those records will be found with the facility, if it still exists. If not, check with the local or state historical society. If your ancestor died while on active duty in the armed forces, he or she would have qualified for burial in a national cemetery. Those with an honorable discharge might also have qualified for burial there. To find someone interred in a national cemetery, use the Nationwide Gravesite Locator (http://gravelocator.cem.va.gov/j2ee/servlet/NGL_v1).

Cemetery records have long been a useful source in articles in periodicals and books published by genealogical and lineage societies. Lineage societies, such as the Daughters of the American Revolution, constantly seek out burying grounds and publish the names found on the tombstones there. The publications are usually given to their state's society and their national repository, if there is one. Duplicate copies are often given to the local library.

I like visiting cemeteries in which my ancestors are buried. I feel a closeness to an individual when I locate his or her grave and spend time in reflection on a life once lived. But it is not always possible to visit every grave of every ancestor. Find A Grave (http://findagrave.com) is a popular website for locating burials and visiting cemeteries virtually. It is a free social-networking site, and anyone who registers can contribute information and photos about any burial. Genealogy information can also be posted there. Figure 4.15 shows an image from Find A Grave that provides not only burial information for Ella Sarah Brown Flora, but also photographs and genealogy information about her.

FIGURE 4.15
Image from Find A Grave that provides burial and genealogical information for Ella Sarah Brown Flora

LESSON NINE

- Select an ancestor on your pedigree chart.
- Find the name and location of the cemetery in which he or she is buried. You may need to look at the death certificate or obituary.
- Find a cemetery reading in a published source, an entry on Find A Grave or another website, or visit the cemetery.
- Obtain a photograph of the tombstone. Does anyone in your family already have a photo of the stone? Do you or does anyone in your family live in proximity to the cemetery so they can take a photograph? Is the photo on Find A Grave?

Other places to find the location of burials are death certificates and obituaries. A caveat for relying upon tombstones for information is the possible inaccuracies they may have. The grave marker may have been placed many years after the burial. Remember, the further in time from an event, the greater the chance of error. One of my husband's ancestors is buried in Vermont. A large stone is on the family plot. The front of the stone shows the name of the mother and father, giving their birth and death years. The back of the stone contains the names of all of the couple's children with their birth and death years. The monument was obviously not in place when the mother and father died, since the names of all the children's death years are also on the tombstone. So the stone must have been incised and placed there many years later. If you find a stone like that, make sure you verify the information with another source.

Finding the physical location of a cemetery, assuming you know its name, is as easy as using Google maps (www.maps.google.com) or MapQuest (www.mapquest.com). Enter the name of the cemetery and the city and state. A map will be displayed pinpointing the location of the cemetery.

If you want more information about researching cemetery records, here is a short list of books:

Bartley, Scott A. *Researching American Cemetery Records.* Toronto: Heritage Productions, 2005.

Carmack, Sharon DeBartolo. *American Cemetery Research.* Baltimore, MD: Genealogical Publishing Co., 2012.

Hansen, Holly T., et al. *Cemetery and Sexton Records: A Research Guide.* Morgan, UT: Family History Expos, 2016.

Passenger Lists and Immigration

The United States is a nation of immigrants. Lists of ships' passengers are a gateway to finding your ancestor's motherland. The number of immigrant ancestors you will find depends on the number of generations backward you need to trace before you find a foreign-born ancestor. On my father's side, I need only to go back to his father to find an immigrant. My paternal grandfather emigrated from Sweden in 1901. But one of my maternal lines goes back to colonial America, leaving me with a much larger number of immigrant ancestors.

There are steps you must take before searching passenger lists: you need to discover the first and last name of the immigrant, his or her age or approximate age upon arrival, and the approximate date of arrival. The closer you can come to a date of arrival, the easier your search will be. Let's pretend that one of your immigrant ancestors was someone with the surname Schmidt. We can't look for all arrivals who have the last name of Schmidt. It would be a futile effort because you would not be able to identify your ancestor among all of those people named Schmidt who are arriving. (Schmidt is a very common German name.) In your research, you will seek to discover his first name. Let's say we find that his first name was Johann. If your Johann Schmidt was born about 1862 and his arrival was approximately 1890, you would be looking for a Johann Schmidt arriving about 1890 who was approximately twenty-eight years old.

How do you determine the approximate year of immigration? If the immigration was recent enough, look at the 1900, 1910, 1920, or 1930 census. If he or she was on a census in one of those years the census will tell you the year of immigration, based on the answer given the enumerator. If you can't pinpoint the immigration year to an exact year, try to find a window in time in which he or she arrived. For an example, let's say your ancestor was born on foreign soil in 1832 and died in the United States in 1885. We know that he immigrated after 1832 and before 1885. If he had a child who was born in the United

States in 1855, then the immigration year would have been between 1832 and 1855. Some questions to ask which, while not necessary, are good to know: Did your ancestor travel alone or with others? Did he bring his family? Did he come as a child? Was someone waiting for him in the United States, or was he the first of his family or friends to arrive?

1820 was a pivotal year in immigration. The overcrowding of immigrant ships was leading to many shipboard deaths en route to the United States. In March 1819, Congress enacted a law that stated there were to be only two passengers for every five tons of a ship's register.[19] The result was an enumeration of all ship's passengers which was to be sent to the secretary of state. These lists are called Customs Passenger Lists. The law took effect in 1820. If your ancestor arrived before 1820, the passenger list will not be an arrival list into the United States. It will be a re-created list that is based on licenses to pass overseas, will records, or land records—any documents that give a date when an immigrant came to this country.

Chapter 3 referenced the *Passenger and Immigration Lists Index* by P. William Filby. References to this book can be found on Ancestry .com. Passenger lists are indexed in this work and are the best places to search for pre-1820 arrivals. Figure 4.16 is an example of what constitutes a pre-1820 passenger list. It is from a chapter of *The Documentary*

OCTOBER; *In the Purmerland Church.*
Claus Paulus, from Delmarsum, and Wife.,
Nicolas du Pui, from Artois, and Wife and three children.
Arnout du Tols, from Ryssel, (Lisle,) and Wife and one child.
Gideon Merlit, and Wife and four children.
Louis Louhman, and Wife and three children.
Jacques Cossaris, and Wife and two children.
Jan de Conchilier, (now, Consilyea) and Wife and five children.
Jacob Colff, from Leyden, and Wife and two children.
Judith Jans, from Leyden, maiden.
Carsten Jansen.
Ferdinandus de Mulder.
Isaac Verniel, and Wife and four children.
Abelis Setshoorn.
Claes Jansen van Heynengen.

FIGURE 4.16
An example of a pre-1820 passenger list

History of the State of New York, entitled "Early Immigrants to New Netherland, 1657–1664."[20] The list is a little disappointing when one is hoping for more information.

The books that have been published to record re-created passenger lists are numerous. Using a bibliography and/or the Filby indexes is a great time-saver. There is another project that deserves mention here. It is a continuing effort by the New England Historic Genealogical Society to identify all immigrants arriving on our shores between 1620 and 1643, and is entitled The Great Migration Study Project. Comprehensive biographical and genealogical accounts can be found in the publications which have resulted from this study: a newsletter entitled *The Great Migration Newsletter* and many book titles. You can obtain subscription information for the newsletter or learn more about the project and its book publications at www.greatmigration.org. One of the project's latest titles is *The Great Migration Directory: Immigrants to New England, 1620–1640.*[21]

If your ancestor arrived at a U.S. port after 1820, there will likely be a passenger list for him or her. The National Archives filmed the passenger lists that were compiled between 1820 and 1954. Most, but not all, arrival lists have survived. The microfilms were digitized and various websites contain those images, such as Ancestry.com and Findmypast. The search will be relatively easy provided you know the name of the immigrant, the approximate year of immigration, the approximate age, and the probable port of arrival. The major ports of entry were Boston, Baltimore, New Orleans, New York, and Philadelphia, but there were also numerous minor ports of arrival. The amount of data collected by the customs agents varied depending on the year of arrival. Like the census records, the more recent the record, the more data was collected. The name of your immigrant ancestor may be recorded differently on passenger lists than you are expecting. It may be as simple as looking for Johann instead of John. But you may be looking for an ancestor whose name was changed after arriving in this country. Contrary to popular belief, names were not changed at Ellis Island or at any other port. (I have heard that story a lot from patrons.) Names were changed by the individuals themselves for various reasons and at many different times.

Figure 4.17 shows a U.S. customs passenger list for arrivals at the port of New York on August 26, 1896, on the ship *Saratoga.*[22] The name of

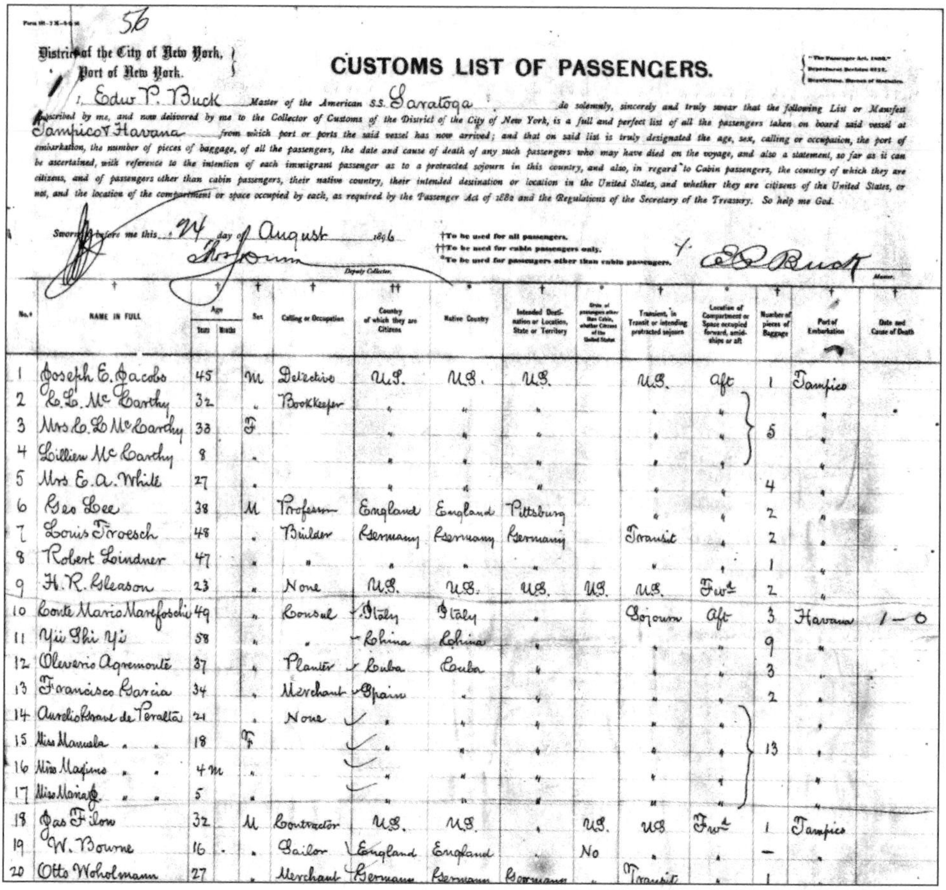

Form … 56

District of the City of New York, Port of New York.

CUSTOMS LIST OF PASSENGERS.

I, Edw P. Buck Master of the American S.S. Saratoga do solemnly, sincerely and truly swear that the following List or Manifest subscribed by me, and now delivered by me to the Collector of Customs of the District of the City of New York, is a full and perfect list of all the passengers taken on board said vessel at Tampico & Havana from which port or ports the said vessel has now arrived; and that on said list is truly designated the age, sex, calling or occupation, the port of embarkation, the number of pieces of baggage, of all the passengers, the date and cause of death of any such passengers who may have died on the voyage, and also a statement, so far as it can be ascertained, with reference to the intention of each immigrant passenger as to a protracted sojourn in this country, and also, in regard to Cabin passengers, the country of which they are citizens, and of passengers other than cabin passengers, their native country, their intended destination or location in the United States, and whether they are citizens of the United States, or not, and the location of the compartment or space occupied by each, as required by the Passenger Act of 1882 and the Regulations of the Secretary of the Treasury. So help me God.

Sworn to before me this 24 day of August 1896

Thos Dunn, Deputy Collector.

† To be used for all passengers.
†† To be used for cabin passengers only.
* To be used for passengers other than cabin passengers.

E P Buck, Master.

No.	Name in Full	Age Years	Age Months	Sex	Calling or Occupation	Country of which they are Citizens	Native Country	Intended Destination or Location, State or Territory	State of passengers other than Cabin, whether Citizens of the United States	Transient, in Transit or intending protracted sojourn	Location of Compartment or Space occupied forward, amidships or aft	Number of pieces of Baggage	Port of Embarkation	Date and Cause of Death
1	Joseph E. Jacobs	45		M	Detective	U.S.	U.S.	U.S.		U.S.	Aft	1	Tampico	
2	C. L. McCarthy	32		"	Bookkeeper	"	"	"		"	"		"	
3	Mrs C. L. McCarthy	33		F		"	"	"		"	"	5	"	
4	Lillien McCarthy	8		"		"	"	"		"	"		"	
5	Mrs E. A. White	27		"		"	"	"		"	"	4	"	
6	Geo Lee	38		M	Professor	England	England	Pittsburg		"	"	2	"	
7	Louis Troesch	48		"	Builder	Germany	Germany	Germany		Transit	"	2	"	
8	Robert Loindner	47		"	"	"	"	"		"	"	1	"	
9	H. R. Gleason	23		"	None	U.S.	U.S.	U.S.	U.S.	U.S.	Fwd	2	"	
10	Conte Mario Marefoschi	49		"	Consul	Italy	Italy	"		Sojourn	Aft	3	Havana	1–0
11	Yiu Shi Yi	58		"	"	China	China	"		"	"	9	"	
12	Oleverio Agremonte	37		"	Planter	Cuba	Cuba	"		"	"	3	"	
13	Francisco Garcia	34		"	Merchant	Spain	"	"		"	"	2	"	
14	Aurelio Grave de Peralta	21		"	None	"	"	"		"	"		"	
15	Miss Manuela " "	18		F		"	"	"		"	"	13	"	
16	Miss Magino " "	4 m		"		"	"	"		"	"		"	
17	Miss Maria " "	5		"		"	"	"		"	"		"	
18	Jas Filow	32		M	Contractor	U.S.	U.S.	"	U.S.	U.S.	Fwd	1	Tampico	
19	W. Bourne	16		"	Sailor	England	England	"	No	"	"	—	"	
20	Otto Woholmann	27		"	Merchant	Germany	Germany	Germany	"	Transit	"	1	"	

FIGURE 4.17

A customs passenger list for arrivals at the port of New York on August 26, 1896 on the ship *Saratoga*

every individual on board the ship was recorded, including their occupation, country of origin, and port of embarkation. Many lists show the place within the ship where each passenger resided. Steerage was a common travel abode. It was a cargo hold and the cheapest accommodation on board ship. Many of our ancestors arrived in steerage.

You may have a family tradition that your ancestor arrived as a stowaway. Figure 4.18 shows a New York passenger list from 1896 with such a designation.[23] Stowaways seldom remained undiscovered.

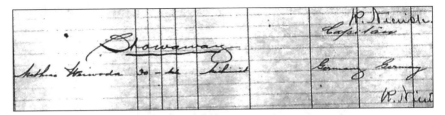

FIGURE 4.18

A New York passenger list from 1896 with a stowaway designation

The number-one processing station and immigrant port of arrival was New York. Before I started doing my own genealogy, I thought all immigrants came through Ellis Island. Not so. Ellis Island was not created as an arrival station until 1892. The earlier processing station in New York, beginning in 1855, was Castle Garden. Eighty percent of all immigrant arrivals in the United States occurred at the port of New York, no matter what processing station was involved. Passenger lists are extant from 1820. New York passenger lists can be searched free at http://castlegarden.org and at the Ellis Island website at http:// libertyellisfoundation.org. The Castle Garden website allows users to search for New York arrivals from 1820 (predating Castle Garden) to 1892. An unexpected source for the arrival date and ship name for many immigrants is the *Emigrant Savings Bank Records, 1841–1945*, which contain passbook savings account records from the Emigrant Savings Bank of New York. Most of the account holders were Irish, but other nationalities are in these records as well. Most of the entries tell the name of the boat upon which they arrived in this country and the date of arrival. Some entries even tell the names of their parents, even if the parents did not emigrate. This is a wonderful source for ancestors who arrived and then stayed in New York. You can find the digital images on Ancestry.com. Figure 4.19 shows a portion of a record from the *Emigrant Savings Bank Records* giving the name, address, and occupation of the passbook holders.[24] On the fourth line, account holder 59527, is Michael Donohue (his mark), who was a laborer.

Figure 4.20 is page two of the *Emigrant Savings Bank Records* entry shown in figure 4.19. The information on this page indicates the place of birth, the date when each person arrived in the United States, and upon what ship. The fourth line is more information about Michael

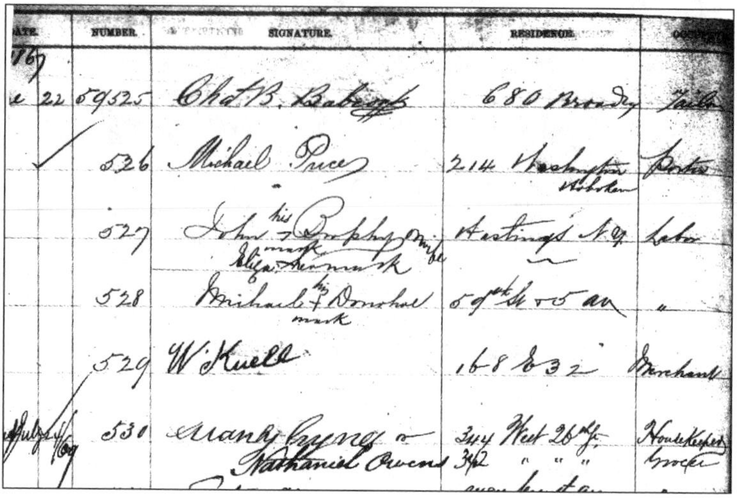

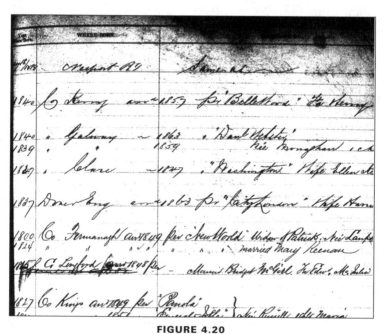

FIGURE 4.19
A portion of a record from the *Emigrants Savings Bank Records*
showing the name, address, and occupation of the passbook holders

FIGURE 4.20
Page two of the *Emigrant Savings Bank Records*
entry shown in figure 4.19

Donohue. He was born in 1827 in County Clare. He arrived in 1847 on the *Washington* (ship). His wife was Ellen Kelly.

In comparisons of the number of passenger arrivals into the United States by various ports of entry, Boston was the second major immigrant port. All of Boston's original customs passenger lists prior to 1883 were destroyed by a fire, leaving only transcripts and copies available, with gaps within the records. However, Massachusetts required a port tax for those arriving there, resulting in lists of passengers. They cover the years 1841 to 1891. You can search the State Lists at www.sec.state.ma.us/arc/arcsrch/passengermanifestsearchcontents .html. Boston was a favored port of arrival for Irish immigrants. After leaving Ireland, many of them became "lost" to friends and family. A newspaper, the *Pilot*, ran frequent advertisements for those looking for missing friends. The names and texts of the advertisements for the years 1831 to 1920 can be found in an eight-volume set of books entitled *The Search for Missing Friends: Irish Immigrant Advertisements Placed in the Boston Pilot*.[25] Figure 4.21 shows an image from volume 3, page 42 of this work. Boston University has created a website of those same advertisements entitled Information Wanted which can be searched at http://infowanted.bc.edu.

Baltimore was the next most active port. Many of Baltimore's customs passenger lists were destroyed by a fire. Quarterly abstracts help to fill the gaps, as do city lists that were gathered between 1833 and 1866. The city lists contain the names of passengers who paid the city a surcharge upon arrival. Philadelphia was the fourth in the number of arrivals in the nineteenth century. Available lists for this port begin as early as 1727. These early enumerations recorded non-English

---

4 March 1854 *INFORMATION WANTED*

REWARD OF FIFTY DOLLARS will be paid for any information that will lead to the whereabouts of THOMAS RATHWELL, who left the city of Albany about two and a-half years ago. He is about five feet ten or eleven inches high; has fair or light hair; with a mole under his right eye; light blue eyes with heavy eye brows; walk straight with stooped shoulders; has a scar of a large cut on left thumb; age is between thirty-one and thirty-four; his appearance is shy or bashful, and speaks childish; is of a solid complexion, has strong black beard, and when last seen wore no whiskers; he now goes under the name of O'Neil; address, JAMES BRICE, Esq, Albany, N Y.

FIGURE 4.21

An image from volume 3, page 42 of *The Search for Missing Friends*

immigrants who were required to sign oaths of allegiance to the British Crown. English arrivals during this period were not recorded, since they were merely going from one British territory to another. Beginning in 1800, the port of Philadelphia began keeping baggage lists, recording the names of passengers who were bringing luggage ashore. Philadelphia's customs passenger lists begin in 1820 and are extant.

New Orleans was the fifth most active port, with less than 800,000 arrivals between 1820 and 1920. The voyage to New Orleans was longer than to other ports, and the threat of disease (due to swampy conditions around the port) soon made this an unattractive port of arrival for nineteenth-century immigrants. Transcripts of baggage lists from 1813 to 1849 exist for this port. Passenger lists also exist beginning in 1820 and they run until 1902, as do quarterly abstracts of passenger lists from 1820 to 1874.

There were many other ports at which immigrant ships landed. Galveston, Texas, was a substantial port. There were also ports in Virginia, Maryland, Maine, North Carolina, Connecticut, Rhode Island, Massachusetts, New Jersey, Florida, Georgia, Delaware, California, and Washington.

What if you still can't find your ancestor's arrival? Look north to Canada. Forty percent of all passengers arriving in Canada were bound for the United States.[26] It was often easier to enter Canada. It had fewer immigration restrictions than U.S. ports and there were no restrictions on crossing the border until 1895, when record-keeping began. The first passenger lists were kept at the port of Quebec City in 1865. Earlier records do not exist. The Library and Archives Canada has a good explanation of Canadian immigration at www.bac-lac.gc.ca/eng. Look for the topic "Immigration." Border crossings from the United States to Canada were first recorded in 1895 with the records kept in St. Albans, Vermont. Both the Canadian passenger lists and the St. Albans lists can be found on Ancestry.com and FamilySearch.org.

Records of Mexican border crossings are also available. The National Archives filmed Mexican border crossings for the years from 1895 to 1957. You can find them on Ancestry.com and FamilySearch .org. Every time a person crossed the border during those years, his or her information was documented. Those recorded were Mexicans coming to the United States, other foreign-born individuals entering the United States through Mexico, and Americans working and/or living

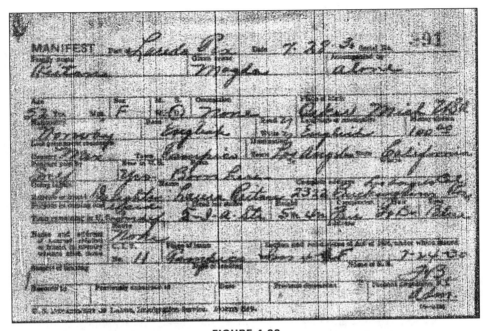

FIGURE 4.22

An image of a card showing Magda Reitan entering the United States
from Mexico on July 29, 1930 in Laredo, Texas

in Mexico who were crossing into the United States for a visit. My
grandmother's sister lived with her husband in Mexico for several
years. I knew very little about her until I discovered her on the Mexican border crossings database. She and her daughters were recorded
several times and her husband, once.

Figure 4.22 is an image of a card showing Magda Reitan entering
the United States from Mexico on July 29, 1930, in Laredo, Texas.[27] The
card indicates that Magda was born in Norway but spoke English. Her
daughter, Laura, is also listed on the card.

The following is a selective bibliography of publications that can
help you understand the immigration process and the records that are
available:

Colletta, John Philip. *They Came in Ships: A Guide to Finding
Your Immigrant Ancestor's Arrival Record*. Orem, UT:
Ancestry, 2008.

Eakle, Arlene, and Johni Cerny, eds. *The Source: A Guidebook of American Genealogy.* Salt Lake City, UT: Ancestry, 1984. Chapter 15, "Tracking Immigrant Origins," includes a list of maritime museums (page 464). In maritime museums you will find ships' logs.

Szucs, Loretto Dennis, and Sandra Hargreaves Luebking, eds. *The Source: A Guidebook of American Genealogy.* Salt Lake City, UT: Ancestry, 1997. See the chapter on "Immigration."

Tepper, Michael, ed. *American Passenger Arrival Records.* Baltimore, MD: Genealogical Publishing Co., 1999.

LESSON TEN

- Review your pedigree chart and identify all of your immigrant ancestors.
- Create a spreadsheet with the name of each immigrant, the year or time frame of arrival, and the port of immigration, if known.
- Begin looking for the passenger arrival list for at least one ancestor.

In this chapter, we have discussed military, church, and cemetery records, as well as passenger lists. All are important records and give you a better profile of your ancestor. They can provide information on births, marriages, and deaths, as well as give added details about your ancestor's life. Finding information about all aspects of your forebears will help you discover who they really were.

NOTES

1. Newton A. Strait, *Alphabetical List of Battles: 1754–1900* (Washington, DC: N. A. Strait, 1905).

2. James C. Neagles, *U.S. Military Records: A Guide to Federal and State Sources, Colonial America to the Present* (Salt Lake City, UT: Ancestry.com, 1994).

3. Virgil D. White, *Index to War of 1812 Pension Files* (Waynesboro, TN: National Historical Publishing Co., 1992).

4. Josephine L. Harper, *Guide to the Draper Manuscripts* (Madison, WI: State Historical Society of Wisconsin, 1983).

5. Draper Papers, 3DD197.

6. Draper Papers, "George Rogers Clark Papers," volume 46, series J, page 39.

7. *Compiled Service Records of Volunteer Union Soldiers Who Served in Organizations from the State of Missouri*, microfilm publication M405, roll 268 (Washington, DC: National Archives and Records Administration).

8. *Card Records of Headstones Provided for Deceased Union Civil War Veterans ca. 1879–ca. 1903*, microfilm publication M1845, roll 4 (Washington, DC: National Archives and Records Administration).

9. *Report of the Adjutant General of the State of Kansas 1861–'65*, vol. 1 (Salem, MA: Higginson Book Co., 1998; originally published Topeka, KS: Kansas State Printing Co., 1896).

10. Ancestry.com, *World War I Draft Registration Cards, 1917–1918* (database online) (Provo, UT: Ancestry.com Operations, 2005).

11. National Archives at St. Louis, "The 1973 Fire, National Personnel Records Center," www.archives.gov/st-louis/military-personnel/fire-1973.html.

12. National Archives and Records Administration, *U.S. World War II Army Enlistment Records, 1938–1946* (database online) (Provo, UT: Ancestry.com Operations, 2005).

13. "First Ten Amendments to the Constitution." *The New American*, 22 May 2017. Student Edition, go.galegroup.com.proxy.mcpl.libmo.us/ps/i.do?p =STOM&sw=w&u=inde80299&v=2.1&it=r&id=GALE%7CA495830121 &asid=3def413eb358eabfe9d0ec2b5a65a05a. Accessed 22 Sept. 2017.

14. "Christen," in *Webster's Third New International Dictionary, Unabridged* (Merriam-Webster, 2002), http://unabridged.merriam-webster.com.proxy .mcpl.lib.mo.us.

15. "Vestry," in *Webster's Third New International Dictionary, Unabridged* (Merriam-Webster, 2002), http://unabridged.merriam-webster.com.proxy .mcpl.lib.mo.us.

16. E. Kay Kirkham, *A Survey of American Church Records*, 4th ed. (Logan, UT: Everton, 1978).

17. Kevan M. Hansen, *Map Guide to German Parish Registers* (North Salt Lake City, UT: Heritage Creations, 2004–).

18. William Wade Hinshaw, *Encyclopedia of American Quaker Genealogy*, vol. 1: *North Carolina* (Baltimore, MD: Genealogical Publishing Co., 1991–).

19. Michael Tepper, *American Passenger Arrival Records: A Guide to the Records of Immigrants Arriving at American Ports by Sail and Steam* (Baltimore: Genealogical Publishing Co., 1993), 63.

20. Edmund Bailey O'Callaghan, "Early Immigrants to New Netherland, 1657–1664," in *The Documentary History of the State of New York*, vol. 3 (Albany, NY: Secretary of State, 1850), 33–42; (Albany, NY: Weed, Parsons, 1850), 60.

21. Robert Charles Anderson, *The Great Migration Directory: Immigrants to New England, 1620–1640: A Concise Compendium* (Boston: New England Historic Genealogical Society, 2015).

22. National Archives and Records Administration, *Passenger Lists of Vessels Arriving at New York, NY, 1820–1896*, microfilm roll number M237_664.

23. Ibid.

24. Emigrant Savings Bank, *Emigrant Savings Bank Records*, roll 10, June 22, 1867.

25. Ruth-Ann M. Harris and Donald M. Jacobs, eds., *The Search for Missing Friends: Irish Immigrant Advertisements Placed in the Boston Pilot* (Boston: New England Historic Genealogical Society, 1989–).

26. Tepper, *American Passenger Arrival Records*, 121.

27. National Archives and Records Administration, *Manifests of Statistical and Some Nonstatistal Alien Arrivals at Laredo, Texas, May 1903–April 1955*, record group 85, microfilm roll number A3437_107, online dataset: Ancestry.com.; *Border Crossings: From Mexico to U.S., 1895–1957* (database online) (Provo, UT : Ancestry.com Operations, 2006).

CHAPTER **FIVE**

Published Sources

P ublished sources of genealogical material in print and online are often easier to access than original records. The courthouse, church, or cemetery that has the record you are seeking may be hundreds of miles away, and unless you are willing to travel, you may have to rely on a professional researcher or contact the record-keeper in that area to help you obtain copies of the original documents you are seeking. But since Americans first began showing an interest in the European origins of their families, researchers have been copying the information held in records repositories and publishing that data. The information may have been published in a book or periodical, and now many compiled records are being published in digital form on the Internet.

Published sources have allowed much greater ease of access to information. You may find exact copies of original documents that are photocopied, microfilmed, or digital, or you may find material that has been transcribed, abstracted, extracted, indexed, or translated from those original documents. Of course, nothing is better than examining an original document; it is the most reliable source of information, and it is easier to tell if the document has been altered. But since it is not always feasible to view the original, what we find in print and online serves as a helpful research substitute. *Transcribed material* is a faithful copy of an original document, including all spelling and punctuation errors in it. The transcription may be typed or handwritten. For a transcription to be correct, the transcriber must both read the original document correctly and make no errors in copying it, such as hitting the wrong computer key or transposing letters. Brackets are added when the transcriber inserts his or her own comments. *Extracted material* is a copy of one or more statements from a document. *Abstracted material* is a summary of the important points of a document. It shortens the original record but retains the important elements such as names, locations, and dates in the same order as the original. Misspellings can be corrected in an abstract except for those same names, dates, and locations. If one is abstracting an original record, one must understand the meaning of the document to correctly give an account of it.

Original documents can also be translated. A *translation* is an accurate transcription from one language to another. An *index* lists the names, subjects, or locations from a document and places them in alphabetical order. As with a transcription, the indexer must be able to read the words being indexed correctly. The biggest complication when viewing a transcription, abstract, extract, or index of a document comes when the original document is handwritten. Names, dates, places, or other important words can be misread as they are written down. Any letter can be misread by an indexer, including capital letters, due to illegible handwriting. The following capital letters are often misread, making an indexed entry wrong: L for S, M for N, and A, or D, for O. If you cannot find a name or word in an index, write it down by hand as sloppily as you can. Then try to guess how it might have been indexed. If a name is not in an index, this does not mean the name is not in the original document; it merely means the name is not in the index.

When looking at published material, remember that there is a difference between original records and anything other than original records, meaning that which is transcribed, abstracted, extracted, translated, or indexed. If it is not an original record, it is in a derivative form. You probably played a game as a child called Telephone. A sentence is whispered from one player to the next. Each player, in turn, whispers the sentence to his or her neighbor, and so on down the line. By the time the last person hears the sentence and says it out loud, it usually has no resemblance to the original sentence. This is also what happens in derivative records. The further you are from the original record, the more deviations you may find. But derivative records are a necessity for the genealogist, for reasons previously stated. Just remember that old saying, "Don't believe everything you read."

Published Family Histories

The goal of a genealogist should be to share that which has been discovered in research. Sometimes the research becomes a published family history or genealogy. Chapter 1 of this book talked about the difference between genealogy and family history. A published genealogy would, in its truest sense, be a pedigree listing the names and dates of a person's ancestry. A family history would additionally include social history, historical events, and family stories. It would truly be a history of one's family.

For example, *The Reams, Reames Family,*[1] privately published in 1956, tells the story of the Reames family. The Reams/Reames family were early settlers in Virginia. One of the Reames family lines moved to North Carolina and were Quakers. At that point they began a connection with the Samuel Colyar family (one of my family lines). From other sources, I learned that the Reames and Colyar families, along with several other families, removed from Wayne County, North Carolina, to Logan County, Ohio, and later to Cass County, Michigan. Moses Reames (1797–1878) married into the Colyar family. He was married four times and predeceased his first three wives. His second wife was Mary Colyar (1812–1884). His third wife was Mary Colyar's sister, Huldah (1815–1900).[2] I have yet to find a book written specifically about my Colyar line, but *The Reams, Reames Family* helps answer some questions about their migration pattern and gives some information on two members of the Colyar family. Therefore, the book aids Colyar researchers, as well as Reames family historians, in their quest for information.

The quality of information found in family histories is varied. Anyone can publish their family's genealogy, but not everyone does quality research. Look for documentation when viewing such a publication. If there are no citations given for the data found within the pages, view it suspiciously. The presentation of the compiled research also varies. Some do nothing more than offer a printout of their family group records (literally a genealogy). Others flesh out the subjects with family stories, social history, and photographs. There are also variations in the quality of printing. Many family histories used to be produced via mimeograph machines or reproduced with carbon paper. Other writers have their work reproduced by a professional printing company. Today, it is easy to duplicate legible pages using one's own computer and printer. You will find family history books hardbound or softcover, stapled or spiraled, or in three-ring binders. There are many variations in quality, appearance, and accuracy, but at least someone took the time to publish and thereby share the research with a wider audience.

Genealogy and family history books are always privately published. Finding a copy can be difficult. Immediate family members are often given notice of the publication, but only at the time of publication and only to those families of which the author is aware. If you are fortunate, the author will have donated a copy to his or her local library or to the Family History Library in Utah. WorldCat is a great way to find copies that have been donated to libraries. Those that are free of copyright protection may have been digitized. Look for digitized books at the following sites:

America's Genealogy Bank, a NewsBank, Inc. database: https://www.genealogybank.com

FamilySearch: http://familysearch.org. Click on "Search" for a dropdown menu and then click on "Books."

Google Books: http://books.google.com

Heritage Quest Online, a ProQuest database: www.proquest .com/products-services/HeritageQuest-Online.html

Internet Archive: http://archive.org

The Library of Congress (LOC) has numerous family histories in its collection. When an author registers a copyright for his or her publication, a copy of the book is given to the LOC. You can search the LOC's catalog at http://catalog.loc.gov. However, the LOC's genealogy material can only be viewed at the library's location in Washington, DC. A somewhat dated publication, *Genealogies in the Library of Congress: A Bibliography,*[3] was produced to enumerate the genealogies held in the LOC. This was prior to the online catalog and was a great help in its time, and it is still a useful publication. Two additional works followed: *A Complement to the Genealogies in the Library of Congress: A Bibliography*[4] and *Genealogies Cataloged by the Library of Congress since 1986.*[5] The latter lists family histories that have been microfilmed. Microfilms can be borrowed from the LOC.

Interlibrary loan collections of genealogy materials are rare, but there are a couple of exceptions:

> The Mid-Continent Public Library's Midwest Genealogy Center (MGC), in Independence, Missouri, has a collection of circulating genealogy books, many of which are family histories. The growing collection has resulted from the donation of the collections of several genealogical organizations: the American Family Records Association (no longer in existence), Missouri State Genealogical Association, Heart of America Genealogical Society (no longer in existence), and the Gann Family Historical Society, as well as donations from individuals. View the catalog at http://mymcpl.org. Look for items that indicate "Adult Non-Fiction" rather than "Reference."

> The National Genealogical Society houses its book loan collection at the St. Louis (MO) County Public Library. The collection of over 20,000 circulating books can be searched from the library's online catalog at http://webpac.slcl.org. Those available for loan do not contain an "R" at the beginning of the call number.

Biographies

Biographies are another genre that can aid a person's quest for genealogical information. Even though you will find out more about what happened during an individual's life from a biography than you will from his or her genealogy, biographies can generate genealogical clues. A biography will usually tell you when and where the individual was born, the names of parents and siblings, and the names of the spouse and children—all of which have genealogical value. You might also find the names of grandparents and earlier progenitors within the work. If your ancestor was a famous person, you will likely find a biography written about him or her. The Gale Corporation publishes the *Biography and Genealogy Master Index* subscription database, which is a comprehensive index of biographical sketches. *Who's Who*,[6] published annually, also gives brief biographical information on selected individuals. You will also find varying publications with similar titles: *Who's Who Among African Americans* and *Who's Who in American History*, to name a few. Each *Who's Who* is published by a different company. *Marquis Who's Who* is a commercial database containing the biographies published in the print version of *Marquis Who's Who* since 1985 and from their historical *Who Was Who* covering the years 1607–1985.

Periodicals

Periodicals are printed materials published at regular intervals: annually, quarterly, monthly, or at other regular (or irregular) intervals. Periodicals have always been an important resource in genealogical research. Much of the information published in them cannot be found elsewhere. In the world of genealogical research, they are published by county, state, and national genealogical and historical societies, lineage organizations, surname organizations, special interest groups, ethnic organizations, and some for-profit genealogy vendors. Periodicals contain the most current research, transcriptions, extractions, and indexing projects taking place within the organizations. Among the types of records you will find reproduced in periodicals are extracts of the federal census for the county or state, census records, cemetery readings, deeds, probate records, and vital records.

Numerous genealogy periodicals have been published over the years. One of the largest public genealogy libraries, the Allen County Public Library (ACPL) in Fort Wayne, Indiana, maintains a collection of over 5,000 active subscriptions of periodical titles as well as some copies of publications that are no longer published. This is a massive amount of information to wade through in order to find an article that may be useful. Accordingly, since 1988 the ACPL has been indexing periodicals and publishing the indexes in the PERiodical Source Index (PERSI). For many years, this was an in-print publication reaching sixteen volumes. It is now online and searchable through the Findmypast website. The database includes some digital copies of original articles and makes the hunt for genealogy periodical content easier.

Other dated, but useful print indexes are:

> Jacobus, Donald Lines. *Donald Lines Jacobus' Index to Genealogical Periodicals*. Newhall, CA: C. Boyer, 1988. Reprint. Originally published: New Haven, CT, 1932, 1948, and 1953. This work is a partial index to eighty-five major genealogy periodicals. Articles are indexed by broad subject.
>
> Rogers, Ellen Stanley. *Genealogical Periodical Annual Index*. Bowie, MD: Heritage Books, 1962–2001. This forty-volume set indexes periodical articles by broad subject, title of article, principal surname, author, and place name.

Most long-running periodicals publish their own annual indexes, and sometimes they publish cumulative indexes. You can find links to genealogical, historical, and lineage societies and more at Cyndi's List (www.cyndislist.com/societies). If the organization publishes a periodical, you will find the information on the society's web page, as well as information on how to subscribe. Often you can purchase back issues to obtain the article you are seeking.

Bibliographies

Bibliographies are published lists of books written for specific subject areas. There are bibliographies of genealogies, geographic areas, wars, genders, occupations, and so on. They will aid in your search for printed material on any given subject. If you are looking for a family genealogy, books such as *Genealogies in the Library of Congress* can help you identify books on genealogy. If you want to find books that help you in your Civil War research focused on the state of Missouri, you might try *Civil War, Slavery, and Reconstruction in Missouri: A Bibliographic Guide to Secondary Sources and Selected Primary Sources*.[7] If you are researching ethnic Germans in colonial America, you might try the *Bibliography on the Colonial Germans of North America*.[8] Knowing the titles of books that have been written can help one immensely in discovering the sources for any research project. It can also aid in collection development in specific subject areas.

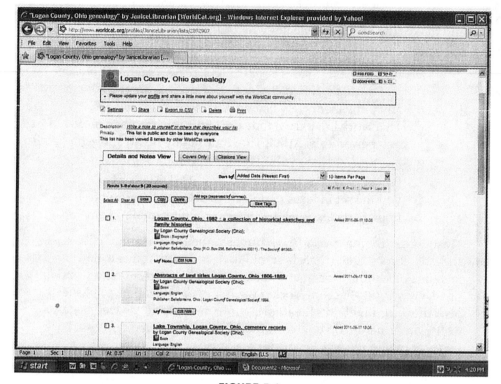

FIGURE 5.1

Screenshot of a simple bibliographic list of Logan County, Ohio, genealogy books

The union catalog WorldCat can also be used as a bibliographic tool. You may have the subscription in your library's database collection, but try using WorldCat.org, which can be found at http://world cat.org. You can create a free account and produce your own set of bibliographies on any subject. The bibliographies you produce may either be kept private or shared with the public. Figure 5.1 is a screenshot of a simple bibliographic list I created of Logan County, Ohio, genealogy books.

Phone Books and City Directories

Would you like to be able to trace an ancestor year by year? Phone books and city directories can enable you to do this. Phone books are becoming a rarity but are still often published. When households had only landline telephones, phone directories would list the names of all householders in a city or other community yearly, along with their phone numbers and addresses. Those telephone owners that are missing from the directory are ones who paid extra to have an unlisted number. Besides private residences, businesses, schools, and government offices are also listed in telephone books. These books are called the "white pages." Businesses that wish to advertise are listed in separate telephone books called the "yellow pages." Phone directories were first published in large cities in the early decades of the twentieth century. Rural community phone books began publication much later. Keeping track of a person's movements can be difficult if they frequently moved, but a phone book can help you trace an ancestor yearly. Knowing where your ancestor lived in a given year can help you find additional records for him or her.

City phone directories called Criss-Cross directories, but usually referred to by genealogy librarians as "city directories," allow you to search in white- yellow- green- and blue-colored paper sections by either name, phone number, or address. Many of them were published yearly by the R. L. Polk Company. You can search for both residents and businesses. The white pages in these city directories, or resident listings, contain a list of adult residents, including students over eighteen years of age, living in the city and residents of other communities employed in the city. In city directories you will find:

- The full name of the resident with his unemployed spouse's name in parentheses. (Employed married women have a separate entry; widows will be listed with their deceased husband's name in parentheses.)
- Occupation
- Complete street address, including the apartment number (if a letter "r" appears before the address it signifies that person is a "roomer")

Businesses listed in the white pages of the directories are listed under the name of the business or the name of the owner of the business or corporation. If the business is a corporation, the corporate officers are listed. Church listings will indicate the name of the pastor.

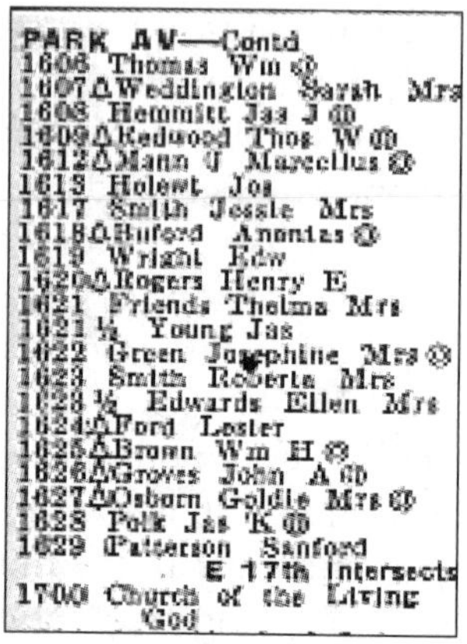

PARK AV—Contd
1606 Thomas Wm
1607 △Weddington Sarah Mrs
1608 Hemmitt Jas J
1609 △Redwood Thos W
1612 △Mann J Marcellus
1613 Holewt Jos
1617 Smith Jessie Mrs
1618 △Buford Ananias
1619 Wright Edw
1620 △Rogers Henry E
1621 Friends Thelma Mrs
1621 ½ Young Jas
1622 Green Josephine Mrs
1623 Smith Roberta Mrs
1623 ½ Edwards Ellen Mrs
1624 △Ford Lester
1625 △Brown Wm H
1626 △Groves John A
1627 △Osborn Goldie Mrs
1628 Polk Jas K
1629 Patterson Sanford
E 17th intersects
1700 Church of the Living God

FIGURE 5.2

Entries from a Criss-Cross directory, listing Individuals living on Park Avenue in Kansas City, Missouri, in 1947

The green pages of the city directories contain the street guide section. Street names are listed in alphabetical order. Numbered streets are listed separately, either before or after the named streets. Under each street name, the house numbers are in numerical order with an indication of cross streets as they occur. After each house number is the name of the resident. If the individual is a homeowner, the status is indicated with an "o" inside a circle. The telephone number follows. If a house was unoccupied, it is listed as vacant. When the building contained separate apartments, each resident was listed separately after the house number. Figure 5.2 shows individuals living on Park Avenue in Kansas City, Missouri, in 1947.[9]

The blue pages of the city directories contain telephone listings in numerical order. The exchange is listed first (for example: CH2 or 242-). Under the exchange are the phone number's next four digits. After each of the four digits, the name of the person or business assigned to that phone number is given.

The city directory also includes yellow pages of classified businesses, or a buyers' guide. In these pages you can find a list of professions, clubs, societies, hospitals, cemeteries, labor organizations, libraries, parks, and schools. Businesses were listed at no charge with their complete address and the owner's name. Another section of paid classified advertisements can also be found in the city directory. If your ancestor was listed as a hospital worker on the 1930 census, a city directory can show you the names of the hospitals existing in the city that year.

City directories offer the genealogist an opportunity to not only search for a person year by year, but also to find out where the person was living, where he or she was employed, who the neighbors were, and the names of the businesses, churches, hospitals, clubs, and other organizations in the community. These directories provide a wealth of information for the researcher. You can find some digitized city directories on Fold3, as well as on some noncommercial Internet sites.

Directories

Directories of organizations, associations, professions, libraries, and so on can help you find information about the who, what, when, where, and why of the organizations listed. In a large research library, you can find various types of directories going back many years. For example, if you find an ancestor's biographical sketch in a county history, you may find that he belonged to the Modern Woodmen of America. A directory of associations will then tell you this was a benevolent society. Benevolent societies provided financial assistance to the widows of their members. They were forerunners of insurance companies. The following is a varied list of a few of the directories found at the Midwest Genealogy Center. You may find similar directories on your own library's shelves:

> *Avondale United Methodist Church* (Kansas City, MO)
>
> *Directory of Alumni*, Clemson University
>
> *Directory of Churches in New Jersey*
>
> *1984 Directory of Dentists, Dental Specialists and Dental Hygienists* (Missouri Dental Board)
>
> *Directory of Family Associations*
>
> *Directory of Higher Education Institutions in Missouri, 1980–81*
>
> *Johnson County, Kansas, Farmers, 1921*

Dictionaries

Dictionaries tell us the definitions of words. Many dictionaries are abridged, containing only the definitions of commonly used words in our language. Alternatively, you may have an unabridged dictionary or the *Oxford English Dictionary* in your library; these contain all the words in the English language, even archaic words. In genealogy, we often find references to words that are unfamiliar to us. You might see a tombstone for Mary Jones indicating she was the "consort" of John Jones. *Consort* is a word meaning "spouse." This tells me that Mary's husband, John, was alive when Mary died. What if a tombstone for Mary Jones said that she was a "relict" of John Jones? *Relict* means "widow," indicating that John Jones preceded Mary in death, and she was a widow at the time of her own death. A death record or obituary may indicate that a person died of "consumption." *Consumption* is nowadays called tuberculosis. Don't bypass an unabridged dictionary when doing genealogical research. Your library may subscribe to databases such as the *Merriam-Webster Unabridged Dictionary* or the *Oxford English Dictionary*. There are other free online sites that give definitions of archaic terms.

"How-To" Books

How-to-do-it information on genealogy is very popular. There are many publications that tell you how to get started doing genealogy, where to go for resources, how to do long-distance genealogy, online genealogy, and more. These books will give you guiding principles for wise genealogical research. You can also find out how to do genealogy from numerous online sites. I recommend you add at least a few of the most useful how-to books to your collection.

Below is a short bibliography of how-to books:

> Christmas, Henrietta Martinez, and Paul Fisher Rhetts. *The Basic Genealogy Checklist: 101 Tips & Tactics to Find Your Family History.* Los Ranchos, NM: Rio Grande Books, 2016. (www.nmsantos.com)
>
> Croom, Emily Anne. *The Sleuth Book for Genealogists: Strategies for More Successful Family History Research.* Baltimore, MD: Genealogical Publishing Co., 2008. (www.genealogical.com)
>
> ———. *Unpuzzling Your Past: The Best-Selling Basic Guide to Genealogy.* 4th ed. Baltimore, MD: Genealogical Publishing Co., ca. 2001, 2010 reprint. (www.gene alogical.com)
>
> Dowell, David R. *Crash Course in Genealogy.* Santa Barbara, CA: Libraries Unlimited, 2011. (www.abc-clio.com/ LibrariesUnlimited.aspx)
>
> Quillen, W. Daniel. *Secrets of Tracing Your Ancestors.* (Place of publication not identified): Open Road Pub., 2017. (available only through Amazon.com)

————. *The Troubleshooter's Guide to Do-It-Yourself Genealogy.*
New York: Cold Spring, 2016. (available only through
Amazon.com)

Simpson, Jack. *Basics of Genealogy Reference: A Librarian's
Guide.* Santa Barbara, CA: Libraries Unlimited, 2008.
(www.abc-clio.com/LibrariesUnlimited.aspx)

Guides to Research

Guides to research differ from self-help books. These books aid your
research in various subject or geographic areas. Every time you begin
research in a new state or country, it is wise to look at a guide for that
area. Searching records in Missouri is entirely different from searching
them in Pennsylvania. A good guide will tell you about the availability
of records and the names and addresses of records repositories. *Ancestry's Red Book* and the *Handy Book for Genealogists,* mentioned in chapter
3, give general information about records in the United States but are
not as thorough as a guide for any one state. Searching for records
overseas can be difficult, but finding a guide to research in a country, such as Germany, will make you aware of the records available
there and how to search for them. Many good guides exist in print. An
online source for research guidance is the FamilySearch Wiki. You can
search by a locality and through the list of results for the topic that best
matches your query.

Gazetteers

A gazetteer is a dictionary of place names. The description of each
locality varies in different gazetteers, but they will often give you the
locality's longitude and latitude coordinates and some historical information. You can find a gazetteer of a state, such as *The North Carolina
Gazetteer: A Dictionary of Tar Heel Places and Their History;*[10] a gazetteer
of the United States, such as *Historical Gazetteer of the United States;*[11]
or of another country, such as *Genealogical Gazetteer for the Kingdom of
Hungary.*[12] A gazetteer will often give the localities of places that no
longer exist. I particularly like the *Omni Gazetteer of the United States*

FIGURE 5.3

Columbia Gazetteer of the World entry on Kirkenes, a village in Norway

of America[13] and refer to it often. When trying to determine the locality of an obscure place, I can often find it in the *Omni Gazetteer*. For instance, in Jackson County, Missouri, there is a place called "Englewood." Those who live nearby know where it is, but it is no longer on any map. In the gazetteer, it is listed as a "population place," the longitude and latitude coordinates are given, and the quadrangle name of the U.S. Geological Survey topographical map where one can find it is listed. I have frequently been able to find a place name listed on the census, but which is no longer on any map, in the *Omni Gazetteer*.

There are also several online gazetteer options. One of these is the *Columbia Gazetteer of the World Online,* which was also published in print until 1998. If I type in "Kirkenes," I first will see a brief synopsis of the locality. As seen in figure 5.3, it is a village in northern Norway, in the region of Finmark. Clicking on the place name, I see that the longitude and latitude coordinates are 69° 43′N 30° 03′E.[14] This information aided in my understanding of the area from which my great-grandfather left in the 1860s.

Another useful series of books for locating localities in the United States, though they are not gazetteers, are post office guides. These are

NORTH CAROLINA.   127

Left-hand column shows compensation of Postmaster.   Right-hand one, net revenue of Office to Department.

Davidson County.

Abbott's Creek	Elisha Raper	$15.31	$9.48
Brummell's	Daniel F. Morris	15.61	9.85
Clemmonsville	Evander McIver	88.58	20.58
Cotton Grove	John Miller	18.98	8.41
Fair Grove	Green H. Lee	6.58	10.88
Healing Springs	William C. Bule	4.00	2.70
Jackson Hill	Edmund B. Clark	11.25	6.62
Lexington (c. h.)	Alexander C. Hege	184.77	166.92
Midway	William G. Beard	18.02	7.98
Pennfield	Jeremiah Piggott	10.06	7.00
Rich Fork	E. D. C. Harris	12.26	4.85
Silver Hill	Thomas Symons	24.19	6.86
Spencer	Seth Ward	5.80	2.91
Thomasville	Henry E. Rounsaville	87.11	5.87
Walser's Mill	William A. Owen	——	——

Davie County.

Clarksville	William O. Smith	6.00	2.50
County Line	Henry C. Eccles	12.68	5.75
Farmington	George W. Johnson	88.79	16.89
Fulton	William R. Sharpe	20.43	8.40
Jerusalem	Joseph W. Hodge	4.58	3.14
Mocksville	Calvin U. Rich	9.28	109.94
Smith Grove	Albert Sheek	14.81	8.92

Duplin County.

Albertson's	Amos W. Simmons	5.61	8.42
Bear Swamp	Luther R. Loftin	11.93	7.93
Branch Store	James G. Branch	8.28	5.43
Bueva Vista	Stephen M. Grady	4.82	2.58
Chinkapin	Julius Scott	12.77	11.54
Faison's Depot	Isham R. Faison	51.62	1u.37
Hallsville	Edward Armstrong	19.55	5.69
Keuansville (c. h.)	Alsa B. Southerland	96.67	191.56
Outlaw's Bridge	John W. Whitfield	5.76	4.54
Reunen	Hugh Maxwell	2.56	2.00
Strickland's Depot	Leonard A. Merriman	94.96	41.47
Teachey's	Cornelius McMillan	86.00	17.00
Warsaw	John B. Southerland	92.02!	17.94

Edgecombe County.

Battleboro'	Isaac W. Ricks	49.23	15.65
Joyner's Depot	William D. Farmer	50.62	9.94
Rocky Mount	Charles C. Bonner	152.70	8u.92
Saratoga	Nathan Webb	7.98	.44
Sparta	James Carney	58.97	50.10
Stantonsburgh	John Wilkinson	54.96	17.56
Tarboro' (c. h.)	David Pender	386.16	504.84
Wilson	Edwin G. Clark	222.25	283.20

Forsyth County.

Bethania	Eugene C. Lehman	88.02	14.85
Flint Hill	John H. Kreeger	1.60	.50
Kernersville	John F. Kerner	27.0	11.00
Lebanon	Daniel Brick	——	——
Muddy Creek	Samuel Atspaugh	6.18	2.22
Old Richmond	Washington Payne	1.44	1.10
Rural Hall	Anthony Bitting	2.58	1.95
Salem	Orestes A. Keehln	425.14	359.95
Sedges Garden	Joseph Waggoner	7.15	5.59
Walkertown	Robert L. Walker	8.77	2.70
Waughtown	Henry M. Lash	18.42	8.14
White Road	George V. Fulp	6.29	4.59
Winston (c. h.)	Peter A. Wilson	65.29	32.69

Gaston County—(Continued).

Dallas (c. h.)	Andrew Hoyl	$67.50	$94.92
Erasmus	Manuel Ford	2.75	2.08
King's Mountain	Benjamin F. Briggs	14.88	6.54
Mountain Island	John Tate	17.00	6.00
Nail Factory	Thomas Darling	11.62	3.72
Old Furnace	John E. White	5.46	3.74
South Point	Samuel W. Craig	9.00	4.49
Stanley's Creek	Valentine Derr	——	——
Stowesville	Edwin B. Stowe	16.50	8.25
White Pine	Benjamin Black	4.91	3.58
Woodlawn	James C. Rudisill	13.93	9.83

Gates County.

Buckland	Samuel E. Smith	17.70	11.37
Gatesville	Shadrach W. Worrell	67.05	49.64
Mintonsville	John C. Trotman	23.29	15.07
Reynoldson	Dempsey Langston	——	——
Sunbury	Coslen Jordan	50.51	16.14

Granville County.

Asylum	John F. Harris	15.94	10.85
Berea	Richard S. Wood	12.57	6.48
Blue Wing	Detron T. Walker	19.05	14.00
Brookville	Samuel H. Cannaday	5.85	4.96
Brownsville	Mary C. Griffin	16.06	8.01
Dutchville	Elijah Hester	15.66	8.00
Fairport	Donalds'n P. Paschall	9.00	8.00
Gregory's Mill	Thomas J. Gregory	8.22	6.77
Henderson	William W. Reaves	187.51	166.60
Kittrell	Elisha H. Overton	29.54	12.55
Knap of Reeds	Logan W. Umstead	11.66	7.49
Millbank	Eaton Davis	3.48	2.74
Oak Hill	William H. Puryear	38.44	22.17
Oxford (c. h.)	A. T. T. Jones	3 5.40	277.16
Sassafras Fork	James A. Satterwhite	15.28	8.73
Tabb's Creek	Thomas D. Harris	4.75	1.20
Tally Ho	Augustus H. Cooke	24.00	15.15
Tar River	Cameron W. Allen	11.00	10.65
Townesville	William B. Hughes	10.88	1.79
Tranquility	Nathan'l E. Cannady	9.41	6.93
Waterloo	William O. Gregory	5.82	5.31
Williamsboro'	Elijah Satterwhite	60.50	22.70
Wilton	Lewis T. Smith	10.88	4.84
Woodworths	James O. K. Paschall	——	——
Young's x Roads	Marcus D. Royster	20.65	13.57

Greene County.

Bull Head	John J. Edmunson	——	——
Hookerstown	Jesse W. Mhore	71.90	27.09
Maysville	George W. Mhore	14.80	4.52
Snow Hill (c. h.)	John T. Freeman	54.47	86.70
Speight's Bridge	William A. Darden	26.22	16.00

Guilford County.

Altemance	William R. Smith	26.82	11.86
Brick Church	Thomas G. Wharton	8.81	3.12
Centre	Andrew C. Murrow	31.71	15.22
Deep River	Cyrus J. Wheeler	12.61	5.46
Fentriss	Frederick Fentriss	6.76	3.89
Friendship	John Hunt	22.48	10.57
Gibsonville	Jerden A. Neese	——	——
Gilmer's Store	Joseph W. Gilmer	14.49	7.55
Greensboro'	Branson G. Graham	254.96	252.92
High Point	Austin H. Welch	31.00	5.00
Hillsdale	Anselom Reed	15.40	8.59

FIGURE 5.4

A post office guide's list of some of the post offices
in North Carolina in 1856

published by the United States Post Office but are often reprinted by others. You can find guides for many different years, such as *Colton's United States Post Office Directory, 1856.*[15] Of what benefit are these postal guides? On nineteenth-century census records, the name of the nearest post office is often listed on each page. Many rural residents did not live in an incorporated city or town thus the name of the nearest post office is a great benefit to the researcher. Many of these post offices have long since disappeared. Knowing more about the post office can help you pinpoint the location where your ancestors were living. Figure 5.4 shows some of the post offices in North Carolina in 1856.

Newspapers

Newspaper research is very beneficial to a genealogist. This type of printed record is now an online resource. Most, if not all, newspaper publications currently have an online presence. The major reason why genealogists use newspapers is to find obituaries, though other items of interest can also be found in them. The obituary may tell you about your ancestor's migration into the area, his or her parents' names, his or her age at the time of death, the names of surviving family members and where they lived at the time, the religious denomination, occupation, name of the funeral home, place of burial, and much more. Or—the obituary may tell you very little. There is no standard when it comes to obituaries. Figure 5.5 shows a very brief obituary for Edmund Harvey, who died in 1899.[16] Even though it is limited, we find that Harvey was a pioneer in the region and was a Baptist by faith.

Edmund Harvey, an old pioneer of Montcalm county, died at his home, three miles southwest of Howard City, Wednesday, Mar. 22, aged 77 years. Funeral services were held at the Baptist church, Friday, Rev. Wm. Templeman officiating.

FIGURE 5.5
A very brief newspaper obituary from the Howard City [MI] Record for Edmund Harvey, who died in 1899

The other items you can find in a newspaper are practically limitless. There are marriage and birth announcements, names of residents temporarily in the hospital, names of visiting relatives and friends, announcements of probate, and events happening within the community. From the information found in figure 5.6, we learn that Charles Campbell had the grippe, the principal Charles Meach was in town, Victor Van Popple sold thirteen new wheels, Mr. and Mrs. Charles O'Donald were going to occupy

Chas. Campbell is a grippe victim this week.

Prin. Chas. Meach, of Lakeview, is in town today.

Victor Van Popple, the Waverly agent has sold 13 new wheels this spring.

Chas. O'Donald and wife will soon occupy the Soules house vacated this week by S. V. Bullock.

Rev. Reed is in Grand Rapids this week assisting Rev. C. S. Wheeler at the Epworth M. E. church in special meetings.

Burt Fraker, formerly employed in the Heath drug store at Hastings, has accepted a position in Nagler's Drug Store.

FIGURE 5.6
Local news and events reported in the Howard City [MI] Record

the vacated S. V. Bullock house, Reverend Reed was in Grand Rapids for the week, and Burt Fraker, formerly of the Heath Drug Store in Hastings, had accepted a position in Nagler's Drug Store.[17]

Your library may have your local newspaper on microfilm. If it does not, hopefully you will be able to tell your patrons where the state newspaper repository is located. Newspapers can often be borrowed on interlibrary loan from various repositories, or they may have online options. Some commercial sources for older newspapers are *America's Genealogy Bank,* Infotrac's *19th Century U.S. Newspapers,* and ProQuest's *Historical Newspapers,* as well as the Library of Congress's *Chronicling America: Historic American Newspapers* at http://chroniclingamerica.loc.gov. See also Wikipedia's list of online newspaper archives at http://en.wikipedia.org/wiki/Wikipedia:List_of_online_newspaper_archives.

Maps

Maps are a wonderful resource for genealogists, and many historic maps are now online. ProQuest has a product entitled *Historic Map Works* which includes many historic and plat maps. A free Internet site is the David Rumsey Map Collection Database and Blog at www.davidrumsey.com. The American Library Association's Map and Geospatial Information Round Table (MAGIRT) offers interesting programming at each ALA Annual Conference. If you wish to learn more about the value of maps, attend one of the programs or join the Round Table.

Finding a map for the time and location in which your ancestor lived will help you determine that person's exact abode. A common type of map that genealogists use is a plat map. It shows the ownership of land at the time the map was published. You may find these maps in a county atlas or plat book. The atlases often have patron lists of the residents and businesses that paid to have the plat book published. There is a lot of detail about these patrons, including their names, their length of residency in the county, previous residency, occupation, names of spouses, and number of children. A plat book of Adair County, Missouri (1919) shows one such patron, W. M. Christensen of Pleasant View Farm. He had lived in the county since 1907. His farm was in section 17, township 62, and range 13. His post office was Brashear. He was born in Iowa in 1884 and married to Odelia Clarkson. They had two children.[18] Figure 5.7 shows Christensen's land in section 17.[19] In addition, many plat books have beautiful line drawings of some of the farms.

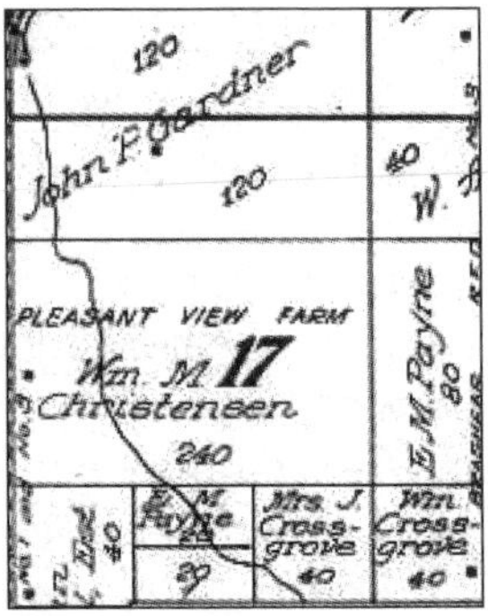

County and Town Histories

Histories of counties and towns are an important component of genealogical research. They take us back in time to when the work was printed and allows us a glimpse of life in that area and the people who lived there.

FIGURE 5.7

Map from a plat book that shows W. M. Christensen's land in Adair County, Missouri

Your ancestor's name may be found in a county history. The information you find may help answer some questions or understand your ancestor better. Unfortunately, not all ancestors appear in county histories. Even so, these works are a good source of information about the localities. Read them and make discoveries.

County histories began to be published after the centennial of the United States in 1876. It is purported that President Ulysses S. Grant asked counties and towns to publish histories of their areas as a celebration of the centennial. Several companies began to respond to the challenge. One of those publishing companies was Goodspeed. They would send a representative into the county and announce that a history was going to be published. If a family wished to prepay to obtain a copy of the book, they were invited to write a biographical sketch about a family member who had lived in the county which would be included in the volume. Since these biographical sketches were written by family members, they were often written in glowing terms. Don't believe everything you read about your ancestor, and verify the information found in a county history. The other content in a county history was contributed by members of the community. These early county and town histories were published as early as 1880 but often not before. This early interest in county histories began to peter out about 1920.

A resurgence of interest in the publication of county histories began with the bicentennial celebration of the United States in 1976 and continues today. In this case, a book committee is usually formed by interested citizens, often members of the local historical society. There are several companies that offer their publishing services, but the content is always written by the citizens of the community.

What is contained in a county history? First look at the date of publication. Was your family in the county at the time it was printed, and thus were they able to aid in the creation of the content? Look at the table of contents to determine what the history contains. In the early county histories, you will usually find a history of the state before finding any county information. The publishing companies included the same content about the state in each county history they published in the state.

The table of contents of the history of Boone County, Missouri, published in 1882, indicates that the first 124 pages are about the history of Missouri: the Louisiana Purchase, description and geography, geology, early settlers, territorial organization, admission into the Union, Missouri as a state, the Civil War in Missouri, an early military record of the state, agriculture and mineral wealth, education and the public school system, and religious denominations. The information included prior to the history of the county is a history of St. Louis, the laws of Missouri, and statistics. It isn't until page 125 that the history of the county begins. This history is broken down into segments: the early history, 1820 to 1830, 1830 to 1840, 1840 to 1850, 1850 to 1860, the Civil War years, 1860 to 1870, and 1870 to 1882. Other information included in the county section is a history of Missouri State University, the geology of the county, township histories, livestock interests, a list of county officials, and a list of illustrations.

The main thing that every genealogist hopes to find in a county history is a biographical sketch of his or her ancestor. Sometimes the biographical sketches were of well-to-do citizens. In figure 5.8 we see a biographical sketch of Samuel Colyar of Cass County, Michigan.[20] The sketch relates Colyar's emigration from North Carolina to Michigan. We see that he was a member of the Baptist church, "a zealous advocate of Christianity," no less, and he had a large family, with three of his children still (in 1882) living in the county.

> Samuel Colyar was raised in North Carolina, from which place he removed to Logan County, Ohio, and from there to Penn, in the spring of 1831, and made a crop on Young's Prairie. In the fall he went after his family, which consisted of his wife and fourteen children, ten of whom came with him, and settled on Section 11. When en route the streams were so swollen that it was necessary to unload the goods and ferry them across and reload them again; on one occasion the wagon-box floated off and was making rapid descent down the river when it was caught by them after a lively pursuit in a pirogue that was near at hand. In November, that year, long before farmers were ready for it, there came an immense fall of snow, burying everything beneath sight, and the cattle, as they wallowed through it, were encased up to their sides; it was finally dissipated by the sun. Mr. Colyar helped very considerably in the development of the country, and was always ready to assist in every good cause. As a christian, he was a zealous advocate of christianity, and assisted very materially in establishing and maintaining the Baptist Church, of which he was a member. He was esteemed by all his neighbors for his many good qualities of mind and heart, and passed away deeply lamented. Of his large family of children, but three remain in the county—Phœbe, Mrs. R. Reams, in Cassopolis; Mary, Mrs. Reams, in Jefferson, and Jonathan, also in Jefferson, he being twenty-one years of age when coming into the county.

FIGURE 5.8

A county history's biographical sketch
of Samuel Colyar of Cass County, Michigan

What if there is no biographical sketch of your ancestor? What else will you find? Here are some examples:

In the *Biographical and Historical Memoirs of Northeast Arkansas* (published in 1889) we find out about the organization of Fulton County. It was established in 1843 from land that had formerly been part of Izard County. Its first town was Salem. The first log courthouse in Salem was destroyed during the Civil War. The next log courthouse was built in 1870.

You may find a list of the cemeteries, early settlements, and names and founding dates of the churches with the names of their charter members, the names of the first settlers and the sections of land they owned, names of the clubs and their charter members, names of the newspapers and who established them, and the names of the ladies in the library association.

The names of the men in military service were usually given. In eastern states, you will often find the names of those who served in the Revolutionary War and the War of 1812. In states further west, you will usually find the names of those who had been enrolled in units of the Civil War.

Natural disasters are often listed. If your family relocated to another state or county, was it due to a drought which destroyed all the crops? Are some of the children in a family missing from one census to another, and you don't know what happened to them? Perhaps there was typhoid fever in the county and the children died. What happened in the county happened to your family as well.

The 1882 *History of Boone County, Missouri,* as shown in figure 5.9, gives a list of the names of men who went to the

---

CALIFORNIA GOLD FEVER.

The discovery of gold in California in 1849 greatly excited the people all over the West, and of course the people of Boone county caught the infection. Early in the spring of that year, but larger numbers of them during 1850, abandoned their homes and business — some of them, alas! never to return — for the gold fields of the new Eldorado. During the month of April the emigrants from this county took up the line of march in wagons and on horseback for their toilsome journey to the Pacific. So far as we have been able to learn, the following are their names : —

Francis T. Russell, R. E. Lusk, Dan'l Grosse, Jerre Orear, Dr. W. B. Lenoir, M. Boyle, Thos. A. Russell, David Guitar, Wm. T. Russell, John Chadwick, Wm. B. Royall, T. A. Garth, Samuel Kennon, A. N. Wilhite, Madison D. Stone, Eli Pulliam, Lawrence Rochford, Rev. Francis Hart, John W. Carter, M. P. Wills, Jr., G. W. Nichols, James M. Wilcox, W. J. Hitt, Nathaniel Torbitt, W. G. Tuttle, ————Elliott, A. E. West, Arch. Goin, W. H. Stone, Samuel R. Tuttle, Thos. A. Sims, Hugh T. Plant, Jas. B. Furnish, James M. Wright, David R. Doyle, Dr. John B. Isbell, G. L. Russell, John M. Willis, Moss P. Foffe, Thomas Orear, John Scott, Chas. R. Thomas, ———— Harris, Samuel D. Lamme, Andrew Trumbaugh, Benj. T. Orear, Lemuel Noble, Thos. J. O'Neal, Wm. Bentley, John H.

FIGURE 5.9

A list in the *History of Boone County, Missouri* (1882) of local men who went to the California goldfields in 1850

goldfields in 1850 during the California Gold Rush.[21] Some of them never returned.

Where to Find County and Town Histories

Most public libraries have the county or town histories that have been published for their area. University libraries, historical societies, and large research facilities may also have copies. If the history was published before 1923, it is free of copyright and is most likely online. Some places to look for county histories online are:

- Google Books
- FamilySearch
- Heritage Quest Online
- America's Genealogy Bank

County histories can provide vast amounts of information on your family. It is like having a conversation with someone who lived long ago, providing you with answers to questions you may have about your ancestors. Knowing the geography and climate may give you an idea of why your ancestors settled where they did. Knowing more about the experiences people had in a county or town will help you know what your ancestor endured. Don't neglect this important part of your ancestor's history.

LESSON ELEVEN

- Look at your library's reference or genealogy collection. Does it have a history of your town or county?
- If you can't find a county history on your library's shelves, check one of the online sources and find your county's history.
- What can you find that is unique in the history you found? List some of those interesting items.
- Find a plat map of your county. If you do not have a map collection in your library, check one of the online sources.
- Who were some of the early residents in your county?

The Internet

Genealogy information can be found almost anyplace: in courthouses, libraries, cemeteries, archives, and attics. The type of information found on the Internet is no different. The World Wide Web is an information resource, and as such it should not be treated any differently than other sources. Evaluation of each website is important. You may find data compiled by a researcher (documented and undocumented), digitized records, transcriptions of records, and indexes. It is impossible to be aware of all the online sources. Moreover, what is on the Web today may not be there tomorrow. What will be placed online tomorrow? One can only hope it is the long-awaited content we are seeking. Websites come and go quickly. Others are tried and true and have lasted, in online terms, for a long time.

Search engines or indexing sites are superb tools for finding one's way in the digital world. One site that is specific to the world of genealogy is Cyndi's List at www.cyndislist.com. It is not a search engine, but it contains categorized links that are specific to genealogical research. Websites are grouped by subject. If you want to find websites for genealogical research in Alabama, Cyndi's List will help you locate them.

Wikis are also beneficial to research. One specific to genealogy is the FamilySearch Wiki. Imagine having the answers to genealogical questions at your fingertips! You will never be alone at the genealogy reference desk if you use the Wiki. If, for example, your patron has a question about doing slave genealogy, you will find helpful answers and links on the site.

There are several online sites that have large quantities of records and other genealogical data; some of these are commercial sites, while others have free content. The list that follows is not an inclusive list. There are many more sites than can conceivably be listed here.

America's GenealogyBank is a Newsbank product. The following information has been shared by Thomas Jay Kemp, director of genealogy products for America's GenealogyBank:

"America's GenealogyBank provides web-based access to nearly 249 million United States core genealogical records from 1690 to the present day. Most of these sources are unique to this collection and are difficult to find on microfilm or in print. Through basic name search or advanced search options, genealogists can find and browse digital images of obituaries, marriage notices, birth announcements, casualty lists, military and government documents, and other essential primary sources. It also provides the full text of modern U.S. newspaper obituaries and death notices from all fifty states, as well as enhanced Social Security Death Index (SSDI) records. The collection also features the entire *American State Papers* (1789–1838) and all items of genealogical value from the *U.S. Congressional Serial Set* (1817–1994). Genealogists can research government and military records, casualty lists, widows' claims, military pension requests, bounty land warrant actions, dispute resolutions, land grant applications, orphans' petitions, and much more."

The information for the following ProQuest databases was provided by William Forsyth, senior product manager for ProQuest:

Ancestry Library Edition

"Since 2004, ProQuest has partnered with Ancestry.com to distribute Ancestry Library Edition, one of the most important genealogical collections available today. It has unparalleled coverage of the United States, including census, vital, church, court, and immigration records, as well as record collections from Canada, United Kingdom, Europe, Australia, Mexico, and many other areas of the world. This collection, with nearly 9 billion records in more than 8,000 unique databases, is essential to having a broad genealogy collection, and its valuable content is a strong complement to HeritageQuest Online."

HeritageQuest Online

"HeritageQuest Online is a comprehensive treasury of American genealogical sources—rich in unique primary sources, local and family histories, convenient research guides, interactive census maps, and more. Now powered by Ancestry, this amazing collection consists of the following core data sets: U.S. federal census records, genealogy and local history books and directories, Revolutionary War pension and bounty-land warrant applications, freedman's bank records with more than 480,000 names of bank applicants, their dependents, and heirs from 1865 to 1874, and the U.S. Serial Set. Remote access is available to your library patrons."

Fold3 Library Edition

"Fold3 Library Edition is distributed to libraries by Pro-Quest and is a premier collection of unique historical military records from the United States, Canada, United Kingdom, Australia, and other countries. Libraries can now offer their patrons this invaluable Ancestry.com resource that brings to life the details of military veterans with stories, photos, and personal documents. Historians, genealogists, and military enthusiasts can access nearly 500 million records beginning with the American Revolutionary War through recent conflicts."

Digital Sanborn Maps

"Digital Sanborn Maps (1867–1970) from ProQuest provides access to 660,000 large-scale digital maps of more than 12,000 American towns and cities, searchable by city and year. Sanborn Fire Insurance Maps are the most frequently consulted maps in public and academic libraries. Founded in 1867 by D. A. Sanborn, the Sanborn Map Company was the primary American publisher of fire insurance maps for nearly 100 years. The maps were originally compiled to help insurers assess the value of property, identify risk factors, and underwrite losses. Historians, urban planners, architects, environmentalists, geographers, genealogists, and others will find the maps a valuable tool for exploring the grid of everyday life in the United States across a century of change."

Historic Map Works Library Edition

"Discover the physical places of the past—from big cities to small farms—with Historic Map Works Library Edition. A distribution and development partnership between ProQuest and Historic Map Works brings this collection to libraries globally. With access to more than 1.5 million maps, genealogists, historians, and researchers can gain insight into how physical and human geographies have changed over time. The core of the collection consists of land ownership (cadastral) maps illustrating the geographic and developmental history of the United States.

Also included are antiquarian maps, birds-eye views, directories and other text documents, and more. This unique content allows users to track the 'residential genealogy' of families and locations over five centuries."

ProQuest Historical Newspapers

"Launched in 2001, ProQuest Historical Newspapers is the definitive newspaper digital archive offering full-text and full-image articles for significant newspapers dating back to the eighteenth century. Every issue of each title includes the complete newspaper cover-to-cover, with full-page and article images in easily downloadable PDF format. The full collection of ProQuest Historical Newspapers contains over 35 million digitized pages from more than forty-five of the most influential and historically respected newspapers in the world."

Newspapers.com Library Edition

"Distributed by ProQuest into library markets worldwide, Newspapers.com Library Edition by Ancestry is an extensive database that provides online access to more than 4,000 historical newspapers. Dating from the early 1700s into the early 2000s, Newspapers.com Library Edition contains full and partial runs of regional, state, and local titles from the United States and other countries."

Findmypast

The following information was provided by Jim Shaunnessy, content marketing manager for Findmypast: "Among the billions of records you can explore at Find mypast, you can find: the U.S. marriage collection (of over 100 million records), Periodical Source Index (PERSI), the Catholic Heritage Archive brought to you in collaboration with the Roman Catholic Church (England, Scotland, Ireland, United States, and Canada), Irish records, British and Irish military records, historic British and Irish newspapers stretching back to the early eighteenth century, early American vital records from the mid-Atlantic states from the Historical Society of Pennsylvania dating back to the 1730s, and United Kingdom parish records. Visit

Findmypast.com today to discover more about the records your visitors can explore."

FamilySearch

The following information was provided by Paul Nauta, public relations manager for FamilySearch: "Family Search.org is a librarian's gold mine for genealogical content—and the vast majority of its original content is not found on the popular paid library-edition sites. Don't be fooled by its totally free access (no license or subscription required). You will find billions of searchable historical records from more than 200 countries, a family-shareable Family Tree feature, and a robust genealogy wiki managed by the online community to help answer general and personal research questions. The wiki includes not only hundreds of thousands of articles, but how-to videos and downloadable guides. It's like having a free genealogy reference library at your constant service. And better yet, FamilySearch adds nearly one-half billion new historical records every year—over 1 million per day. Check it out. Bookmark it. Add the FamilySearch.org link prominently on your library's desktop with your premium, licensed services. No contract is required. Your patrons will love you."

RootsWeb
(http://rootsweb.ancestry.com)

The primary purpose and function of RootsWeb is to connect people so they may help each other and share genealogical research. This free website is owned by Ancestry.com. Genealogists may submit records they have transcribed for inclusion in their user-contributed databases. Because the content is user-driven, there is a myriad of sources. Users may also download their family trees, giving secondary source information to the genealogical community.

Genealogy Connect

Genealogy Connect is a subscription database offered by Gale (a Cengage Company). It contains a collection of digitized, online books that have been published by the

Genealogical Publishing Company and Clearfield Press. The books are both audible and readable. The fully searchable publications contain research guidance as well as transcribed and extracted genealogy data.

In this chapter, we have looked at printed and Internet sources of genealogy material. Since original records are not always easily accessible, one can discover information through published sources in print or online. But as you have seen, not all the resources you might use are considered true genealogy material. Finding information about your ancestors can take many varied paths. I hope you venture onto some new ones.

NOTES

1. Harry Clyde Smith, *Reams, Reames Family and Allied Families* (Glendale, CA: H. C. Smith, 1956).

2. Ibid., 105.

3. Library of Congress, *Genealogies in the Library of Congress: A Bibliography* (Baltimore, MD: Magna Carta Book Co., 1972).

4. Marion J. Kaminkow, *A Complement to the Genealogies in the Library of Congress: A Bibliography* (Baltimore, MD: Magna Carta Book Co., 1981).

5. Library of Congress, *Genealogies Cataloged by the Library of Congress since 1986: With a List of Established Forms of Family Names and a List of Genealogies Converted to Microform since 1983* (Washington, DC: Cataloging Distribution Service, Library of Congress, 1991).

6. *Who's Who . . . an Annual Biographical Dictionary* (New York: St. Martin's, 1849–).

7. Gary W. Shearer, *Civil War, Slavery, and Reconstruction in Missouri: A Bibliographic Guide to Secondary Sources and Selected Primary Sources* (Angwin, CA: G. W. Shearer, 2000).

8. Emil Meynen, ed., *Bibliography on the Colonial Germans of North America: Especially the Pennsylvania Germans and Their Descendants* (Baltimore, MD: Genealogical Publishing Co., 1982); originally published as *Bibliography on German Settlements in Colonial North America* (Leipzig, Germany, 1937).

9. *Polk's Kansas City (Jackson County, Missouri) Directory, Kansas City, Mo.* (Gate City Directory, 1947).

10. William Stevens Powell, *The North Carolina Gazetteer: A Dictionary of Tar Heel Places and Their History* (Chapel Hill, NC: University of North Carolina Press, 2010).

11. Paul T. Hellmann, *Historical Gazetteer of the United States* (New York: Routledge, 2005).

12. Jordan Auslander, *Genealogical Gazetteer for the Kingdom of Hungary* (Bergenfield, NJ: Avotaynu, 2005).

13. Frank R. Abate, ed., *Omni Gazetteer of the United States of America* (Detroit, MI: Omnigraphics, 1991).

14. *Columbia Gazetteer of the World Online*, s.v. "Kirkenes," www.columbiagazetteer .org/main/ViewPlace/70830.

15. Theron Wierenga, *Colton's United States Post Office Directory, 1856* (Muskegon, MI: T. Wierenga, 1985), reprint: originally published under the title: *Post Office Directory or Business Man's Guide to the Post Offices in the United States. Compiled by D.D.T. Leech* (New York: J.H. Colton, 1856).

16. *The Howard City [MI] Record*, March 30, 1899.

17. Ibid.

18. *Standard Atlas of Adair County, Missouri: Including a Plat Book of the Villages, Cities and Townships of the County, Map of the United States and the World, Patrons' Directory, Reference Business Directory and Departments Devoted to General Information, Analysis of the System of U.S. Land Surveys, Digest of the System of Civil Government, Etc., Etc.* (Chicago: Geo. A. Ogle, 1919).

19. Ibid.

20. *History of Cass County, Michigan: With Illustrations and Biographical Sketches of Some of Its Prominent Men and Pioneers* (Chicago: Waterman, Watkins, 1882), 369.

21. *History of Boone County, Missouri: Written and Compiled from the Most Official and Private Sources; . . .* (Cape Girardeau, MO: Ramfre, 1970), reprint; originally published St. Louis, MO: Western Historical Co., 1882.

Advanced Genealogy

U ntil now, we have been learning about basic genealogy research and methodology in the United
States. Patrons can and will bring genealogy
questions to you that will truly have you stumped. That is okay. It
is good to be challenged because that is how we learn. But don't be
afraid to refer them to a professional researcher at this point. You can
do a search for a certified professional on the Board for Certification of
Genealogists website (www.bcgcertification.org/). In this chapter, we
will talk about some of the advanced subject areas you may encounter.

Foreign Research

Eventually genealogical research will take you out of America and
onto foreign soil. Census records may tell us the country of origin of
our ancestors, but that is not enough. It is necessary to know the name
of the town or parish within another country to continue the pursuit
of family history. A biography in a U.S. county history may tell you the
exact location of foreign origin of your immigrant ancestor. You might

also find that information in birth and death records, church records, marriage and probate records, passenger lists, or family Bibles. But don't count on it. The information can be extremely hard to come by. But continue your pursuit of every U.S. record you can find for your immigrant ancestor, and talk to family members. Occasionally, when asked to provide a country of origin on a document, someone will also include the town or parish he lived in there.

Look for books and websites that tell you how to research ancestors in the country in question. Use the FamilySearch Wiki for easy, online assistance. Printed guides to research can also help you discover the types of records available. The more detailed and specific the guide, the better. In European countries, you will often be looking at church records to determine the names of parents and the dates of births, deaths, and marriages, rather than civil documents. Let's look at some of the countries you and your patron may encounter.

Germany

Historically, German country and state borders shifted constantly. A series of feudal lords, dukes, princes, barons, and ecclesiastics ruling over specific areas resulted in various kingdoms, principalities, duchies, states, and estates. To find out what area your ancestors lived in any given time, you must look at a map for the time considered. Germany is now divided into states, with each state divided into parishes, then towns or cities. Records were recorded and kept at the parish level, so it is vital to know where your ancestor resided. Knowing someone was from the state of Bavaria is not good enough. It is too large a region. Use the *Map Guide to German Parish Registers*[1] and *The Atlantic Bridge to Germany*[2] to assist in your research. There are over fifty volumes of the *Map Guide*, each giving the names of the Lutheran and Catholic parishes in each area. *The Atlantic Bridge to Germany* is a multivolume set of books showing the different German states with maps and lists of city and parish names. For the serious researcher, one who doesn't mind trying to decipher the language and old German script, you can try *Meyers Gazetteer*.[3] Though technically it has a longer name, it is generally called *Meyers Gazetteer* or *Meyer Orts*. This publication gives detailed information on every German place name, the type of place, whether Lutheran or Catholic, and the types of commercial services (such as a bank or metalworks) available. It is based on data from the early twentieth century. You can find a free online version of Meyers Gazetteer at https://www.meyersgaz.org. The site gives an image of the original book entry as well as a translation of each page.

German research involves using both civil and church (parish) records. Parish records include births, baptisms, marriages, deaths, and burials recorded by the church. Many records were recorded as early as 1650, but the effects of war, weather, and neglect have left some records damaged and destroyed others.[4] But don't despair—records do exist. Many digital records can be found on FamilySearch and Ancestry.com. Records kept by the German government are called civil registrations. They are also records of births, deaths, and marriages. The beginning of civil registrations varied by area, but most had begun by 1876. A guide to available online German records can be found at https://www.germanroots.com/germandata.html. Sometimes you may have to write churches or towns for copies of records. An excellent guide to writing for German records is called *Writing to Germany* by Kenneth L. Smith.[5]

Below is a selected bibliography to aid in your German research:

Beidler, James M. *Trace Your German Roots Online: A Complete Guide to German Genealogy Websites.* Cincinnati, OH: Family Tree Books, 2016.

Humphrey, John T. *Finding Your German Ancestors: A Practical Guide for Genealogists.* Washington, DC: Pennsylvania Genealogy Books, 2009.

Meitzler, Leland K. *German Genealogy Research Online: Tips and Links.* Bountiful, UT: Family Roots, 2012.

Riemer, Shirley J., et al. *The German Research Companion.* Sacramento, CA: Lorelei, 2010.

Schweitzer, George Keene. *German Genealogical Research.* Knoxville, TN: G. K. Schweitzer, 2003.

Italy

Italy is divided into regions, provinces, and municipalities. Records in Italy are recorded at the town level. Since it is a Catholic country, church records are excellent and sometimes go back into the sixteenth century. You will find records of births, deaths, marriages, and confirmations. Italy also has civil registrations (government records), many of which have been microfilmed by the Family History Library and predate 1870. Each province and town has archives for searching more recent registrations. Your search must begin at this local level. Below is a selected bibliography of books you might find useful in researching your Italian roots:

Adams, Suzanne Russo. *Finding Your Italian Ancestors: A Beginner's Guide*. Provo, UT: Ancestry, 2008.

Colleta, John Philip. *Finding Italian Roots: The Complete Guide for Americans*. Baltimore, MD: Genealogical Publishing Co., 2008, ca. 2003.

Holtz, Melanie D. *Finding Your Italian Ancestors*. Toronto, ON: Heritage Productions, 2014.

Nelson, Lynn. *A Genealogist's Guide to Discovering Your Italian Ancestors: How to Find and Record Your Unique Heritage*. Cincinnati, OH: Betterway Books, 1997.

Great Britain

Researching British records has one advantage over other records in foreign countries: they are in English. However, the laws, the records, and the history are not the same as they are in the United States. First, a little bit of history regarding the name. What is this country called? Is it England, Great Britain, or United Kingdom? Paul Milner, in *A Genealogist's Guide to Discovering Your English Ancestors,* describes it perfectly. In 1536 England and Wales united, and in 1707 Scotland joined their union, and the three countries became known as Great Britain. In 1801 Ireland united with Great Britain, and the name was changed to the United Kingdom of Great Britain and Ireland. By 1921, Ireland was not too happy with England, and so most of Ireland separated itself from the United Kingdom. The remaining countries of England, Wales, Scotland, and Northern Ireland are now called the United Kingdom of Great Britain and Northern Ireland, also known as the U.K. The "British Isles" is an informal name that embraces England, Wales, Scotland,

Northern Ireland, the Republic of Ireland, the Channel Islands, the Isle of Man, and all other surrounding islands.[6]

In researching British roots, again we look to both parish and civil records. Parish record-keeping began at the time of King Henry VIII in the early sixteenth century. That king broke with the Roman Catholic Church and established the Church of England, also called the Anglican Church. A law was established in 1538 for recording christenings, burials, and marriages within parishes. England is organized by county, parish, and town. Until the nineteenth century, the parish church was the center of both religious and civil administration within a geographical region. During this time the parish took care of the poor, administered justice, and raised militias when needed; in fact, the parish did it all, and you will find the records for these activities in the parish records. A dated source which I still find useful in determining English parishes is *Parish Maps of the Counties of England and Wales.*[7] In addition to giving the dates that parish records exist for each parish, the *Parish Maps* book gives the Family History Library film numbers. Many of those filmed records have been digitized. Since the book's publication in 1977, additional records have most likely been filmed. Another helpful guide is *Researching English Parish Records.*[8]

England also has public or county records offices where civil records are recorded. In these repositories you will find land, church, tax, and probate records. Sometimes the records offices have indexes to local people and/or places. *Record Offices: How to Find Them*[9] can guide you in locating an office near your ancestor's home. You may also want to try *Parishes & Registration Districts in England & Wales.*[10] England had its first national registration of vital records in 1837, its first census in 1801, and probate records since 1858.[11] You will find various English records on Ancestry.com/ALE, Findmypast, and FamilySearch. A free website for finding records of births, marriages, and deaths in the United Kingdom is www.freebmd.org.uk. Gen-Uki (UK and Ireland Genealogy) has free content, made possible by a charitable trust and volunteers, at www.genuki.org.uk.

Some additional books to aid in your discovery of your British roots are:

> Annai, David, and Audrey Collins. *Birth, Marriage, and Death Records: A Guide for Family Historians.* Barnsley, UK: Pen & Sword Family History, 2012.

Baxter, Angus. *In Search of Your British and Irish Roots: A Complete Guide to Tracing Your English, Welsh, Scottish, and Irish Ancestors.* 4th ed. Baltimore, MD: Genealogical Publishing Co., 2006, ca. 1999.

Ireland

When considering Irish research, right away you have a problem: were your ancestors a part of what is now Northern Ireland or the Republic of Ireland? Most of Ireland broke away from the United Kingdom in 1921 to form the Republic of Ireland, leaving only Northern Ireland to remain part of the earlier union with Britain. This section about Irish research is focused on records in the Republic of Ireland.

Census records were taken in Ireland, but the earliest surviving schedule is 1901. Earlier census records were either destroyed by fire or destroyed by the government after the data was collected. All record-keeping in Ireland has been determined by the political or administrative divisions of the land. The country is divided into counties called shires. It is also divided into the ecclesiastical provinces (or archdioceses) of Armagh, Tuam, Dublin, and Cashel, and then divided into dioceses. The country is also divided into parishes: civil and ecclesiastical. Irish counties are divided into townlands. Townlands are the smallest administrative division in the county, and their main purpose is to distinguish between different geographic locations. But not all townlands are "towns." Some are farmlands. There are approximately 62,000 townlands in Ireland and they vary in size. Irish parishes often ignore the borders of townlands and counties. Townlands are not record-keeping entities, so look for records of birth, death, and marriage in civil and ecclesiastical parishes.

Ireland was historically known for its linen trade. The Board of Trustees of the Linen and Hempen Manufactures wanted to encourage the growth of flax and hemp seed in Ireland. In 1796 spinning wheels were given to those involved in this agricultural venture in proportion to the acreage of flax sown. Lists were kept of those making claims for the spinning wheels. A result was the *Spinning Wheel Records of 1796*. The index to those receiving free spinning wheels can be found on Ancestry.com.

One of the most important nineteenth-century Irish resources is *Griffith's Valuation*. Between 1847 and 1861 properties in Ireland were

		MONASTEREVIN-BOG. (Ord. S. 26.)	Immediate Lessor	Description	A R P	£ s d	£ s d	£ s d
1		William M'Dermott,	Marquis of Drogheda,	Land,	11 1 29	5 0 0	—	
—	a	Michael Duffy,	Same,	House and garden,	0 1 24	0 5 0	0 10 0	
2		John Harris,	Same,	Land,	19 1 17	8 0 0	—	
—	a	Thomas Gavin,	Same,	House and garden,	0 0 12	0 1 0	0 5 0	
3		Christopher Cusack,	Same,	House and land,	5 0 12	1 10 0	0 5 0	
4		James Deering,	Same,	Land,	13 0 25	6 5 0	—	
—	a	Martin Doolan,	James Deering,	House and garden,	0 3 34	0 15 0	0 5 0	
5		James Brennan,	Marquis of Drogheda,	House and land,	7 1 30	2 15 0	0 5 0	
6		Robert Gorman,	Same,	Land,	8 1 1	3 0 0	—	
7		Patrick Gorman,	Same,	House and land,	3 2 0	1 5 0	0 5 0	
8		Marquis of Drogheda,	In fee,	Land (bog),	55 3 14	4 10 0	—	
9		Charles Deegan,	Marquis of Drogheda,	House and land,	6 0 10	2 5 0	0 5 0	
10		Thomas Kelly,	Same,	Land,	10 1 24	4 0 0	—	
11		Michael Murray,	Same,	House and land,	11 0 32	3 15 0	0 5 0	
				Total,	153 0 24	43 6 0	2 5 0	
		MOOREABBEY DEMESNE. (Ord. S. 26.)						
1		Marquis of Drogheda,	In fee,	House, offices, steward's and farm houses, office, and land,	1267 0 5	600 0 0	110 0 0	
—	b	Joseph Fleming,	Marquis of Drogheda,	House,	—	—	0 5 0	
					1267 0 5	600 0 0	110 5 0	
		OGHIL. (Ord. S. 37.)						
1 A, B		Marquis of Drogheda,	In fee,	Land (bog),	56 2 22 / 223 1 25	0 5 0 / 3 10 0	—	
—	A G	Thomas Dowd,	Marquis of Drogheda,	House and garden,	0 2 3	0 5 0	0 5 0	
2		John Hyland,	James Behan,	House and land,	5 2 5	1 15 0	0 5 0	
3 A, B		James Behan,	Marquis of Drogheda,	House, offices, and land, / Land,	247 0 10 / 39 0 13	107 0 0 / 9 0 0	5 10 0	

FIGURE 6.1

Example of an Irish valuation list

assessed and taxed, with the monies used to support the poor. The valuations list the name of the head of the household, the name of the landowner, the amount of acreage, the value of the property, and the amount of the tax assessed. Maps are also found in the records. The Ask About Ireland website has a free search of *Griffith's Valuation* at www.askaboutireland.ie/griffith-valuation. It can also be searched on Ancestry.com. Figure 6.1 is an example of an Irish valuation list.[12]

The following is a selected bibliography of guides to Irish research:

Carlberg, Nancy Ellen. *Beginning Irish Research.* Anaheim, CA: Carlberg, 1996.

Collins, E. J. *Irish Family Research Made Simple.* Indianapolis, IN: Summit Publications, now published by Ye Olde Genealogie Shoppe, 2001.

Morris, Gary L. *Handy Irish Genealogy Handbook.* United States: Gary Morris, 2015.

Stewart, Alan. *My Ancestor Was Irish: A Guide to Resources for Family Historians.* London: London Society of Genealogists Enterprises, 2015.

France

Prior to the French Revolution in 1790, France was divided into provinces, and some administrative jurisdictions still use the names of the former provinces. But since 1790 France has been divided into departments. You need to know the department that your ancestor's town was located in to find that ancestor's records. Church records of births, marriages, and deaths extend as far back as the sixteenth century. The Catholic Church was the official church until 1787, so when looking at pre-1787 church records you will look at Catholic records, no matter what religion the ancestor may have been during or after that date.

But not all French citizens were Catholic. Many were Huguenots, that is, members of the *Protestant Reformed Church of France* during the sixteenth and seventeenth centuries. After the seventeenth century they were called French Protestants. In 1560 King Charles issued an amnesty to Huguenots, allowing Protestant baptism in 1562. In spite of the change in laws, there was still religious persecution that caused many Huguenots to relocate to other majority Protestant countries. Among these countries were England, Denmark, Switzerland, and the North American colonies.

State registrations of vital records began in France in 1792. Prior to this, the Catholic Church kept records of all vital events. From 1792 to the present, civil registers are the best source for finding vital records. After 1792 the church was only concerned with the sacraments of baptism, marriages, and burials. Marriages after 1792, to be officially recognized, had to occur in the town hall. Look for marriage records from this point on in both civil and church records. Notarial records, those records of events recorded by a notary, may be found as early as the fourteenth century. Notaries were used to record contracts. The types of notarial records you may find are marriage contracts, wills, property divisions among heirs, inventories of property after death, and guardianship agreements. Notarial records may be found in departmental archives, but most are not indexed. A useful book for guiding your research into French records is *Ancestral Research in France: The Simple Guide to Tracing Your Family History through French Records.*[13]

Scandinavia

Many aspects of researching ancestors are similar among all of the Scandinavian countries—Norway, Sweden, Finland, Denmark, and Iceland. Naming patterns are one common thread throughout these countries. Surnames could be patronymic, occupational, characteristic, or military. Patronymic names are surnames that derive from the first name of the father. (For example, the surname Johnson/Johansen ("Johann's son") meant that the father's name was Johann.) Occupational surnames were given to those in trade, while characteristic surnames could have been used to designate a physical characteristic. Military names were chosen by a man when he entered military service. (You can imagine how difficult it would be to have an army of many Johann Johannsens.) Upon leaving service, a man could keep his military name or resume his patronymic name. My maiden name, Lindgren, means "green linden tree" in Swedish and is a military name.

Another common element of Scandinavian countries is the Lutheran church as the state church. Administratively, you were considered Lutheran, even if you belonged to another religion. The Lutheran church was in charge of keeping records of christenings, marriages, and burials. As with other European countries, knowing the parish is vital to finding records for your ancestor in Scandinavian countries.

Danish records include census, church records, civil registrations, and court records. Census records began in 1787 and are available through 1911. The enumerations were sporadic until 1840, when they were taken every five years. From 1860 to 1880 they were taken every ten years. Civil registrations began in 1874, but the records are generally not available to the public, except that part of Denmark that came under German rule for a time. These are available from 1865 to 1920. Court records include cases regarding land rights, inheritance, and crime. Some useful websites are:

Tracing Your Danish Ancestors: http://denmark.dk/en/
practical-info/tracing-your-danish-ancestors.

Genealogy Research Denmark: http://aurelia-clemons.dk.

Some useful guidebooks for Danish genealogical research are:

National Danish-American Genealogical Society. *Searching for Your Danish Ancestors: A Guide to Danish Genealogical*

Research in the United States and Denmark: Including Danish Letter-Writing Guide & Updated Uniform Resource Locators (URLs). Minneapolis, MN: National Danish-American Genealogical Society, 2016.

Smith, Diana Crisman. *Finding Your Danish Ancestors: A Primer for Research & History.* Toronto, ON: Heritage Productions, 2015.

Smith, Frank. *Genealogical Guidebook & Atlas of Denmark.* Bountiful, UT: Thomsen's Genealogical Center, ca. 1998.

Finland has two official languages: Finnish and Swedish. The Finnish language is closely related to Estonian and is distantly related to Hungarian. Census, church, and passport records are available to aid in your Finnish research. Selected records can be found on Ancestry.com, Findmypast, FamilySearch, and MyHeritage.com. You can also find information and records at:

Institute of Migration: www.migrationinstitute.fi/en/

Finland Gen Web: www.rootsweb.ancestry.com/~finwgw/index.html

Norway has census records available beginning in 1664, and they are available through 1910. Church records began in 1668 and civil registrations in 1876. Emigration lists of passengers, lists of those leaving the country, began in 1867. The major exit ports were Oslo, Bergen, Trondheim, and Stavanger. If your ancestors were farmers, you might try locating *Bydgebøker* (farm books) on used book websites. These books contain a history of the families that owned a particular farm. The farms were named, and while a family lived on that farm they would use that name as a surname. Selected online records can be searched at Ancestry.com, FamilySearch, Findmypast, and MyHeritage.com. Some other useful websites are:

Norway Genealogy: www.rootsweb.ancestry.com/~wgnorway

Ancestors from Norway: http://homepages.rootsweb.ancestry.com/~norway/index.html

Norwegian American: www.lawzone.com/half-nor/ROOTS.HTM

Digital Archives from National Archives of Norway: http://
digitalarkivet.uib.no/cgi-win/WebFront.exe?slag
=vis&tekst =meldingar&spraak=e

The following is a selected bibliography of guidebooks for Norwegian
research:

> Flom, George T. *A History of Norwegian Immigration to the
> United States: From the Earliest Beginning Down to the
> Year 1848.* Baltimore, MD: Reprinted for Clearfield Co.
> by Genealogical Publishing Co., 2002.

> Gregerson, Merle Winton. *Norway Family Farm Surnames,
> 1589–1989: Research Lists for Norwegians in USA.*
> Onalaska, WI: M. W. Gregerson, 1989.

> Herrick, Linda M., and Wendy K. Uncapher. *Norwegian
> Research Guide.* Janesville, WI: Origins, 2004.

Swedish records include parish records beginning in 1750. Included
in the parish records are emigration records. These were sent to the
government annually, beginning in 1865, by the parish minister and
included the names of those arriving from or departing to another
country. In addition, the parish records include clerical survey records,
which were yearly examinations by the parish minister to determine if
everyone in the household could read and understand the catechism.
Census records exist from 1630 to 1860. Selected Swedish genealogy
records are available online on Ancestry.com, FamilySearch, Findmypast, and MyHeritage.com.

Some books to help you in your Swedish research are:

> Clemensson, Per, et al. *Your Swedish Roots: A Step by Step
> Handbook.* Provo, UT: Ancestry, ca. 2004.

> Johansson, Carl Erik. *Cradled in Sweden.* Sandy, UT:
> Everton, 2002.

> Pladsen, Phyllis J., et al. *Swedish Genealogical Dictionary.* St.
> Paul, MN: Swedish Genealogical Group, Minnesota
> Genealogical Society, 2000.

Records in Iceland go back to the ninth century. This island was settled largely by Danes, but there is also a large segment of the population with Scots and Irish ancestry. The country was under Danish rule
until 1918. Records prior to 1800 may be in Danish or Latin. Selected

Icelandic records can be searched on Ancestry.com, Findmypast, and MyHeritage.com. If you desire to use a print guide to research, the options are limited:

> Hart, Annie. *Tracing Your Baltic, Scandinavian, Eastern European, & Middle Eastern Ancestry Online: Finnish, Swedish, Norwegian, Danish, Icelandic, Estonian, Latvian, Polish, Lithuanian, Greek, Macedonian, Bulgarian, Armenia, Hungarian, Eastern European, & Middle Eastern Genealogy (All Faiths)*. New York: ASJA, 2005.

Canada

Many Americans had immigrant ancestors who came through Canada or lived in Canada prior to settling in the United States. Canada was originally organized as six separate colonies. The Province of Canada was divided into Upper Canada (Ontario) and Lower Canada (Quebec). Later, Ontario became known as Canada West and Quebec as Canada East. Eventually the Dominion of Canada was divided into provinces. The order in which they were formed is Ontario, Quebec, Nova Scotia, New Brunswick, Manitoba, Northwest Territories, British Columbia, Prince Edward Island, Yukon, Saskatchewan, Alberta, Newfoundland, Labrador, and Nunavut.

Like the United States, Canada was settled by people from many different countries. The French settled in Canada early, starting in 1604. During the first 150 years of settlement, almost 10,000 French immigrants came to Canada. Many former American colonists settled in Canada during and after the American Revolution. Those who were loyal to the British Crown, the Loyalists, fled to Canada in fear for their lives and are called the United Empire Loyalists. The first group of Loyalists left Boston for Canada in March 1776.

Before European settlement, native tribes lived in Canada. They are called the First Nations. Those of mixed Indian and European blood are called the Métis. The Métis are ancestors of French, Scottish, or English fur traders and Cree, Ojibway, or Saulteaux women. Records of Métis land claims from 1870 to 1924 are on microfilm at Library and Archives Canada. In 1982 the Métis were given aboriginal status.

Ontario land records are called Crown land records, or original land grants. Crown land records pertain to property owned by the

British Crown. When land was sold after being granted, it was considered land registry. The Land Purchase Act of 1853 allowed tenants to purchase their land from the government. A series of payments resulted in a deed which was recorded in township ledgers. Those who were Loyalists were given land grants for being true to the British Crown. In Quebec, landed estates held by feudal tenure were called *seigneuries*. The landholder was called a *seigneur*.

If you are researching Canadian probate records, or any court records, you must remember that Canadian law contains aspects of both the English and French legal systems. As a British colony, acts passed by the British Parliament affected the procedure of wills in Canada. In Quebec before 1760 the will of a deceased person was distributed by a *notaire* (notary).

Lists of immigrants arriving into Canada generally did not begin until 1865, though there are a few earlier records, some as early as 1745. They are housed in the Library and Archives Canada (LAC). Passenger lists for the port of Quebec from 1865 to 1900 are on microfilm but are incomplete. Records for the port of Halifax from 1881 to 1899 are on microfilm and, again, are incomplete. Records for the port of Saint John, New Brunswick, began in 1900. Lists for Victoria and Vancouver in British Columbia, North Sydney in Nova Scotia, and Montreal begin in the early twentieth century. For those arriving in Canada and going to the United States, there are records on the St. Albans lists, as discussed in chapter 4.

Canadian census records, as well as various other Canadian records, can be found online at Ancestry.com, Findmypast, MyHeritage.com, FamilySearch, and the LAC at www.bac-lac.gc.ca/eng/Pages/home.aspx. The first Canadian census took place in Quebec in 1666. When Canada underwent confederation in 1867, another census was taken. Beginning in 1871, a census was taken in Canada every ten years. The most recent enumeration available to researchers is the 1921 census.

Canadian vital records are sketchy before 1920. A marriage act in Ontario in 1831 allowed the civil registration of marriages and validated all marriages that had been performed prior to that date. Before civil registrations, look for church records. A set of books that can help you find Canadian ancestors in vital records, histories, and censuses is *The Atlantic Canadians*[14] (people in Nova Scotia, New Brunswick, Prince Edward Island, and Newfoundland), *The French Canadians*,[15] *The*

Central Canadians[16] (people in Ontario and Manitoba), and *The Western Canadians*[17] (people in Alberta, British Columbia, Saskatchewan, Yukon Territory, Nunavut, and the Alaska Territory). The volumes are an index of names that were found in various sources, with citations to the sources. If you are looking for all records in which your Canadian ancestor may be found, this is an excellent first step.

The LAC (Library and Archives Canada) is the major repository for Canadian records. Its holdings include family histories, parish registers, census records, passenger lists, naturalization records, land records and grants, newspapers, Métis land claims, and an increasing number of online databases. For information about researching French Canadian families, use *French and French-Canadian Family Research.*[18]

Native American Genealogy Research

Nothing can shake an inexperienced genealogy librarian more than a patron who says, "My ancestor was Native American." Native American genealogy research can be very difficult, but always have your patron show you what he or she has already searched. If they haven't even begun to search basic records, start them on the beginning path. Native Americans must have been in the right place at the right time to find them in printed records. They had to be living with a tribe on Indian land to be recorded on a document. The basics of Native American research are the same as in searching for any ancestor. Begin with yourself and move backward in time until you find someone you feel is the Native American ancestor. You must know the name of the ancestor before you can explore his or her Indian affiliation. Don't assume anything—you need to find the facts and be able to separate fact from fiction or family lore. But do listen to the family stories and use them as your guide.

Next, you will need to do some background research into the history of the suspected tribe. Use the *Gale Encyclopedia of Native American Tribes.*[19] This work has historical information on each tribe and where they were located. The locations of tribal land have changed from time to time. Look at maps of the areas in which your ancestors lived and compare them with maps that show tribal lands. Was your ancestor living in an area where Indian tribes were known? Many of these maps are available on the Internet. The U.S. Geological Survey (at https://

nationalmap.gov/small_scale/mld/indlanp.html) has printable and downloadable maps of Indian lands.

Use census records to identify someone as "Indian." All censuses beginning with 1870 show the possible race of "Indian" (I). The 1910 federal census, for states with reservations, had additional Indian schedules. The enumeration asked for the Indian name, nativity, blood quantum (the degree of Native American blood), marital status, citizenship, and type of dwelling. The 1930 federal census showed the name of the tribe in the space where you would find the place of the father's birth, and showed the blood quantum where you would find the birthplace of the mother. Indian Census Records, 1885–1940 are special census records taken of tribal members. These special schedules include the name (Indian and/or English), gender, age, birth date, the person's relationship to the head of family, marital status, name of the tribe, and the names of the agency and reservation. Please note that there is not a census for every reservation or group of Indians for every year. Only persons who maintained a formal affiliation with a tribe under federal supervision are listed on these census rolls.

You can sometimes find Native Americans in church records. The Catholic Church did a lot of missionary work among the native tribes. A book that will help you in this area is *History of the Catholic Missions among the Indian Tribes of the United States, 1529–1854.*[20] This book has been digitized. You can find it on Google Books and read it in its entirety online. The areas encompassed by the early archdioceses were larger in the time of the early Catholic missions than they are today. For instance, the Archdiocese of Detroit has records for Indians in the upper Midwest, especially Wisconsin, Michigan, and the lower part of Ontario, while the Archdiocese of San Antonio has Indian records for Texas and the northern part of Mexico. Other religious bodies that gave ministry to the tribes were Baptist, Presbyterian, Dutch Reformed, Mormon, and Moravian. The records of the Moravian Church have been filmed and are available through the Family History Library. In print, see also *Records of the Moravians among the Cherokees.*[21]

For the most part, American Indians did not have a written language. The exception was the Cherokee. With no written language, there were only oral traditions, which is what makes Native American research so difficult. You must look for entities that recorded the names of American Indians. The preceding paragraph mentioned church records. The federal government is another entity which recorded names. When our government interacted with native people, records were created. Searching federal documents is vital for the Native American genealogy researcher. When treaties were signed, the principal chief, braves, and warriors were to sign. For a list of treaties, see *Documents of American Indian Diplomacy: Treaties, Agreements, and Conventions, 1775–1979.*[22] The U.S. Serial Set has many documents dealing with interactions with Native Americans, including information on their treaties with the U.S. government. When land was being allocated, enrollments were created. Annuity payments as a result of compensation from treaties created lists of recipients. Citizenship rolls and land allotments from the Dawes Act (1887) created more records. When the government decided that Native American children needed to be educated in "civilized" ways, Indian schools were created and thus, more records were created. Many of these documents are housed at NARA or its field branches. The field branches house archival documents created in their region.

Many of the disagreements between the U.S. government (and its citizens) and the Native American tribes dealt with land. White settlers wanted to find new opportunities for land on which to build a new life. Frequently, that land was Indian land. Settlement areas in the east were becoming scarce without using tribal land, and this led to the removal of Native Americans from all of the land east of the Mississippi River. President Andrew Jackson signed the Indian Removal Act on May 28, 1830. Each tribe was asked to sign a removal treaty. This included all Indian tribes, but the tribe most closely associated with the removal and the Trail of Tears was the Cherokee tribe. Many records exist that document the Cherokee nation's protest of the removal, some of which can be found in the U.S. Serial Set.

In 1887 the Dawes Act was passed. It provided for the division of tribal lands into individual allotments for Indians and extended the protection of federal laws to those individuals. The heads of families received 160 acres, single individuals over the age of 18 received 80 acres, orphans under the age of 18 were given 80 acres, and others under the age of 18 received 40 acres. Citizenship was promised to those Indians registering for land, provided they gave up their allegiance to the tribe in favor of allegiance to the U.S. government. Extensive documentation for the application of the Dawes Act and subsequent legislation to the Five Civilized Tribes (Choctaw, Chickasaw, Cherokee, Creek, and Seminole) exist. The records can be found online on Fold3 and AccessGenealogy.com.

For more information about researching Native American ancestors, see:

> Carpenter, Cecelia Syinth. *How to Research American Indian Blood Lines: A Manual on Indian Genealogical Research.* Bountiful, UT: Heritage Quest, 2000.
>
> Native American Genealogy: Reconnecting with Your American Indian Heritage (www.native-languages .org/genealogy.htm) gives steps for beginning your search for Native American ancestors.
>
> Native American Nations (www.nativeculturelinks .com/nations.html) is a website that contains links to the home pages of various Native American tribes. Look at each Native American website for a link to "genealogy" or "enrollment." You might have to search long and hard to find the right link, but you should be able to find one.
>
> Ocean, Suellen. *Secret Genealogy IV: Native Americans Hidden in Our Family Trees.* Grass Valley, CA: Ocean-House, 2014.
>
> Southwest Oklahoma Genealogical Society. *American Indian Family History Research.* Lawton, OK: Southwest Oklahoma Genealogical Society, 2008.

African American Research

African American research is another difficult subject area that arouses fear in the novice genealogy librarian. Researching this ethnic group can be daunting at best. The first thing to remember is that tracing African Americans after 1870 is like searching for any other ancestor. So, start with yourself and work backward in time, using all the usual sources. Pay particular attention when you get to the 1870 federal census. This is the first census that recorded the names of former slaves. Before this date, they were only recorded on the slave schedules as statistics, but not by name. Only the slave owner was named. Knowing the name of the slave owner will help you immensely in your research. If your ancestor was a "free black" (a non-slave black person), he or she will continue to be recorded by name on the census as you go backward in time.

One way to find the names of slaves is to research church records. These names will most likely be found in the records of the church that their slave owners attended, which is one good reason to discover the name of the slave owner. The Catholic records of New Orleans contain many names of slaves. If your ancestor was a free black or a slave who was allowed to attend the church of his or her choice, look in the records of the following religions: African Methodist Episcopal (A.M.E.), African Methodist Episcopal Zion (A.M.E. Zion), Baptist, Catholic, Methodist, Presbyterian, Protestant Episcopal, and Quaker. The oldest black church in America was founded in Philadelphia in 1787 and was called the Mother Bethel A.M.E. Church. Many early church records acknowledged if the individual was a free black or a black slave.[23]

Military records also listed the names of slaves. African American participation in the military goes back to the Revolutionary War. You can find the names of some of those men in *Forgotten Patriots: African American and American Indian Patriots in the Revolutionary War: A Guide to Service, Sources and Studies*[24] and in *Black Courage, 1775–1783: Documentation of Black Participation in the American Revolution.*[25] The Civil War also saw much participation by African Americans on the side of the Union, especially after the Emancipation Proclamation in 1863. Fold3 and Ancestry.com have service records of those serving in the Colored Troops and other volunteer Union units.

African Americans also participated in the Indian wars fought on the Great Plains and elsewhere after the Civil War. The black soldiers in the U.S. 10th Cavalry Regiment, formed on September 21, 1866, at Fort Leavenworth, Kansas, were nicknamed Buffalo Soldiers by the Indian tribes they fought against.[26] The term "Buffalo Soldier" later became synonymous with all African American regiments formed in 1866, and the term was used in other, later military conflicts as well. Similar black regiments served in the Spanish American War, the Philippine Insurrection, World War I, and World War II. You can search for records in the *Register of Enlistments in the U. S. Army, 1798–1914* at FamilySearch,

Ancestry.com, Findmypast, and Fold3. Records of black soldiers can also be found at the National Personnel Records Center in St. Louis, Missouri. Desegregation of the armed forces began during President Harry Truman's term of office with Executive Order 9981, signed on July 26, 1948. A timeline, digitized documents, and photographs regarding the desegregation can be found on the Truman Library and Museum website, www.trumanlibrary.org/whistlestop/study_collec tions/desegregation/large/index.php?action=chronology#1953.

The records of African Americans who were slaves are not consistently available, but they do exist. You will find information in records of deeds, wills, plantations, manumissions, the Freedman's Bureau and the Freedmen's Savings Bank, slave manifests, and newspaper advertisements. Unfortunately, we must think of slave ancestors as property when searching for them. When slaves were sold, the deeds of sale were registered in the local courthouse. When a slave was inherited through the death of the owner, he or she was mentioned in a will. A slave could buy his or her own freedom or an owner could set a slave free. Those records of manumission were also filed in a courthouse. Ancestry.com has a collection of emancipation and manumission records.

Many, but not all, slaves lived on plantations. Plantation owners kept diaries that often mentioned slaves. They also kept deeds of sale and lists of slaves. These records can be found in university repositories, and some have been microfilmed. Check your local university library or check WorldCat.org. If you use the search term "southern plantation records" and limit to "archival materials," you will find a list of some of the microfilmed records and a list of the libraries that have copies of them. Figure 6.2 shows a list of the slaves owned by Wm. B. Turnbull, taken from the Turnbull family papers and published in a collection of plantation documents.[27]

The Freedman's Bureau was an agency created by the federal government in 1865 to help former slaves adjust to freedom. The agency helped legalize slave marriages, provided food, clothing, and transportation, helped in legal matters and relocation, and operated hospitals. This was never meant to be permanent aid, and in 1872 the bureau was deemed to have met its goal. The records of the bureau's field offices have been filmed by NARA and can be found on Ancestry .com. The Freedmen's Savings and Trust Company, also known as the

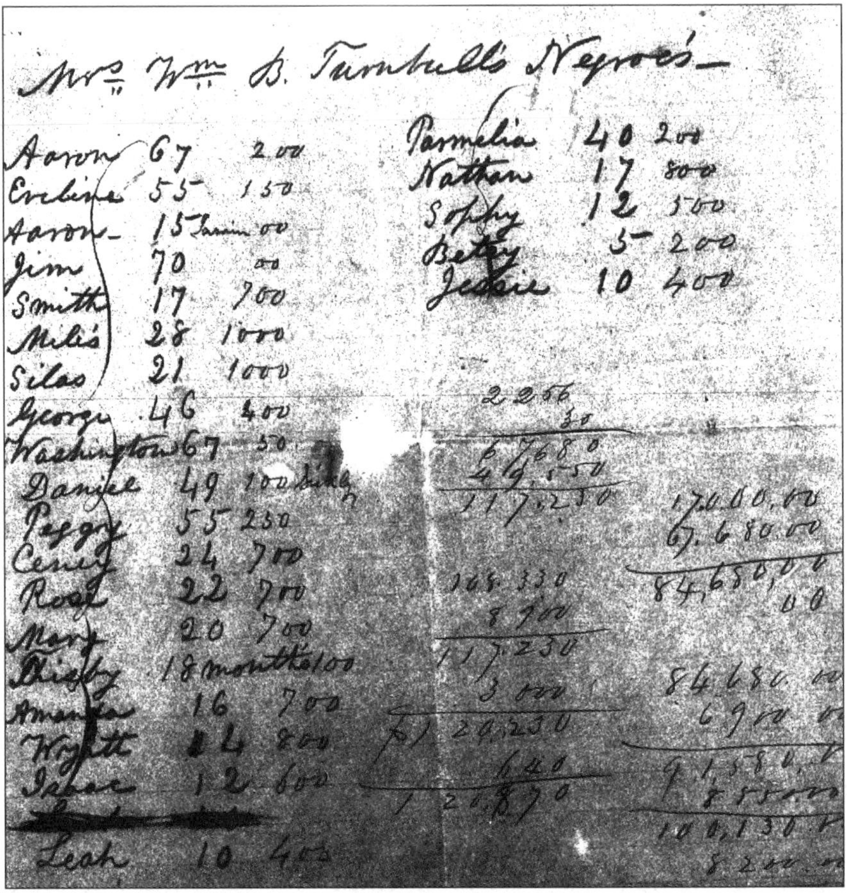

Mrs. Wm. B. Turnbull's Negroes—

Aaron	67	200
Eveline	55	150
Aaron	15	00
Jim	70	00
Smith	17	700
Miles	28	1000
Silas	21	1000
George	46	400
Washington	67	50
Daniel	49	100
Peggy	55	250
Ceney	24	700
Rose	22	700
Mary	20	700
Phillis	18 months	100
Amanda	16	700
Wyatt	14	800
Isaac	12	600
Leah	10	400
Parmelia	40	200
Nathan	17	800
Sophy	12	500
Betsy	5	200
Jessie	10	400

FIGURE 6.2

A list of "Wm. B. Turnbull's Negroes"

Freedman's Bank, was a savings bank for freed slaves which operated in thirty-three Southern cities from 1865 through 1870. Its records were also microfilmed by NARA and can be found on Heritage Quest Online.

Records of the slaves that were brought to this country from Africa are few. Congress ordered a halt to the importation of slaves in 1807, but slaves could still be bought and sold within the country. The port of New Orleans was a major hub for buying and selling slaves. Scholarly Resources microfilmed the Outward Bound Slave Manifests

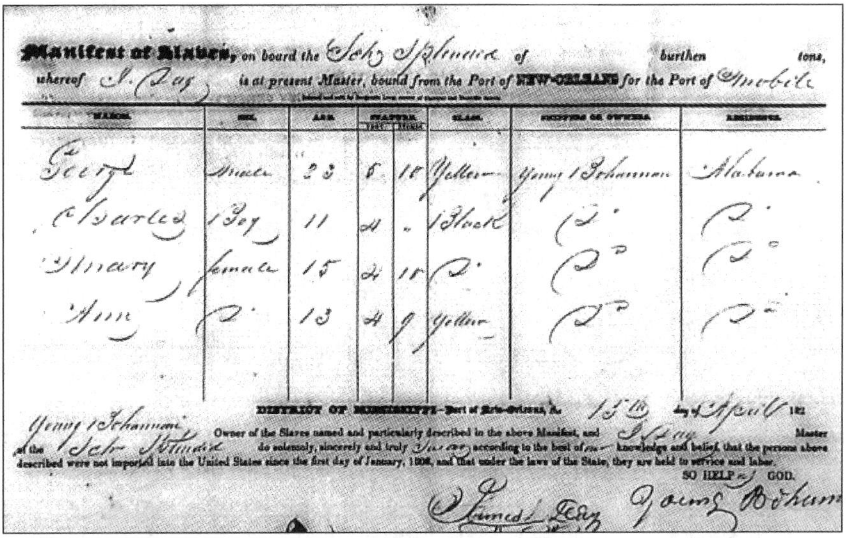
Manifest of Slaves, on board the ... of ... burthen ... tons, whereof ... is at present Master, bound from the Port of NEW-ORLEANS for the Port of ...

DISTRICT OF MISSISSIPPI—Port of New-Orleans, ...

Owner of the Slaves named and particularly described in the above Manifest, and ... Master of the ... do solemnly, sincerely and truly swear according to the best of our knowledge and belief, that the persons above described were not imported into the United States since the first day of January, 1808, and that under the laws of the State, they are held to service and labor.

SO HELP us GOD.

FIGURE 6.3

An outward-bound slave manifest for April 1828

(1812–1856), a record of purchased slaves leaving New Orleans, and the Inward Slave Manifests (1807–1860), a record of the slaves being brought into New Orleans for sale. The microfilm for these records can be found in some libraries, and digitized images are available on Ancestry.com. Figure 6.3 shows an outward-bound slave manifest for April 1828. The first line lists a twenty-three-year-old slave named George who was five feet ten inches tall and of yellow complexion.[28] Figure 6.4 shows an inward-bound manifest for December 1821 that lists slaves some of whom have last names, which is quite unique.[29]

A helpful website for searching African American ancestors is www.afrigeneas.com. It is a free website containing names, photographs, and links to other websites.

The following is a selected bibliography of African American research guides:

Burroughs, Tony. *Black Roots: A Beginner's Guide to Tracing the African American Family Tree.* New York: Fireside Books, 2001.

Hait, Michael. *Finding Your African American Ancestors.* Toronto, ON: Heritage Productions, 2014.

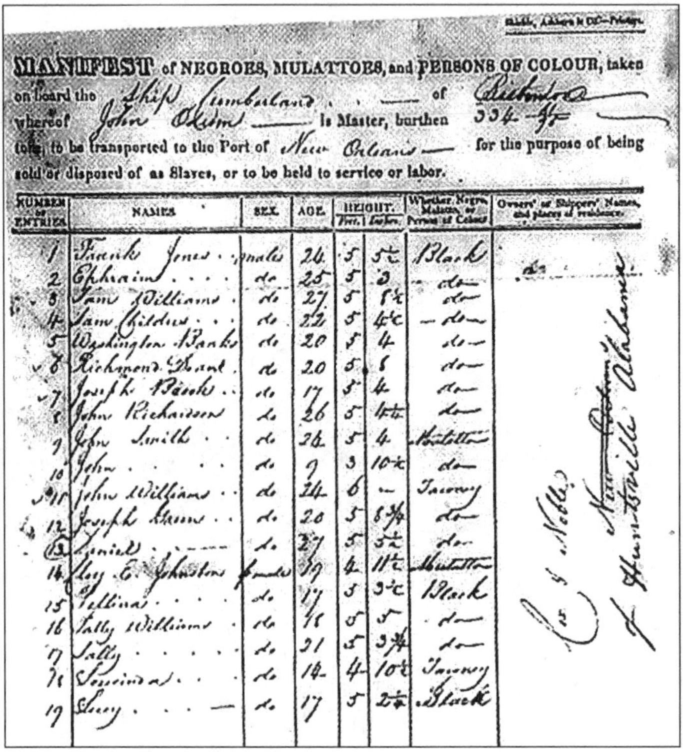

FIGURE 6.4

An inward-bound slave manifest for December 1821

Thackery, David T. *Finding Your African American Ancestors: A Beginner's Guide*. Orem, UT: Ancestry, 2000.

The following is a selected bibliography of research guides for other ethnic groups:

Chorzempa, Rosemary A. *Polish Roots = Korzenie Polskie*. Baltimore, MD: Genealogical Publishing Co., 2014.

Jensen, Cecile Wendt. *Sto Lat: A Modern Guide to Polish Genealogy*. Rochester Hills, MI: Michigan Polonia, 2010.

Mokotoff, Gary. *Getting Started in Jewish Genealogy: 2016–2017 Edition*. New Haven, CT: Avotaynu, 2016.

Ryskamp, George R. *Finding Your Mexican Ancestors: A Beginner's Guide*. Provo, UT: Ancestry, 2007.

Schmal, John P., and Donna S. Morales. *Mexican-American Genealogical Research: Following the Paper Trail to Mexico.* Westminster, MD: Heritage Books, 2007, ca. 2002.

Yan, May. *Research Guide to Chinese Genealogy.* New Westminster, BC: Global Research and Archival Management, 2010.

You might find the following websites useful:

www.chineseroots.com/ (Chinese)

http://feefhs.org/ (Federation of East European Family History Societies)

http://belgium.rootsweb.com/index.html (Belgium)

www.hispanicgs.com (Hispanic)

http://freepages.genealogy.rootsweb.ancestry.com/ ~irishancestors (Ireland)

www.jewishgen.org/ (Jewish)

Ethnic Periodicals

Ethnic genealogical societies exist and are good sources of information. The following organizations publish a newsletter or journal in an area of ethnic research. This is a selected list of periodical publications.

African American

Journal of the Afro-American Historical & Genealogical Society, www.aahgs.org/journal.htm

Black History Bulletin (Foundation for the Study of African American Life and History), http://asalh.org/bhb.html

Belgium

Belgian Laces, www.rootsweb.ancestry.com/~inbr/belgian_laces.htm

Flemish American Heritage, http://rootsweb.ancestry.com/~gsfa/ gsfainfo.html#publications

Canada

American-Canadian Genealogist, http://acgs.org/

British Columbia Genealogist, www.bcgs.ca/

Generations (Manitoba Genealogical Society, Inc.),
    www.mbgenealogy.com/

Generations (New Brunswick Genealogical Society), www.nbgs.ca/

Czech

Nase Rodina "Our Family" (Czechoslovak Genealogical Society
    International), www.cgsi.org

England

Essex Society for Family History, www.esfh.org.uk

Your Family History, www.yourfamilyhistorymag.co.uk/

Genealogists Magazine (Society of Genealogists), www.sog.org.uk/

France

Acadian-Cajun Genealogy (Acadian Genealogy Exchange),
    www.acadian-cajun.com/

Germany

American/Schleswig-Holstein Heritage Society Newsletter,
    www.ashhs.org/

American Historical Society of Germans from Russia, www.ahsgr.org/

Palatine Immigrant/Palatine Patter (German Genealogical Society
    Palatines to America), www.palam.org/

Hispanic American

Hispanic Genealogical Society Journal,
    www.hispanicgs.org/journals.html

Ireland

The Septs (Irish Genealogical Society),
    www.irishgenealogical.org/page/septs

Irish Roots Magazine, www.irishrootsmedia.com

American Irish Historical Society, www.aihs.org/

Italy

Italian Genealogical Group, www.italiangen.org/

Jewish

Avotaynu, www.avotaynu.com

Lithuanian

Lithuanian Heritage Magazine, www.draugas.org/lh/

Native American

Goingsnake Messenger, www.goingsnake.org/

Norway

Norwegian-American Studies,
www.naha.stolaf.edu/pubs/nastudies.htm

Poland

Eaglet (Polish Genealogical Society of Michigan), www.pgsm.org
Rodziny (Polish Genealogical Society of America), www.pgsa.org

Scotland

Highlander, www.highlandermagazine.com/highlandermagazine.htm

Sweden

Swedish American Genealogist, www.augustana.edu/x13918.xml

LESSON TWELVE

1. List the names of the countries from which your ancestors immigrated.
2. Select one of those countries and research its history. Search your library collection for a general history of the country.
3. Discover when record-keeping began. This will help you prepare for the research adventure to come. The FamilySearch Wiki should be able to give you an idea of available records.
4. Review the country's available records on AncestryLibraryEdition, FamilySearch, and other websites.

The search for your ancestors gets more and more fascinating as you continue on your journey. As we begin to discover the rich cultural heritage of our families, we begin to appreciate the struggles they had to overcome to reach this land and the struggles they had to endure after their arrival. As we discover our heritage, we truly discover the world around us.

Building Solid Evidence

Sometimes in our genealogy research we discover information that just doesn't sound right or may conflict with other sources. How do we determine the correct information? How do we make sure that we are compiling a reliable genealogy? The Board for Certification of Genealogists (BCG) has developed a standard for building a credible pedigree. It is called the Genealogical Proof Standard (GPS). As already stated, much genealogical information can be found in books and on the Internet. Some of the conclusions you reach using these sources, without further research, can look pretty good. You might conclude that because you found information in a printed source, it is correct. But wait a minute—look at that research carefully. You might find that it is only partially correct. The research is only as good as the researcher. Mistakes are made every day in genealogical research. Citing your sources and drawing sound conclusions are the only way to ensure a solid pedigree.

I once bought a jigsaw puzzle which was truly a puzzle. The picture on the box did not relate to the pieces I was pulling out of the box. Let us liken this puzzle to a genealogical problem. We want to eventually make the puzzle look like the picture on the box. In genealogical research we will call this defining the problem and thinking of a possible solution. As I took pieces out of the box, I began my foundation or border. We always need a foundation or a plan before we begin. But I hit my first problem. There were too many border pieces, and I could not tell which pieces I should use. Have you ever had that problem with your genealogy? Maybe you have too much information and are having trouble analyzing where it all fits in. My other problem with the jigsaw puzzle was that I couldn't tell the top from the bottom and the bottom from the sides. I was very confused.

Then I came upon another problem. I began pulling pieces of blue sky out of the box, but there was no hint of blue sky in the picture on the lid. I was getting pieces that did not belong in the puzzle. This is often our genealogy problem. We find information that just doesn't fit. The Genealogical Proof Standard is a solution for that. The GPS is used when there is no direct evidence to prove a conclusion, or to resolve a case where evidence conflicts. All evidence must point to the same direction, and contrary data must be resolved.

The GPS is a standard of credibility. Can you proudly say that your genealogical research is free of errors? A speaker at a national genealogy conference I attended asked, "Wouldn't it be nice if we could proudly say 'I found my information on the Internet'?" Wow! The speaker did not have a high opinion of information found online. More and more information can be found on the Internet, and much of it is correct. But compiled pedigrees found there are often not correct— at least not totally. Not all genealogists are good researchers, and some will accept anything they find. A good genealogical researcher will look to the Genealogical Proof Standard as a guide to proper research no matter where it is found.

I was helping a friend, Judith, with her genealogical research. She did not know very much about her maternal line. Her mother had abandoned the family when Judith was four years old. Though she reconnected with her mother in later years, Judith did not have the privilege of hearing family stories at reunions, weddings, and funerals as she was growing up. Finding the family in genealogical records began to mean a lot to her as she discovered upstanding citizens among her maternal line. One of Judith's ancestors was William H. Burns. Hundreds of pedigrees for William H. Burns exist on Ancestry.com and other websites containing compiled pedigrees. Here is an example of some of the discrepancies found online:

Name:	William H. Burns; William Harrison Burns
Birth:	May 1835; 25 May 1835; about 1835; 22 April 1834
Place of birth:	Kentucky; Washington County, Kentucky
Death:	18 February 1896; 1906
Place of death:	Washington County, Kentucky; Kansas City, Missouri; Kashmir, Pakistan
Spouse:	Martha Burns; Martha Stumpff; Martha McKittrick; Emeline Smock
Parents:	Matilda Prier/Pryor; William M. Burns and Sarah Catherine Fowler

The steps in GPS are a reasonable and exhaustive search; complete, clear, and accurate source citations that allow others to replicate the steps taken in research; an analysis of the evidence and correlation of the evidence from each applicable source; a resolution of any conflicting evidence; and a soundly reasoned proof conclusion with an explanation as to how the evidence led to a conclusion.[30]

To create a credible pedigree, begin with an analysis and definition of the genealogical problem. You should determine what information you hope to find, and you should review what you already know. Your pedigree chart is your road map. Your family group records are supplemental road maps. They chart your course and keep you on the right track in your genealogical research. The blank spaces on your pedigree chart or on your family unit charts are the problems to which you hope to find a solution. In the case of William H. Burns, the first problem to solve is: when and where did he die?

We have defined the problem and reviewed what was known. The next step is to find out what sources are available. A thorough research of an ancestor should try to reveal every record generated in his or her lifetime. If there are birth records available, find the birth record. If your ancestor lived from 1835 to 1906, you should find him or her on every census record from 1840 through 1900. There will be different sources, depending on when and where your ancestor lived. You should thoroughly research the area in which your ancestor lived, and you should know what resources are available there. Then identify those sources that may be useful and can provide reliable information relevant to the problem or the solution.

Let's return to the question of when and where William H. Burns died. Judith and I reviewed her pedigree and went back step by step until we came to him. His daughter lived in Kansas in her adulthood, but we found the family on the 1900 census in Kansas City, Jackson County, Missouri. Family lore said he was buried in Mount Saint Mary's Cemetery in Kansas City, Missouri. Judith and I visited the cemetery and found his tombstone, which stated that Wm. Harrison Burns died in 1906. It also gave his wife's name (buried next to him) as Martha Stumpff. An online search of Missouri death records indicated that William died in Kansas City on February 16, 1906 and Martha died on February 6, 1906. His physical burial in Kansas City and his death record indicating Kansas City as the place of death gave us assurance that this William Burns died in Kansas City, Missouri, in 1906.

It is helpful to keep a research log or calendar of the sources you have searched. You can create a simple log by creating an Excel spreadsheet or Word document, or you can find a template online. A couple of examples can be found at https://familysearch.org/wiki/en/File:Research_Log.pdf or www.familytreemagazine.com/info/researchforms. At the top of the sheet write the surname of the person you are researching, one log per individual or surname. Below that, state the problem or research focus. Then list every book, periodical, and Internet site searched, as well as recording visits to cemeteries and courthouses. Next to each source record the date, the information you found (or did not find), and the place you found that source—the name of the library with the call number of the book, or the URL and name of the website. The benefit of keeping a log is that you will not look at the same publication or Internet site more than one time for each problem, unless you discover more information and desire to search the source again. There is nothing more frustrating than realizing you have already looked at a book previously for the same problem.

Conduct a reasonably exhaustive search. Look at every source imaginable. Think about your ancestor's life or the locale in which he or she lived. Determine the laws that were in place for record-keeping. Check history books or websites to determine if a war was taking place during your ancestor's lifetime or if there was another requirement for military duty. Look at research guides to determine what records are available. Look at every record that your ancestor could have generated in his or her lifetime. By using many sources, you eliminate the possibility of reaching a too-hasty conclusion.

During your research, you must create clear, complete, and accurate source citations. Where did you find this information? How do you know it is true? A guide to citing genealogy sources is *Evidence Explained: Citing History Sources from Artifacts to Cyberspace*[31] by Elizabeth Shown Mills, which, as the title suggests, explains everything you need to know about citing a source. Citing your sources allows others to replicate your steps and evaluate the quality of your research.

You will be making conclusions based on the information or evidence you find. You must analyze the evidence from each source to ensure that the conclusion reflects the evidence. Evaluation leads to additional sources or facts you may want to research. The evidence you find will be either direct or indirect. Let's say we are looking for the parents of James Smith. On his birth certificate it states that his parents are John and Mary Smith. That is direct evidence. But what if there is no birth certificate for James? Let's say you find that James Smith has a brother named Ethan, and you find documentation that Ethan Smith is the son of John and Mary Smith. Indirectly you have linked James to John and Mary. Just make sure your assumption is sound.

The evidence will also be either primary or secondary and original or derivative. A death certificate has both primary and secondary evidence. The primary information is taken at the time of the event (name, death date, location, cause of death) and is provided by the attending physician. The secondary evidence is the age, birth date, birth location, and parents' names. The informant was usually someone who was not present at the time of birth, unless the informant was the mother or father. Each segment must be reviewed and analyzed for accuracy. More information is usually needed to back up secondary evidence. An original piece of evidence is the exact document that has not been copied or altered. A derivative document is a photocopy or digital image. A derivative is given less weight than the original but is still considered primary evidence if the original was primary evidence. You should build a case for accuracy with direct evidence or a combination of direct and indirect evidence. If there is no direct evidence, indirect evidence may be used. The important thing to remember in building a case for accuracy is that you must do an exhaustive search and all evidence must point in the same direction. If there is any opposing evidence, it must be researched and either negated or explained.

What should you do if the evidence conflicts? Conflicting evidence, even when it is primary evidence, must be resolved by carefully considering each piece or segment of the document. The search must be exhaustive. When was the document created? Who created the document? Why was it created? A document created close in time to an event usually carries more weight. Assess the information's quality as to whether or not it can be evidence. For example, digital images, microfilm copies, and photocopies carry more weight than transcripts or abstracts. A photo of a tombstone carries more weight than notes taken from the inscription. Evaluate every piece of information you have.

You should also put your ancestors into the correct historical setting. Using a timeline helps a great deal. We discussed timelines in chapter 2. It helps to determine if an event could have happened in the way it is presented. If you feel your ancestor fought in the Revolutionary

War, look at a timeline of the war and one of your ancestor's life and compare the two. If you notice he was nine years old at the end of the war, there is not a high probability that your information is accurate. Your ancestor's birth date may be wrong, or the problem could be his supposed participation in the war. You want an honest portrayal of individuals, their relationships, their records, and all related data.

What do you do if you have conflicting evidence? You must resolve it. There must be a soundly reasoned proof that explains how the evidence has led to a conclusion. Create a document in Excel or Word compiling your data in a logical sequence, with all the source citations and repositories searched. Outline the negative and positive research results and analyze the information. Evaluate the results of the search and determine if you should continue the plan, modify it, or develop a new one. This may sound like a lot of work, but genealogical research is a constant process of gathering, compiling, and evaluating evidence. The GPS is considered the minimum requirement in genealogy research.

Let's return to our example of William H. Burns. The pedigree my friend inherited indicated that William's spouse was "Martha Stumpff [McKittrick??]." Most of the online pedigrees indicated that Martha's maiden name was Stumpff, as did most of the sources we discovered. But her daughter's death certificate indicated that the mother's name was Martha McKittrick. (Remember, in an earlier chapter I mentioned that death certificates can be wrong.) Martha's marriage record stated that her name was Martha Stumpff. Judith and I were unsure which source to believe, and we wondered if there had been an earlier marriage to account for the different surnames. We did a search of the Kentucky 1850 census (Martha's location of birth) and could not find anyone named Martha Stumpff who was approximately eleven years old. Since there was a Missouri connection, we searched the 1850 Missouri census and found an eleven-year-old Martha Stumpff in Johnson County. Could this be Judith's ancestor? We searched Johnson County marriage records and found that Martha Stumpff married about the same time that Martha married William, but this was a different man. We searched 1850 Kentucky census records for Martha McKittrick and found an eleven-year-old girl in Washington County (the anticipated county). We also found William and Martha's marriage record in the same county. Next, we searched through every Washington County,

```
McKITTRICK, THOMAS - Will - W: 3 Jun 1846 - P: 19 Aug 1856                                    J-384
    Leg: Wife, Francis and to her two youngest children, William & Martha Stumpff.
    W: Robert S. Mitchell, James Long                              Signed: Thomas McKittrick
```

FIGURE 6.5

An extraction of Thomas McKittrick's will naming the legatees as Frances McKittrick
and her two youngest children, William and Martha Stumpff

Kentucky, book in the Midwest Genealogy Center. After much searching we had an "aha" moment. In volume 1 of *Washington County, Kentucky Wills* we found a guardianship record for William and Martha Stumpff, and the guardian being named was Thomas McKittrick.[32] In volume 2, we found an extraction of Thomas McKittrick's will naming the legatees as Frances McKittrick and her two youngest children, William and Martha Stumpff.[33] (See figure 6.5.) Judith and I felt we had solved the conflict of evidence.

Below is a selected list of articles by authors who have used the Genealogical Proof Standard successfully:

> Bockstruck, Lloyd D. "Who Was Mary, the Wife of George Archer?" *Virginia Genealogist* 43 (January-March 1999): 42–47. (Mary's maiden name was believed to be Kennon based on previous research by others. Confusion began when a wrong definition was applied to "dower." All available records were searched, and the author concluded the maiden name was actually Bevill.)

> Haines, Jeffrey L. "Under a Spreading Chestnut Tree: Parents for the Village Blacksmith, Nathaniel F. Sullivan of North Carolina." *National Genealogical Society Quarterly* 89 (March 2001): 16–28. (No document specifically names Nathaniel's parents. A search of all available deed and tax records was conducted. The evidence pointed to William and Nancy Sullivan as the parents.)

> Jones, Thomas W. "A Conceptual Model of Genealogical Evidence: Linkage between Present-Day Sources and Past Facts." *National Genealogical Society Quarterly* 86 (March 1998): 5–18.

Leary, Helen F. M. "Resolving Conflicts in Direct Evidence: Identity and Vital Dates of Mary Kittrell." *National Genealogical Society Quarterly* 87 (September 1999): 199–205.

The following is a selected bibliography for learning more about the GPS:

Ancestry.com (firm); Board for Certification of Genealogists. *Genealogy Standards.* Nashville, TN; New York: Ancestry.com, 2014.

Christensen, Penelope Janet. *How Do I Prove It?* Toronto, ON: Heritage Productions, 2008.

Jones, Thomas W. *Mastering Genealogical Proof.* Arlington, VA: National Genealogical Society, 2013.

Meriman, Brenda Dougall. *About Genealogical Standards of Evidence: A Guide for Genealogists.* Toronto, ON: Ontario Genealogical Society, 2008.

Rose, Christine. *Genealogical Proof Standard: Building a Solid Case.* San Jose, CA: CR Publications, 2014.

Genetic Genealogy

I do not profess to be a scientist or even slightly knowledgeable about genetic research. I started genealogical research when it was all about site visits and book and microfilm research. Then came the Internet. And now we even have genetic genealogy. I have not submitted my DNA for testing, but many have. DNA testing is not a replacement for genealogical research, but it can help answer questions that have long been mysteries. It is a tool, but to be effective it must supplement diligent traditional research.

Genetic genealogy will help you identify those who share your DNA: your relatives. You inherit DNA from your parents, and they inherit DNA from their parents, and so on. How much DNA you share with someone depends on how far back you share a common progenitor. Genetic genealogy will help verify the paper trail, break through brick walls, and enable you to learn more about your deep ancestry.

There are several types of chromosomal testing. Y-chromosomal (Y-DNA) testing traces the male line only. You inherit two sex chromosomes from your parents. A male receives a Y chromosome from his father and an X chromosome from his mother. Females have two X chromosomes. Since a female does not inherit a Y chromosome, this test will not work for her. The Y chromosome inherited by men is almost entirely unchanged from their fathers.[34]

Another test is mitochondrial DNA (mtDNA) testing, which traces the maternal line. Mitochondria are organelles that are found in almost every cell in the body; they break down nutrients and produce energy from them. The mtDNA is passed from a mother to her male and female children. Only the daughters will pass the inherited mtDNA to their children.[35] But all of the mother's children inherit her mtDNA, so all descendants, male and female, can benefit from this type of test.

The third genetic test is autosomal DNA (atDNA) testing. Autosomal refers to the non-sex chromosomes in your body. They are numbered from 1 to 22. AtDNA is inherited from both parents, about 50 percent from each parent. AtDNA allows one to determine how much DNA someone is likely to share with a close relative.[36] Family studies are often done with atDNA testing. A patron of mine was in a surname genealogy association. The group made a concerted effort several years ago to have all its members tested. The results showed everyone sharing a relationship except one person. He had traced the paper trail back to the common progenitor, but most likely there was an adoption that occurred somewhere in the lineage that did not show up in documents. It was an eye-opener to the non-relative and everyone in the association.

Several companies advertise their genetic testing services. To use DNA studies for genealogical purposes, you must submit a pedigree chart. The following selected list is not intended to be an endorsement of DNA testing companies. As with any company, they will come and go, so be sure to do a thorough search of the options. A vendor fair at a large genealogy conference is a good place to compare options.

Those offering autosomal testing only are:

23 and Me, https://23andme.com; AncestryDNA, https://www.ancestry.com/dna; and MyHeritage, https://www.myheritage.com/dna

FamilyTree DNA, https://familytreedna.com, which offers autosomal, mtDNA, and Y-DNA testing

The following is a selected bibliography of sources that discuss genetic genealogy:

Bettinger, Blaine T. *The Family Tree Guide to DNA Testing and Genetic Genealogy.* Cincinnati, OH: Family Tree Books, 2016.

Dowell, David R. *NextGen Genealogy: The DNA Connection.* Santa Barbara, CA: Libraries Unlimited, 2015.

There are both beginning and advanced areas of genealogy with which your patrons may need assistance. Unless you are a professional genealogist, there will always be certain areas that will cause you to stumble. This chapter was intended to give you an idea of the advanced subjects you might encounter. You don't have to know all the answers, but being able to point your patron in the right direction is essential. The next chapter will give you suggestions for additional training in genealogical research.

NOTES

1. Kevan M. Hansen, *Map Guide to German Parish Registers* (North Salt Lake, UT: Heritage Creations, 2004–).
2. Charles M. Hall, *The Atlantic Bridge to Germany* (Logan, UT: Everton, 1974–).
3. Raymond S. Wright, *Meyers Orts- und Verkehrs-Lexikon des Deutschen Reichs: With Researcher's Guide and Translations of the Introduction, Instructions for the Use of the Gazetteer and Abbreviations* (Baltimore, MD: Genealogical Publishing Co., 2000).
4. Chris Anderson, *A Genealogist's Guide to Discovering Your Germanic Ancestors: How to Find and Record Your Unique Heritage* (Cincinnati, OH: Betterway Books, 2000), 14.
5. Kenneth L. Smith, *Writing to Germany: A Guide to Genealogical Correspondence with German Sources* (Columbus, OH: K. L. Smith, 1984).
6. Paul Milner and Linda Jones, *A Genealogist's Guide to Discovering Your English Ancestors: How to Find and Record Your Unique Heritage* (Cincinnati, OH: Betterway Books, 2000), 13.
7. Institute of Heraldic and Genealogical Studies, *Parish Maps of the Counties of England and Wales* (Logan, UT: Everton, 1977).

8. Penelope Janet Christensen, *Researching English Parish Records* (Toronto, ON: Heritage Productions, 2001).

9. Jeremy Sumner Wycherly Gibson, *Record Offices: How to Find Them* (Baltimore, MD: Genealogical Publishing Co., 2002).

10. Penelope Janet Christensen, *Parishes & Registration Districts in England & Wales* (Toronto, ON: Heritage Productions, 2001.)

11. Milner and Jones, *Genealogist's Guide*, 21.

12. Ask About Ireland, www.askaboutireland.ie/search.xml?query=griffiths &radio_filter=images.

13. Patrick Pontet, *Ancestral Research in France: The Simple Guide to Tracing Your Family History through French Records* (Andover, UK: P. Pontet, 1998).

14. Noel Montgomery Elliot, *The Atlantic Canadians, 1600–1900: An Alphabetized Directory of the People, Places and Vital Dates* (Toronto, ON: Genealogical Research Library, 1994).

15. Noel Montgomery Elliot, *The French Canadians, 1600–1900: An Alphabetized Directory of the People, Places and Vital Dates* (Toronto, ON: Genealogical Research Library, 1992).

16. Noel Montgomery Elliot, *The Central Canadians: An Alphabetized Directory of the People, Places and Vital Dates* (Toronto, ON: Genealogical Research Library, 1994).

17. Noel Montgomery Elliot, *The Western Canadians: An Alphabetized Directory of the People, Places and Vital Dates* (Toronto, ON: Genealogical Research Library, 1994).

18. J. Konrad, *French and French-Canadian Family Research* (Indianapolis, IN: Ye Olde Genealogie Shoppe, 1998).

19. Sharon Malinowski, *The Gale Encyclopedia of Native American Tribes* (Detroit, MI: Gale, 1998).

20. John Dawson Gilmary Shea, *History of the Catholic Missions among the Indian Tribes of the United States, 1529–1854* (New York: J. P. Kennedy, 1854).

21. C. Daniel Crews and Richard W. Starbuck, *Records of the Moravians among the Cherokees* (Tahlequah, OK: Cherokee National; Norman, OK: distributed by University of Oklahoma Press, 2015, ca. 2010).

22. Vine Deloria and Raymond J. DeMallie, *Documents of American Indian Diplomacy: Treaties, Agreements, and Conventions, 1775–1979* (Norman, OK: University of Oklahoma Press, 1999).

23. Deloris Kitchell Clem, *Tracing African American Roots* (Las Vegas, NV: Gator, 1999), 79.

24. Eric G. Grudset, *Forgotten Patriots: African American and American Indian Patriots in the Revolutionary War: A Guide to Service, Sources and Studies* (Washington, DC: National Society Daughters of the American Revolution, 2008).

25. Robert Ewell Greene, *Black Courage, 1775–1783: Documentation of Black Participation in the American Revolution* (Washington, DC: National Society of the Daughters of the American Revolution, 1984).

26. William H. Leckie, *The Buffalo Soldiers: A Narrative of the Black Cavalry in the West* (Norman, OK: University of Oklahoma Press, 2003), 26, 27.

27. "Turnbull-Bowman-Lyons Family Papers," in *Records of Ante-Bellum Southern Plantations: From the Revolution through the Civil War,* series I, part 4, reel 36, frame 444.

28. *Outward Bound Slave Manifests, 1812–1860* (Farmington Hills, MI: Scholarly Resources), roll 3 (April 1828).

29. *Inward Slave Manifests 1807–1860* (Farmington Hills, MI: Scholarly Resources), roll 2 (December 1821).

30. Board for Certification of Genealogists, *The BCG Genealogical Standards Manual* (Orem, UT: Ancestry, 2000), 1.

31. Elizabeth Shown Mills, *Evidence Explained: Citing History Sources from Artifacts to Cyberspace* (Baltimore, MD: Genealogical Publishing Co., 2007).

32. Faye Sea Sanders, *Washington County, Kentucky Wills* (Louisville, KY: F. S. Sanders, 1987–), 1:127.

33. Ibid., 2:9.

34. Blaine T. Bettinger, *The Family Tree Guide to DNA Testing and Genetic Genealogy* (Cincinnati, OH: Family Tree Books, 2016), 70.

35. Ibid., 52.

36. Ibid., 92–94.

CHAPTER SEVEN

Collection Development and Training

L ibraries have many different types of customers, and genealogists are just one of them. One of the first places genealogists used to go once they developed an interest in the subject was libraries. Today they often think of Internet sites first, but libraries continue to be a good location for beginning a genealogy project. You might not work in a genealogy department, but your library probably has historical and other records for your local community. Those records might be tombstone readings of the local cemetery, marriage records for the county (transcription or otherwise), a history of your county, or vertical files.

Perhaps you work in an academic library. Your main priority is to help your students, but you may also have materials that would interest a genealogist. The history books, census abstracts and demographics, archival collections, and databases in your collection can be helpful to those seeking information about their ancestors.

Committees and sections of the American Library Association prepare guidelines for their areas of expertise. The Genealogy Committee of the History Section of the Reference and User Services Association (RUSA) has prepared "Guidelines for Developing a Core Genealogy

Collection."[1] I was fortunate to be a part of the committee that revised these guidelines in 2007. I consider it a good source for those who are managing genealogy departments as they attempt to develop a solid collection. For those who do not work in a genealogy department, the guidelines will help you discern the materials you already have that could be of help to genealogists.

The guidelines stress that "public libraries have a responsibility to service the needs of patrons interested in genealogy research by providing basic genealogy reference materials in print, microform, and digital, and how-to-do-it books in the library."[2] I would like to add that a knowledge of how to use those materials is imperative. There can be a gray line of separation between what is consider genealogy content and what is considered local history, but the following discussion will, hopefully, help you determine the types of books and records you should collect.

"Genealogy collections should begin with available local history materials and local records for the community which the library services. As funds allow, collections should branch out to include materials for the county, state, border states, and states along the migration patterns leading into the state."[3] If you don't know the migration patterns leading into the state, look at an early census record for your county, perhaps 1850. Make note of the states recorded under place of birth for each person. You will notice a pattern of those states that is repeated often. They are the mother states of your county.

Your library's collection should include available local history records and materials. A dedicated genealogist is one who travels to locations in which his or her ancestors lived. If those ancestors lived in your community, the traveling genealogist will want to look at those unique items of local history that your library has collected. This can include a history of your county. It doesn't have to be a new history to be useful to your patrons. You may still have vertical files or scrapbooks containing local history content. Unfortunately, space often becomes a consideration, and many vertical files have been discarded. If you still have them, think about ways in which you might preserve their content.

Local genealogists may offer you their compiled family histories or genealogies. These are useful, especially if they contain information about local families. You should certainly accept them when they are offered as donations, assuming they are books rather than a collection of papers. If you are offered raw genealogy research papers or computer discs, and the materials are copies or transcriptions of records or undocumented pedigree charts, accept them only if you have room and time available to process them. The uncompiled data will not often be used by local patrons unless you have good online finding aids. Having said that, the exception would be pedigree charts of local families. One of my former staff members did some research on local families and created pedigree charts and family group sheets which we kept in a notebook. As a result, when someone wanted to have ready data about local families, it was easily accessible. Online indexes are imperative if the charts are going to be useful.

Local vital records of births, deaths, and marriages are very useful. These may be copies (print or microform), transcriptions, indexes, or links to online sources. The number of government websites that now have digital images or online indexes to vital records is impressive. These websites may be those of the city or county government or the state archives. Making sure you know how to access the online records is necessary.

Cemetery readings for local burial grounds should be a part of your collection. The local genealogical society has probably published books of cemetery readings. Make sure you know the location of all your area's cemeteries, both active and historic. This may take some research on your part. It is amazing how many cemeteries, both pioneer and recent, can be in a county. We were fortunate in my county that the local DAR chapter published a list of vital historical records, including cemetery readings, in the 1920s. Many of those cemeteries no longer exist. The local genealogical society subsequently updated that list giving their locations, when known.

Local church records, those that exist, can be a wonderful addition to your library's collection. Historical records can usually be provided by your local genealogical society, historical society, or DAR chapter. When our library began receiving donations of church directories, which included photographs of the members, we realized we had a unique resource. The photographs usually had pictures of family units.

Other county records, as they are available, should be a part of your collection: naturalizations, probate and will records, land and deed records, and military records. These records may be microfilm, indexes to records, transcriptions, or extractions. Genealogical and historical societies publish local records in various formats and are a good source for acquiring this material. "The genealogy collection should be developed and maintained to support the basic research needs of the community serviced by the library. An assessment should be made concerning the ethnic background and countries of origin of the members of the community . . . in order to determine the scope of the genealogy collection. The scope of the collection should represent, at least, the majority of the community but not be limited to it."[4]

Guides to researching records in your state should also be included. As space and money permit, add guides for your border states. Guides to researching specific topics should also be part of your library's collection, such as naturalization research. The Genealogical Publishing Company and the Newberry Street Press both offer guides for sale.

If you don't have a genealogy collection in your library, or the genealogy room is manned by volunteers and open only for limited hours, you may have to rely on your general reference collection to give assistance to genealogy patrons. Take a good look at your reference collection. You may be surprised by what it contains.

Atlases, incorporating county, state, federal, and international levels, give help in finding place names and locations found in census records, obituaries, marriage announcements, and so on. Histories of organizations within your community are another source. This may include information in your vertical files. The yearbooks of high schools and various organizations can help genealogists discover photographs of family members. City directories are an excellent resource if you have had space to keep a historical collection. Many older directories are available online. Old phone books are also excellent resources for finding ancestors. If you have kept older issues of your state's official manuals, these are another unique resource for helping genealogists.

Local newspapers should not be forgotten. Your library may have older issues on microfilm. Newspapers allow you to put ancestors into historical context with the daily happenings in the community and are fascinating reading. You will find death information about your ancestor in many ways in newspapers: obituaries, death notices, necrologies, lists of dead (particularly war dead), death anniversaries, probate notices, social items indicating an illness or death, information from other localities (some obituaries will state "other newspapers, please copy" when the decedent had family elsewhere), and notices of thanks.

Newspapers also contain marriage notices. The types of information you may find are the names of immediate family, names of guests, names of attendants, attire worn by the bridal party, decorations, gifts, occupations of the bride and groom, and residences of the bridal couple, party, and family. Look also for lists of individuals obtaining marriage licenses at the courthouse, which often occurred weekly. Marriage notices may be found immediately after the wedding or several weeks or months later.

Look also for birth information in newspapers. The notices are usually provided by the parents, but they may be provided by the hospital with the parents' permission. Births of illegitimate children are seldom listed. In the past, you could find births mentioned in the society column. Look also for milestones of anniversaries and birthdays, such as the fiftieth anniversary of a marriage or the commemoration of a 100th birthday.

Newspapers will give you the essence of life in the community. News of local disasters, droughts, storms, and accidents can be found, as can social items of happenings in the schools, churches, organizations, and reunions. You will soon notice the names of prominent people as you peruse the newspaper, and you will find the advertisements of local businesses. Look for legal notices and classified ads for land and sheriff's sales, title changes, property transfers, land records, tax lists, appointments to political office, lists of jurors, name changes, guardianship, notices of divorce, and notices of runaway slaves and missing persons.

Surprisingly, another good resource is juvenile reference books. Someone wanting a brief but concise synopsis of a historical event can find that information in the juvenile section. I was preparing a lecture on colonial immigration and found excellent information about the beginning of each American colony in juvenile reference books. One does not feel overwhelmed with information, but learns the pertinent explanation sought.

This chapter has discussed the types of materials that should be a part of your library's collection. Many resources are now offered online which, in the past, needed to be books or microforms within our libraries. You and your staff should be aware of how to use the genealogy databases within your library's collection and how to find local and state records online. If collections are retained by other repositories in your area, you should be aware of their location.

LESSON THIRTEEN

1. Review the genealogy collection in your library. Is it adequate for your community?

2. If you do not have them in your library's collection, where might you find (online or in another repository) local

   - births
   - deaths
   - newspapers
   - will and probate records
   - county histories
   - church records

   Note: these records may be found on Ancestry Library Edition or FamilySearch.

Continuing Education

As you have discovered in the course of reading this book, genealogy is a unique subject that can be very complicated. You and your staff should be trained and periodically updated in genealogy research methods, document analysis and evaluation, protocols, and available resources. Proper research methods don't change, but genealogy resources change all the time. Websites change, the availability of online records constantly changes, and newly compiled print documents are increasingly published. So how do you become trained, and how do you stay current?

Become involved with your local and state genealogical societies. Avail yourself of their classes and conferences. They have so much to offer, and as you reach out to them, you will be able to share information about your facility and resources. Often you will find other library professionals attending the events, allowing you the opportunity to network.

National genealogy conferences are another way to receive genealogy education. The National Genealogical Society usually holds its conferences in the spring at various cities around the United States. Visit its website at https://www.ngsgenealogy.org to find the location of the next conference. The Federation of Genealogical Societies (FGS) holds its conferences in the fall, usually near Labor Day. Again, these are held at various cities around the United States. The FGS's website, http://fgs.org, will tell you when and where the next conference is being held. There are librarians' days at both conferences and they are normally free, one-day educational opportunities. The conferences themselves encompass three or four days, depending on the conference. Each day you will be able to select from the many available classes, and by the time you leave you will feel as if you have immersed yourself in genealogy. The opening session of each conference is followed by the opening of the exhibit hall. This is a time to get an overview of the available vendors, but not a time to have a quality visit with any of them. Make note of those you want to visit later. After the initial opening, you will have ample time to return to the hall during session and lunch breaks. If there are certain vendors with which you would like to have an in-depth conversation, make an appointment to talk with them while others are in classes. Be sure to take advantage of these events.

ALA conferences are a great way to learn about the world of genealogy. Genealogy pre-conferences are usually held at both the Midwinter and Annual Conferences. Often these are free but are not well advertised in advance. Therefore, your travel preparations may be made before the pre-conference is advertised. Within RUSA, there is a History Section which has a Genealogy Committee, Local History Committee, and Genealogy and Local History Discussion Group. These are open meetings and available for all to attend. They are fantastic ways to network with other librarians who are working with genealogists. Check out the Genealogy Committee's Facebook page (https://www.facebook.com/search/top/?q=rusa%20hs%20geneal ogy%20committee) to stay informed.

To find out about educational opportunities, or anything genealogical on a professional level, subscribe to GENEALIB—a discussion list for the Librarians Serving Genealogists website. The list administrator is Drew Smith, who is academic advisor to the Pathway Program at the

University of South Florida and adjunct for the USF School of Information. Smith has shared the following when asked about the founding of the discussion list: "GENEALIB resulted from a meeting between Pam Cooper [retired librarian, Vero Beach, Florida], Curt Witcher [director of Special Collections & Genealogy at the Allen County Public Library, Fort Wayne, Indiana], and myself at the 1996 annual conference of the Federation of Genealogical Societies in Rochester, NY. At the time, ALA was not offering any kind of e-mail list specifically for genealogy librarians, and I volunteered to administer one hosted at the University of South Florida. Over time it has grown to over 1,100 subscribers, who are primarily genealogy librarians at public libraries, but other subscribers include library science students, retired librarians, volunteers at Family History Centers, archivists, and vendors who want to listen in on what issues genealogy librarians are facing with their products or in general. It is often the case that genealogy librarians are alone at their libraries (no colleagues to share problems with), and GENEALIB allows them to ask about problems and policies at other libraries. They get lots of great ideas that they can apply at their own libraries. It has also been especially good when it comes to libraries sharing duplicate materials that other libraries might want."

RootsTech (https://www.rootstech.org) is a unique offering among genealogy conferences. Held each winter in Utah, it not only focuses on traditional genealogy sessions, but also highlights the latest in genealogy technology. Librarians' days are also offered prior to the opening of RootsTech each year—another opportunity to network. If you can't make it to the venue, it offers streaming of select sessions at its website after the event and until the next conference.

Another educational opportunity is the Genealogical Institute on Federal Records (Gen-Fed). The institute is held annually at the National Archives in Washington, DC with a focus on researching federal records. However, it is not for the novice. It is geared for experienced genealogists, archivists, historians, and librarians who are interested in using federal records for genealogical research. The institute is held each July at the National Archives. The institute sells out quickly, so plans must be made early to attend.

The Institute for Genealogy and Historical Research is an intense five-day institute incorporating education and research. Formerly held at Samford University in Birmingham, Alabama, it has been relocated to the University of Georgia's Athens campus. The classes are taught by nationally known genealogical and historical experts. The course chosen, which can range from beginning to specialized topics, lasts throughout the week. The institute is a great opportunity to learn about genealogical research and methodology, research skills, evaluation of resources, and critical analysis of documentation.

Self-paced learning online is available from the National Genealogical Society's educational courses entitled American Genealogical Studies, https://www.ngsgenealogy.org/cs/educational_courses/ameri can _genealogical_studies. There are multiple course tracks available, ranging from genealogy basics, documentation and source citation, to beyond the basics and "Branching Out." Each course module is graded and certificates are given upon successful completion. Members of the NGS are given a discount on the class tuition.

Boston University's Genealogical Research Program is another online course of study. Current genealogical technologies and research methods are taught by experienced genealogy professionals there. The program is not for the novice and requires previous genealogy experience. This intense program has proven to be excellent preparation for those seeking genealogical certification. For more information, go to http://professional.bu.edu/programs/genealogy.

If cost is an issue (and even if it's not), free online learning is available at the Ancestry Academy (https://www.ancestry.com/Academy/ courses/recommended), Brigham Young University free online courses (http://isreg.byu.edu/site/courses/free.cfm#), and the FamilySearch Learning Center (https://familysearch.org/learningcenter/home.html).

There are so many options available to you for beginning or continuing education. All staff who have contact with patrons should become knowledgeable about the basics of genealogical research. If patrons interested in genealogy visit your library, you have a duty to help them in every way you can. It is my hope that you have learned enough in these pages to whet your appetite for further study and research. Genealogy has stimulated people of all ages to learn more about the history of their families and determine how they fit into the history of our country. What a great opportunity you have in assisting them in their journey. Enjoy!

NOTES

1. Reference and User Services Association, "Guidelines for Developing a Core Genealogy Collection," www.ala.org/rusa/resources/guidelines/guidelinesdeveloping.
2. Ibid., 1.1.
3. Ibid., 3.1.
4. Ibid., 3.3.

INDEX